Also By Harvey Frommer

Holzman on Hoops *(with Red Holzman)*

Behind the Lines *(with Don Strock)*

It Happened in the Catskills *(with Myrna Frommer)*

Running Tough *(with Tony Dorsett)*

Growing Up at Bat: The Official 50th Anniversary of Little League Baseball

Throwing Heat *(with Nolan Ryan)*

Primitive Baseball: The National Pastime in the Gilded Age

150th Anniversary Album of Baseball

Red on Red *(with Red Holzman)*

Olympic Controversies

City Tech: The First Forty Years

Baseball's Greatest Managers

National Baseball Hall of Fame

The Games of the XXIIIrd Olympiad: Official Commemorative Book *(Editor & Principal Author)*

Jackie Robinson

Baseball's Greatest Records, Streaks, and Feats

Sports Genes *(with Myrna Frommer)*

Baseball's Greatest Rivalry: The New York Yankees and the Boston Red Sox

Rickey and Robinson: The Man Who Broke Baseball's Color Line

Basketball My Way—Nancy Lieberman *(with Myrna Frommer)*

The Sports Date Book *(with Myrna Frommer)*

New York City Baseball: 1947–1957

The Great American Soccer Book

Sports Roots

Sports Lingo: A Dictionary of the Language of Sports

The Martial Arts: Judo and Karate

A Sailing Primer

A Baseball Century

Shoeless JOE AND Ragtime Baseball

Harvey Frommer

Taylor Publishing Company
Dallas, Texas

Published by Taylor Publishing Company
1550 West Mockingbird Lane
Dallas, Texas 75235

Photos courtesy of the National Baseball Hall of Fame, the Library of Congress, and the Chicago Historical Society.

Designed by Hespenheide Design

Library of Congress Cataloging-in-Publication Data

Frommer, Harvey.
    Shoeless Joe Jackson and ragtime baseball / Harvey Frommer.
        p.   cm.
    Includes index.
    ISBN 0-87833-784-9 : $19.95
        1. Jackson, Joe, 1888–1951.   2. Baseball players—United States—
Biography.   3. Chicago White Sox (Baseball team)—History.
4. Baseball—United States—History—20th century.   I. Title.
GV865.J29F76   1992
796.357'092—dc20   91–43040
    [B]   CIP

Printed in the United States of America

10   9   8   7   6   5   4   3   2

For my son, Freddy, with much love.
One day, I know, he will dedicate a book to me.

Acknowledgments

At the top of the list is my severest critic and greatest ally—my wife Myrna. This book has her deft touch and writing insights on each and every page.

A tip of the hat goes to my excellent editor at Taylor, Jim Donovan. He was there from start to finish, capably coaching away.

Others who make the list: Virginia Stannard of the Greenville County Library, Bill Jenkinson, Wayne Cunningham, *The Sporting News,* and the National Baseball Hall of Fame.

Finally, special thanks to my son Freddy for his careful proofreading and on-target queries.

Contents

Sixteen pages of photographs follow page 114

. . . And let me speak to the yet unknowing world
How these things came about: so shall you hear . . .
Of accidental judgments, casual slaughters;
Of deaths put on by cunning and forc'd cause,
And, in this upshot, purposes mistook
Fall'n on the inventors' heads;
All this can I
Truly deliver.

William Shakespeare, Hamlet

Jackson's fall from grace is one of the real tragedies of baseball. I always thought he was more sinned against than sinning.

Connie Mack

Shoeless JOE AND Ragtime Baseball

Prologue

Sometime in the late 1940s Ty Cobb and sportswriter Grant-land Rice stopped off at a liquor store in Greenville, South Carolina, on their way back from the Masters Golf Tournament in Augusta, Georgia.

Cobb greeted the heavyset man behind the counter. "I know you," he said. "You're Joe Jackson. Don't you know me, Joe? I came by especially to say hello."

"I know you," said the man behind the counter, "but I wasn't sure you wanted to speak to me. A lot of them don't."

When the two men had last met more than a quarter of a century earlier, it was on a baseball field. Both were celebrants then, close competitors in the rush to be the best. But life had proscribed vastly different paths for each. Cobb had become a baseball Hall of Famer, a hailed legend, a millionaire entrepreneur, while Jackson had lived in the ignominy of tarnished glory, winding down his life not far from the small town where he was born.

"Joe," said Cobb, "you had the most natural ability, the greatest swing I ever saw."

Jackson nodded and looked away for an instant.

"Could I get an autographed baseball from you?" Cobb continued. "I always wanted one."

Jackson hesitated. "I'll get you one, but you'll have to come back tomorrow if that's all right."

"Well, we're just passing through . . . we'll do it some other time."

There was never another time. It would have been easy for Jackson to get a ball that same day, but still, after all the years, he had not learned to sign his name.

1

[1]

Greenville

The era 1900–1920 was one of great transition for the United States. It was coming of age and becoming a world power. It was a time when baseball gave America, a land of brief history and limited mythology, a cast of characters, a saga of adventures, a substitute for the newly closed frontier. It was also when baseball high-stepped out of its nineteenth-century roots, through the era of ragtime into its role as the national pastime, from an agrarian ethos into a ritual that would become part of American life.

In doing so, it echoed the new ragtime music that was capturing the nation's attention. The first organized music to become part of the world of jazz, ragtime utilized two coronets, a trombone, a clarinet, a banjo or guitar, a tuba or string bass, and drums. It was based on formal composition, the parts flowing into the whole—yet its appeal was unmistakably modern, a sense of something new. Baseball was likewise a formal and deliberate composition, its diverse parts contributing to a regulated whole, a game of a nation on the move.

Baseball's evolvement mirrored the larger transformations of the nation: the abandonment of the restraints of the Victorian period, the closing of the frontier, mass immigration, the development of cities, growing attention to entertainment and leisure-time activities, mass production and the development of scientific management, emergent American imperialism and military might. The population of the United States increased

3

from 76 million to 106 million during that era, and the population of its large cities escalated from 30 to 54 million.

Change and newness were everywhere. A five-cent piece featuring the buffalo and Indian head came into being. The Boy Scouts of America were formed. George Eastman built the first Kodak camera and sold it for $25. The Sears & Roebuck catalogue was introduced (one of its first products was an organ in a solid oak case that sold for $37.35) and included a money-back guarantee for any dissatisfied customers.

Average annual earnings climbed from nearly $500 at the start of the century to almost $1,500 by the end of its second decade. The workweek dropped from 57.4 hours to 50.4 hours.

Technological advances, improvements in newspaper printing, the camera, the telephone and telegraph, the motion picture—all of these brought information and entertainment more quickly to more people. You could see *The Great Train Robber*—a twelve-minute film—for five cents in a nickelodeon in 10,000 stores.

It was the time of poets like Carl Sandburg and Robert Frost, a time when people went to see such performers as Tom Mix, Charlie Chaplin, John Barrymore, Gloria Swanson, Douglas Fairbanks, and Mary Pickford, a time when Irving Berlin, Victor Herbert, and Sigmund Romberg were writing America's favorite songs.

In 1910, two billion copies of sheet music were sold. A couple of favorites were "A Bird in a Gilded Cage" and "Shine on Harvest Moon." Baseball players as composers, singers, speakers—all were part of the popular musical scene.

"The Red Sox Speed Boys," a little ditty that appeared in the mid-1900s, did very well. The title was wishful thinking, because the Sox were at or near last in stolen bases throughout those years. The "American League Two Step" was dedicated to the pennant-winning 1905 Philadelphia A's. The "White Sox March" was published in 1907 to celebrate the '06 World Champions. "Cubs on Parade," a march two-step by H.R. Hempel, was dedicated to Chicago's 1907 World Champions. A song called "Between You and Me," allegedly written by Johnny Evers and Joe Tinker, was referred to as "the catch of the season." The sport's anthem, "Take Me Out to the Ballgame," was published in 1908.

During the ragtime era Cornelius Vanderbilt built what he called a "small cottage"—a 70-room mansion that cost $5 million. William Vanderbilt spent $6 million more for a marble house. The spendings of the Vanderbilts were the exception.

In that America of forty-five states at the turn of the century there were no radios and no refrigerators; eggs were twelve cents a dozen, a complete turkey dinner cost twenty cents. At the Squirrel Inn at 131 Bowery in New York City, a family of six could eat for $1.00 and still have change left over. A steak, beef stew, or three fried eggs cost ten cents at the Squirrel Inn while for five cents you could order coffee, tea, milk or cocoa, and pie. Barber shops featured shaving mugs individually emblazoned with the names of customers. A shave was fifteen cents. You could purchase a made-to-order suit from a skilled tailor for ten dollars, a frontier 44-caliber revolver for $3.75, a Homan sewing machine for $7.58, a pocket watch for fifty-nine cents, a standard stethoscope for twenty-eight cents, an Armorside corset for eighty-five cents.

That America of 1900 was shocked by the assassination of President William McKinley. Teddy Roosevelt succeeded him, becoming the youngest president of the United States in history. He was forty-two years old.

Although Henry Ford had popularized the "Tin Lizzie" and the $5-a-day wage scale for a full eight-hour day, there were less than 10,000 cars in America of the early 1900s. Many of those who did have cars were subjected to the cry of "Get a horse" whenever there was a rainstorm and they had to struggle to get their cars out of muddy ditches in the roads.

Changing demographics altered the appearance and feel of America. The falling price of cotton, rising costs, and a public outcry against the use of child labor sent Northern mill owners south. There they built mill towns with mill stores and mill churches and mill homes. Countless small towns were overrun by the booming new industry.

Greenville, South Carolina was just such a town.

Joseph Jefferson Wofford Jackson was born on July 16, 1889 in Pickens County, not more than fifteen miles outside of Greenville, the first of five boys and two girls brought into the world by George Elmore and Martha Ann Jackson. The Jacksons were Baptists but not religious. Still, Martha Jackson, a big woman who kept her jet-black hair tied back in a knot and who was skilled in making hot biscuits and jelly from apples, refrained from cooking on Sunday.

When Joe was six years old, the family moved to Brandon, a town of about 13,000 people ringed by textile mills. There, like the others his age, Joe was put to work sweeping floors in the mill. The long stultifying hours of working as a cleanup boy, or "linthead," depressed him.

By 1902, when Joe Jackson was thirteen years old, he was working a dozen hours a day in the cotton mill along with his father and a brother and all the other mill workers who outnumbered the citizens of Greenville two to one.

The boy's sole escape from the whirring machinery and the din, dust, and danger of the mill took place out in the fields, playing baseball.

Because Southern mill workers frequently moved from town to town, job to job, the owners of the mills introduced measures to try and keep a hold on their workers, to literally "keep them in their place." Cows, organs, expensive merchandise was made available—all on credit. Organized social gatherings were staged weekly to create a sense of community. And there was also baseball. The Textile League provided a rooting interest for workers and a sense of belonging. All mill cities were interconnected by a railroad called the Belt Line. Saturday afternoons teams and their fans went from town to town for baseball. Those who played for the Textile League teams were given the easiest jobs, some time off for practice, and lots of prestige.

The managers of the Brandon Mill team had observed the gangly Joe Jackson playing baseball in pickup games or in those moments he stole away from mill work. Impressed with his natural ability, they asked Joe's mother for permission to allow him to play for their team.

The teenager was a natural right from the start, pounding homers with a baseball that was fat and soft and scuffed and heavy. "Joe's Saturday Special" was how fans referred to a Jackson home run. Each time Joe smacked a home run, his younger brothers—David, Jerry, Earl, Ernest, and Luther—would race into the stands. In a businesslike manner they would pass the hat and collect money from the fans. There were times Joe's brothers picked up as much as $25—about a good month's pay at the mill. This, coupled with the $2.50 paid to each player for the Saturday games, netted the young Joe Jackson a tidy sum, which he passed on to his mother and father.

Katie Wynn, four years younger than Jackson, was one of his most ardent fans. She rooted for Joe at the games and spent time with him at Harrison's Drugstore in Greenville. It was there that he would often order his favorite drink—"dope and lime"—a beverage whose name was far more deadly than its actual contents: Coca-Cola and a squirt of lime.

Good quality baseball gloves of the time could be purchased for about two dollars, but they were used more as protection against the ball rather than anything else. The bat was the baseball player's real tool of his trade.

Charlie Ferguson, the local batmaker, was a follower and a fan of Joe Jackson. The two would often talk bats and the art and science of fashioning the right kind. When Joe was fifteen, Charlie presented the youth with a bat that he had created from a well-seasoned four-by-four that had once been part of a strong hickory tree. The bat was ash white when it was completed, but Charlie Ferguson knew that Joe liked black bats. So the batmaker busied himself adding the finishing touches to the 36-inch long, 48-ounce bat that he shaped to the fit of Joe's large and growing hands. A couple of coats of tobacco juice transformed the bat into a glistening piece of wood with the look of ebony about it. Joe Jackson called the bat "Black Betsy."

Ferguson gave specific instruction on the care of the bat—the rubbing with sweet oil, the wrapping in a clean cotton cloth when not in use. And Joe Jackson followed these directions to the letter.

Joe's long gangling arms that had so much power in them convinced Brandon Mill officials to tinker with playing the youth at catcher. But Jackson's catching career was aborted when a pitch from a burly mill hand dented his catcher's mask into his forehead, scarring him there for life. He played a bit of third base and pitched a little. But the outfield was where he finally settled, where he was able to use his running speed and powerful arm to the greatest advantage.

It was the custom of the time for mill teams to raid and outbid each other for gifted players. That was how Joe wound up playing for Victor Mills, located in Greer just south of Greenville. Then, Lawrence Lollie Gray, who had played football for Clemson and was the organizer of the "Near Leaguers," a semiprofessional team, noticed Jackson enthusiastically pounding away with Black Betsy. Gray signed him up for his team. Some days Jackson played for that team; other days he performed for Victor Mills.

At that time, Joe was obsessed with the two passions of his life: baseball and Katie Wynn. The two teenagers spent many soft southern evenings talking of the future: of their getting married and of Joe's dream of a career in the booming sport of professional baseball.

Faced with no challenge from any other sports, delighted at rising attendance, and averaging nearly seven million fans a season, baseball was truly king of the hill. In the early 1900s there were 400 leagues in Chicago alone. All over the south, hundreds of semiprofessional and professional "barnstorming" teams traveled about offering challenges to local teams. Communities vied with each for the right to have a professional team represent them. For several years, Greenville civic leaders had labored to obtain one. So it was a matter of much pride when Greenville officials announced that their city would have a baseball franchise in the new Class D Carolina Association when the 1908 season got under way.

The New York Times had reported in 1900, "Rowdyism by the players on the field, syndicalism among the club owners, poor umpiring and talk of rival organizations . . . are the principal reasons for baseball's decline." But the report flew in the face of the reality that baseball in that America was all the rage. The game had only to be seen to be loved, a writer of the time noted. Other writers like Grantland Rice, Ring Lardner, and Hugh Fullerton romanticized and publicized the sport and the players who had names like Babe, Ping, Rube, Wahoo Sam, Mugsy, Chief, Muddy, Kid, Dummy, Hooks, Hod.

In 1900, the National League cut down from a dozen teams to eight: Boston, Brooklyn, Chicago, Cincinnati, New York, Philadelphia, Pittsburgh, and St. Louis. It was a pattern that would remain intact for fifty-three years—those eight teams of the National League whose names virtually every schoolboy was able to recite by heart. That year home plate became a 17-inch, 5-sided figure, replacing the 12-inch square.

On Opening Day of the new century the Philadelphia Phillies defeated the Boston Braves, 19–17, in ten innings, setting a record for most runs scored by two teams on the first day of the season. On October 20, 1900, the Cardinals withheld paying the final month's salary to all but five players, claiming that the team tied for fifth place because of gambling, late hours, and general dissipation.

In ballparks all over the country, Bull Durham signs decorated outfield fences. And those players lucky enough to bat a ball that hit the sign were rewarded with a fifty-dollar check by the tobacco company.

Fields of play were often oddly shaped and erratic. Many times outfield walls were formed by the contours of fans standing shoulder to shoulder. On June 9, 1901, 17,000 fans jammed in to watch a game in Cincinnati. The overflow crowd ringed the outfield and crowded close behind the infield. There were so many ground-rule doubles hit in that game that it was finally declared a forfeit.

Those who were unable to see the games at major league ballparks congregated at the local general stores of small towns and for a dime or fifteen cents listened to an operator recreate the play-by-play that came in on a telegraph wire. Baseball matinees, they were called, and those who listened reacted with cheers and jeers just as if they were at the actual game.

When catcher Roger Bresnahan began the practice of wearing shin guards in the early 1900s, grumblings came from the *New York Sun:* "The latest protection for catchers looks rather clumsy, besides delaying a game while the guards are strapped behind the knee and around the ankle, and it is doubtful if the fad will ever become popular."

In 1903, the American League gained recognition as a major circuit, banding together with the National League and the minor leagues into a framework called "Organized Baseball" under the supervision and jurisdiction of the National Commission. In mid-August of 1903 president Ban Johnson ordered all gambling and betting to cease at American League parks. No one paid any attention to his orders.

With their teams headed towards pennants, Pittsburgh's Barney Dreyfuss and Boston's Henry Killilea agreed to have their teams play a best-of-nine playoff after the season ended for the "Championship of the United States."

> The minimum price of admission shall be 50 cents and the visiting club shall be settled with by being paid 25 cents for every ticket sold.
>
> —World Series contract

The first World Series game was played at Boston's Huntington Street Park on October 1, 1903. The Pirates, who had won their third straight National League pennant and were one of the original franchises dating back to 1876, won the game 7–3, to the dismay of the hometown fans. Boston had entered the American League in 1901. The team was called the Americans, then the Somersets, then the Pilgrims. They became the Red Sox in 1907 because their owner's son John Taylor liked the color of the stockings the players wore. Pirate fans had earthier names for the Boston players who defeated them in the World Series. It was a victory that gave the American League a sense of legitimacy.

Throughout baseball's brief history, umpires had generally used long-handled brooms to dust off home plate and then discarded the brooms. But in 1904, outfielder Jack McCarthy of the Cubs hurt his ankle when he accidentally stepped on a broom trying to score from third base. League officials ordered all umpires to switch to a whisk broom, which they were to keep at the ready in their back pocket. That 1904, season Orator Jim O'Rourke, who had recorded the first hit in National League history, was employed as a catcher by McGraw. At age fifty-two O'Rourke became the oldest man in National League history to get a hit.

There was no World Series in 1904 because John McGraw's New York Giants refused to play against Boston, the American League repeat champion.

JOHN McGRAW: "Why should we play this upstart club or any other American League team for any postseason championship? We are champions of the only real major league."

McGraw's boycott was motivated by his anger at the American League for placing the Highlanders franchise in New York to compete against the Giants for fans. McGraw also harbored hostility towards Ban Johnson for what he called "unjust treatment" during his American League days as a member of the Baltimore Orioles.

By 1905, McGraw's ruffled feelings had been smoothed. The World Series resumed. New York's Christy Mathewson pitched three shutouts against the Philadelphia Athletics, and McGraw's Giants took the title in five games. The Series was an economic shot in the arm for baseball, and an image-enhancing moment for John J. McGraw, the man they called "Mugsy."

Young Joe Jackson, playing in a Textile League game, also had an image-enhancing moment. He was fortunate that a writer from the local newspaper and a scout from the newly formed Greenville Spinners saw it. The hyperbolic newspaper report recalled the moment: "In the final inning with three on and two out Joe cracked the horse hide a swat that carried it into the next township and won the game."

After the game the scout signed Jackson to a $75-a-month contract. Joe Jackson began his professional career, playing under manager Tommy Stouch for the Greenville Spinners in 1908. In his first game, an exhibition contest against the Boston Nationals, he homered, tripled, and doubled. Stouch announced that when the season began, Jackson, the only ex-millhand on a Spinner team composed primarily of middle-class youths from various states, would bat third in the batting order and play center field.

With the beginnings of a career in professional baseball seemingly secured, Joe Jackson and Katie set a marriage date: July 19, an off day for the Spinners.

The 1908 official Opening Day game saw Greenville pitted against the Anderson Electricians. Grandstand seats were 40 cents. Bleachers seats cost two bits. And the left-field foul line was crowded with cars, buggies, and carriages, all at 50 cents per vehicle. Black fans sat in the restricted colored section and cheered on the Spinners, who wore ice-cream-white home uniforms.

It was a wonderful day for the home team—a 14–1 victory. And it was a wonderful day for Joe Jackson—two doubles and a triple and a dazzling, grasping catch that got the fans on their feet. That was how he began in pro ball, a nineteen-year-old in the full bloom of his talent.

As the Carolina season moved into the middle of May, there was little doubt in the minds of all who saw him that Joe Jackson was the most outstanding player in the league. Batting .350, hitting home runs, and making big plays in the field, he was a natural.

Joe was recommended by a writer friend to Joe Cantillon, former manager of the Washington Senators, who came down to check out the phenom. But Cantillon was not impressed.

JOE CANTILLON: "He's simply a bush leaguer flash in the pan and will prove a farce in the big leagues."

But Tommy Stouch knew what he had. As the story goes, he called his friend Connie Mack, owner of the Philadelphia Athletics, and told him about all "this natural talent." Mack dispatched injured A's outfielder Socks Seybold to check out Jackson and his Spinner teammate Hyder Barr in a game the Spinners played against the Charlotte Hornets. A double, a triple, and a home run by Jackson. Seybold was sold.

Another version of the Joe Jackson discovery comes from Connie Mack himself: "An apothecary down in that burg who had previously written me some good tips in regard to young prospects kept urging me to give this fellow a trial. But what intrigues me most was that this prodigy played without shoes. 'He doesn't wear spikes or in fact any kind of covering for his feet,' came the tip. He's so fast that he can tear around those bases without any such help. They call him 'Shoeless Joe.'"

They did call him "Shoeless Joe," and he became a baseball myth, a mix of fact and fantasy.

One oft-repeated account has him playing in the outfield sans shoes amid the debris of stubble, glass, and rocks.

"I'm quittin'," he supposedly told Tommy Stouch.

"Are the rocks and glass cutting your feet?"

"Naw. But they're fuzzin' up the ball and I can't throw it."

Another account comes from Carter "Scoop" Latimer, former sports editor for the *Greenville News*. In Anderson, South Carolina, according to Latimer, Jackson was called in from the outfield to pitch a game. The next day Jackson was back in the outfield nursing a very sore foot. When his time came to bat, he slipped off his shoe and stepped into the batter's box. He then slammed a home run. "As he rounded third base, a fan shouted out 'You shoeless son of a bitch!'" said Latimer. "As a cub reporter free-lancing for a Greenville paper I picked it up and tagged him Shoeless Joe, and the nick-name stuck."

Then there is the October 1949 *Sport* magazine account by Jackson of how he was tagged with the "Shoeless Joe" nickname.

JOE JACKSON: "We had only twelve men on the roster. I was first off a pitcher, but when I wasn't pitching I played in the outfield. I played in a brand new pair of shoes one day and they wore blisters on my feet. The next day we came up short of players, a couple of men hurt and one missing. Tommy Stouch, the manager, told me I'd just have to play, blisters or not.

"I tried it with my old shoes on and just couldn't make it. He told me I'd have to play anyway, so I threw away the shoes and went to the outfield in my stockinged feet. I hadn't put out much until the seventh inning. I hit a long triple and I turned it on. The bleachers were close to the baselines there. As I pulled into third some big guy stood up and hollered.

"'You shoeless sonofagun you!'

"They picked it up and started calling me Shoeless Joe all around the league, and it stuck. I never played the outfield barefoot, and that was the only day I ever played in my stockinged feet, but it stuck with me."

A person who would stick with Joe Jackson through the high moments and the low became his bride on Sunday, the nineteenth of July, 1908; the nineteen-year-old star of the Carolina Association married fifteen-year-old Katherine Wynn. The *Greenville News* reported the event: "Joe Jackson made the greatest home-run of his career on Sunday. The home-run was made on Cupid's diamond and the victory was a fair young lady."

On August 22, the Philadelphia Athletics announced that they had purchased Joe Jackson's contract from the Spinners for $325. He was expected to report to Philadelphia after the Carolina Association season ended.

That same day two of the most exciting major league pennant races in baseball history played out. The New York Giants and the Chicago Cubs went head-to-head in the National League. In Chicago and New York electric bulletin boards with electric diamonds chronicled the race. At the Gotham Theater and at Madison Square Garden in New York City hundreds lined up to watch "Compton's Baseball Bulletin," described in newspapers as "a wonder of its time."

Chicago would win the pennant on the basis of what would forever be known as "the bonehead play"—Giant player Fred Merkle's failure to touch second base on what should have been the game-winning hit. The Giants and the Pirates would tie for second place, a game off the pace. In the American League, Detroit, Cleveland, and Chicago battled through the humid heat of August. The Tigers would win the pennant on the last day of the season with a bare .004 margin of victory over Cleveland.

Those northern cities were lit up by the exciting pennant races, and Greenville was aglow over the batting exploits of its native son. In its first year of operation, its fledgling franchise had produced a batting champion. Joe Jackson had hit for a .346 average to lead the Carolina Association.

His time of celebration was brief, for a couple of days after the season ended, Jackson was a reluctant passenger on a train headed north to Philadelphia to report to the Athletics. Hyder Barr was with him and so was Tommy Stouch, as part guide, part nursemaid, part jailer. Stouch listened patiently as Jackson drawled out his misgivings and uncertainties, his fears about big-city life and city slickers. As the train moved north, Jackson's complaints grew. Three times he managed to slip away from Stouch only to be rounded up and re-routed north.

CONNIE MACK: "He was the town hero on the mill team and thoroughly satisfied with his lot. He was the center of attraction at the village store in the evening and the whole town rang with his exploits. The trouble was that Jackson didn't want to come to the big leagues."

2

Philadelphia

Philadelphia was a new world for Joseph Jefferson Jackson. It was also a new world for thousands upon thousands of immigrants who arrived from southern and eastern Europe. Jews, Russians, Poles, Irish, and Italians, jammed into booming and crowded old cities like Philadelphia. Baseball, a game without a clock, was a way to escape the shrillness of factory whistles and time-clock punching, and immigrants flocked to it as they assimilated into the culture and learned the ceremonies of America.

The new world of major league baseball that Jackson entered was one of the "dead ball," high batting averages, low earned runs averages, big hit totals, and small run totals. Pitchings was dominant.

Prior to 1906, home teams supplied baseballs. Many were frozen, scuffed, or scraped. Numerous complaints resulted in switching the responsibility and control of supplying balls to the umpires. Directed by owners, umpires attempted to ration the use of baseballs to two or three a game. Fans were required to return balls hit into the stands. After just a couple of innings of use the baseballs became softer, sometimes lopsided and speckled with the stains of licorice, dirt, grass, tobacco juice, and any other substances pitchers had the nerve and imagination to apply.

Overmatched as they were against hurlers and oft-invisible trick pitches, batters compensated with nuance and guile.

17

Games were rarely decided on a single swing but on the cumulative efforts of teams working together—the parts creating the whole. Bunting, sacrificing, and placement of the ball were fashioned into art forms by players like Ty Cobb, Nap Lajoie, Willie Keeler, Honus Wagner, and other legends.

Joe Jackson's new world was one where first-class hotels were off limits to ballplayers, where waiters used the code words "baseball steaks" for poor-quality meat, where superstition, cussing, crashing, and crass pranks characterized the behavior of players.

In 1908, as Jackson entered the major leagues, owners had agreed to a new rule change. A batter was credited with a sacrifice fly and not a time at bat if the runner scored on a fly ball that was caught. 1908 was the final major league season of nineteenth-century throwback "Iron Man" Joe McGinnity, who pitched both games of a doubleheader a record five times in his career. A remarkable physical specimen, McGinnity would continue to pitch in the minor leagues and finally end his career at age fifty-four.

For the Athletics of Philadelphia, 1908 was a rebuilding season. The team would play its final season in Columbia Park and wind up in sixth place, twenty-two games behind the pennant-winning Tigers.

The look of the country was flush on the 6'2", 180-pound Jackson, whose coal black hair was parted in the middle and flattened down. He gathered himself together and stepped off the train in Philadelphia along with Hyder Barr. Dizzied by the swirling crowds of people, the fast movement, and the bigness of it all, Jackson and Barr checked their bags at the station and reported to Columbia Park at 29th Street and Columbia Avenue in Brewerytown, the famed beer-producing section of Philadelphia.

Just twenty years old, homesick, and totally out of his element, Jackson was a stark counterpoint to another twenty-year-old baseball player of that time, a pitcher for the Washington Senators named Walter Johnson. On September 7, 1908, Johnson would shut out the New York Highlanders for the third time in a four-game Labor Day series played in New York City.

The enormous press buildup that Jackson had received was something that Philadelphia had not experienced for many years. All around the city baseball fans talked about the new kid from the Carolinas.

Jackson played center field and batted cleanup in the first game he played. Columbia Park seated almost 15,000, but only 3,000 fans were there on August 25, 1908, a dank day. One can only wonder what Joe Jackson thought, being in a major league ballpark for the first time. Did he smell the aroma of barley, hops, and malt that wafted in the air from the breweries located close by the little ballpark as he stepped into the batter's box with two outs and two on base for the first of his 4,981 major league at bats? The crowd rose to cheer him.

In 1908, the rule that banned discoloring of the baseball by rubbing it with soil was in effect. But there was no ban on the spitball, and that was the specialty of Heinie Berger, Cleveland's pitcher that day, who was on the way to a 13–8 record.

Berger looked in for the sign and delivered the ball to Jackson out of an exaggerated windup. Jackson sliced the ball down the right-field line. It went foul. But he measured the next pitch carefully with his eyes and bat and lined the ball to left for the first of his 1,774 hits, and the first of his 785 runs batted in. An over-the-shoulder catch, a throw from the fence in left center field that was nearly 400 feet, and some fine baserunning— Joe Jackson showed off the whole package that August day in Philadelphia.

CONNIE MACK: "If nothing happens to him, he should develop rapidly into one of the greatest players the game has yet produced. But give the boy time to learn and develop and don't expect too much of him from the start. Remember he is only a boy and this is his first year out."

That night, Barr, well known as a ladies' man, took up with a girl. He convinced Jackson to go back to the train station alone to recover both their bags. At the station Jackson heard the announcer call out: "Baltimore, Washington, Richmond, Danville, Greensboro, Charlotte, Spartanburgh, Greenville,

Anderson. . . ." The words sent Jackson to the window, where he purchased a ticket for Greenville. But club officials, already aware of the rookie's previous aborted attempts at flight, felt that Joe Jackson and a railroad station were nothing but trouble. They were right. They rushed down to the depot and were able to round him up just before his train came in.

JOE JACKSON: "It wasn't anything I had against Mr. Mack or the ball club. Mr. Mack was a mighty fine man, and he taught me more baseball than any other manager I had. I just didn't like Philadelphia."

It was not only Philadelphia. It was a lot of the players on the Athletics.

CONNIE MACK: "My other players didn't know what to make of him. He was a regular sphinx, never entered into conversation with anyone."

The Tigers came to Philadelphia for a four-game series. The first two games were rained out. With time on their hands and no games to report on, the Philly writers devoted much space to what they said was going to be a great individual baseball rivalry—the new star in town, Joseph Jackson, and the four-year pro Ty Cobb, who was on his way to winning his second of a dozen American League batting titles.

Some of the Athletics resented the extensive press coverage given to Jackson. Moreover, they were turned off by his dour demeanor and obvious illiteracy. Alternately ignoring and abusing him, they seemed to delight in playing practical jokes at his expense. Perhaps the lowest prank they devised was tricking the young player into drinking from a finger bowl after dinner.

Fed up and feeling foolish and out of place, Jackson once again made his way to the train station. This time he managed to board the train back to Greenville.

CONNIE MACK: "He packed his old fashioned 'war bag' and hit the rattlers for home. I think the big city and the big crowds scared him. I found out later that he was in love with a Greenville belle and couldn't stand for the separation."

Newspaper reports of Jackson's absence attributed it to fear of a head-to-head confrontation with Ty Cobb. His mother denied such reports and claimed he'd returned home to be with his wife, who was ill, and to pay a final visit to an uncle who was not expected to live. "Joe is game and has always been game," the robust matriarch said.

The Athletics and Tigers played two doubleheaders to make up for the earlier rainouts. Cobb managed just one hit in fourteen at bats in those games. Perhaps he had Joe Jackson on his mind. For ten days Joe remained in Greenville. There was no public comment. It seemed that his major league career would be concluded after one game because there was talk in the newspapers that Connie Mack was planning on having him blacklisted from major league baseball if he did not return to Philadelphia.

On September 7 he returned, played in four more games, and fumed in silence all the time at the continuing abuse dumped on him by some of his Philadelphia teammates. Finally, unable to take any more, the humbled and homesick rookie once again hopped a train and returned to South Carolina. Mack suspended him.

In five games Jackson had batted just .177. Joe Cantillon's prophesy that he was just a busher and would prove a farce in the big leagues seemed to be coming true.

The patriarchal Connie Mack offered to get a teacher to work with Joe during the off season so he could learn his ABCs. But Jackson refused. "It don't take no school stuff to help a fella play ball," he said.

Instead, during the off-season he worked in the butcher shop that he had helped his father purchase. The oldest child and the favorite of his mother, he spent a lot of time helping her with the household chores, peeling apples and baking bread.

CONNIE MACK: "I sent Socks Seybold down after him the following spring. It took two days of earnest argument before Socks could induce him to make a try for the big league again."

In the spring of 1909, Jackson wrapped Black Betsy up carefully in a long piece of white cotton cloth and reported to

Atlanta, where the spring training camp of the rebuilding Philadelphia Athletics was located.

The sportswriters around Philadelphia dubbed the bright young players on the Athletics "Yannigans," a term for rookies that had been in use for several years. The group consisted of Joe Jackson, Stuffy McInnis, Amos Strunk, Eddie Collins, Home Run Baker. As the Athletics barnstormed north, it was plain to all that the confident and capable Yannigans, especially Jackson, were much more than a match for the veteran players.

CONNIE MACK: "He made the headlines in Montgomery and New Orleans, but this didn't mean anything to him because praise and censure was all the same to him. He never knew what was in the papers because he couldn't read. At Louisville, he hit a ball over the right-field fence, one of the longest homers ever hit in that neck of the woods. He became an overnight sensation . . . but he did not want to go to Philadelphia. . . . I had him under the escort of the entire team as we headed north."

The train carrying the Athletics stopped at Reading, Pennsylvania. On the opposite railroad siding, more than fifty large milk cans stood in a row all with red destination labels. Jackson stared at the milk cans, transfixed by the sight.

Jackson turned to Mack. "I wish that you'd put a red tag on me and ship me along with the milk cans down south."

"Where would you like to go?"

"Savannah."

On March 28, Connie Mack optioned Joe Jackson to Savannah in the South Atlantic League.

In 1909, the United States was a nation of 90 million people. Electric streetcars, trolleys, had made ballparks much more accessible for fans. Railroad systems linked city to city and made it possible for teams to play opponents over a wider geographical region. On baseball's Opening Day, President William Howard Taft threw out the first ball, beginning what would become an American tradition.

WILLIAM HOWARD TAFT: "The game of baseball is a clean,

straight game and it summons to its presence everybody who enjoys clean straight athletics."

It is ironic that Taft, one of the least athletic presidents of the United States, established this precedent while Theodore Roosevelt, who was one of the most athletic presidents, disdained what would become the American pastime.

ALICE ROOSEVELT LONGWORTH: "Father and all of us regarded baseball as a molly-coddle game. Tennis, football, lacrosse, boxing, polo, yes. They are violent, which appealed to us. But baseball? Father wouldn't watch it, not even at Harvard."

The Athletics in 1909 moved into brand-new Shibe Park at 21st Street and Lehigh, baseball's first steel-and-concrete ballpark. The sod was transplanted from Columbia Park. Named for Athletics majority stockholder Ben Shibe of the baseball manufacturing firm of A.J. Reach, the park would be the home of the Athletics for forty-five years and a lucky charm for Connie Mack, who would win four pennants and three world championships in his first six years there. An almost churchlike French Renaissance dome, where Connie Mack's office was located, topped the exterior roof behind home plate. One especially modern feature was the installation of water plugs in the stands of the single-decked facility. They were there in case of fire and to expedite hosing down and cleaning. Colorful six-foot-tall signs advertised products such as "Regal Shoes" and "White Rock" on the outfield walls. A ladder in front of the left-field scoreboard went all the way to the top. It was 360 feet down the lines, 515 feet to the center-field fence, and almost 400 feet in the power alleys—all custom-ordered by Mack to accommodate the needs of his team. The pitcher's mound was twenty inches high—also especially designed for the Athletics. Later that season, when landlords rented space to fans on the rooftops of buildings adjacent to the ballpark, Connie Mack ordered the stadium wall raised.

Opening Day at Shibe Park was April 12, 1909. Vendors arrived early and sold lemonade, popcorn, peanuts, and A's pennants. A huge crowd of 30,000 came out, mostly men sporting derby hats and wearing suits and ties. There were seats available for only 20,000; the other 10,000 purchased standing-room-only tickets. Most of them congregated in the outfield behind ropes. As late as 1900 some clubs allowed fans to park their automobiles or carriages in the outfield, although the practice had since been discontinued. But there was such a collection of horses and buggies parked outside of Shibe Park for the 3:15 game that the scene resembled a cavalry camp.

Throughout the world of major league baseball there was change that 1909 season. Several new rules were in place. One credited a catcher with a putout on a bunt on a third strike. Another took away credit to a runner for a stolen base on an attempted double steal if either runner was thrown. The New York Highlanders were called "Yankees" by headline writers in newspapers for the first time in 1909. The name would prove popular with fans. It would also be a blessing for layout editors who had struggled for years to squeeze the eleven-letter word "Highlanders" into headlines.

Down in Savannah, Joe Jackson delighted in his new surroundings. He was in his element: down-home cooking, freedom from taunting teammates, enjoying the friendship and encouragement of manager Bobby Gilks. It all proved a tonic for him. Jackson rapped out thirty-six hits in his first eighty at bats for a .450 average.

One moment in that season in the South Atlantic League is part of the stuff that made Joe Jackson a legend. Savannah played Chattanooga. Going into the top of the ninth inning, the Tennessee pitcher, Prince Gaskill, had given up but just one hit and led 1–0. He walked the Savannah leadoff batter in the ninth, and that brought Jackson to the plate. Bobby Gilks walked out from the bench in his civilian clothes and told Jackson, "Swing away. Kill it."

The first pitch came in and Jackson slugged the ball over the right-field fence.

Everything was going well for Jackson, but the same could not be said for Savannah. With the team losing, Gilks paid the price of failure. He was fired.

Although Jackson did not talk about how much he missed Gilks, his body language expressed his feelings. His mopey demeanor and sluggish movements on the field underscored a dropping batting average. When the season finally came to an end, his average had dropped almost a hundred points from his season high. Yet Jackson still managed to wind up batting .354 in 136 games. That made it two minor league seasons for Jackson and two batting titles.

On September 4, 1909, the man the newspapers called "Home Run Joe" and "Stonewall" rejoined the A's. The previous year when Jackson was originally called up by Philadelphia, the team was just playing out the string. This time it was different. The emerging Athletics were in the midst of a tough pennant race in second place behind the Tigers.

CONNIE MACK: "We brought him and his missus up. We tried to teach them our way of doing things, but it still was difficult for them to get adjusted. Our players played pranks on Joe, and he regarded them with suspicion."

Jackson's first major league appearance in 1909 was against New York.

JOE JACKSON: "I hit the first pitch Jack Warhop threw me for a double. I had a single later and had two for three."

The box score of the time does not confirm Jackson's memory. In all, he played in just five games for the 1909 Athletics, managing five hits in seventeen at bats. And then he went back home to South Carolina, fretting about the limited opportunity he had been given.

That year the new National League President was Thomas Lynch. He succeeded Harry Pulliam, who had committed suicide the previous summer. In 1910, the rubber-centered baseball was replaced by one with a cork middle for "occasional" play. Then the ball was given a thinner leather cover and yarn that was more tightly wound and had less protrusion to the seams. All of this made the baseball more resilient than it had been, thus generating more offense, however sparingly.

On April 20, Addie Joss of Cleveland pitched the second no-hitter of his career, beating Chicago 1–0. On May 4, 1910, both the Browns and Cardinals played home games in St. Louis. President Taft, always the polite politician, saw parts of both games at Robison Field and Sportsman's Park and grumbled a bit about the lack of power and slugging exhibited in major league games. The White Sox that season would personify what Taft was talking about, as they posted the lowest team batting average in baseball history. Their seven home runs as a team were also a record low. The other Chicago team, the Cubs, would win their fourth championship in five years, and F.P. Adams in the *New York Mail* would publish his Tinker-to-Evers-to-Chance refrain.

Player salaries averaged about $2,500 by 1910, with some superstars receiving as much as $12,000. At the end of the pay scale, though, were those who made just a thousand dollars a season.

The rebuilt Athletics began their domination of baseball of that time—a string of winning four pennants in five years. They had star pitchers like Jack Coombs, Chief Bender, and Eddie Plank. Their $100,000 infield consisted of Stuffy McInnis at first base, Eddie Collins at second base, Frank "Home Run" Baker at third base, and Jack Barry at shortstop. With players such as these available to Connie Mack, Joe Jackson was the odd man out.

The roster of the Athletics showed Mack's touch in being able to match a player with the right position. It also reflected his preference for college-educated players.

CONNIE MACK: "These boys, who knew their Greek and Latin and their algebra and geometry and trigonometry, put intelligence into the game."

The 1910 Athletics were probably the most highly educated team in history to that point: Eddie Collins of Columbia University, Jack Barry of Holy Cross, Jack Coombs of Colby, and Eddie Plank of Gettysburg. "Connie Mack's college boys," they were called.

The former millhand on the team, the only illiterate, sullen, and out-of-place ballplayer, Jackson posed a problem for Mack. He did not want to trade the young ballplayer, yet he couldn't seem to fit him into the dynasty he was carefully building. So the manager they dubbed the "Grand Old Man," sometimes shortened to GOM, simply assigned Jackson in 1910 to the minors once again—this time to the New Orleans Pelicans of the Southern League.

The Pelicans had a close working relationship with the Cleveland Naps, and played several spring training games against the major league team. Throughout that spring, as Jackson unleashed Black Betsy against the Naps, Cleveland owner Charles Somers looked on in envy. He then made a decision that would affect the direction of young Jackson's life.

The big Opening Day headline in the major leagues was Walter Johnson's shutting down the Athletics on one hit. "The Big Train" was off in high gear. But so was Joe Jackson. There was an electronic scoreboard in the New Orleans ballpark, and it lit up time after time like a pinball machine as it recorded Jackson's batting pyrotechnics. After fifteen games as a member of the Pelicans, he was batting over .500.

New Orleans was a cosmopolitan city with many different nationalities, friendly fans, and supportive media—all of which buttressed Jackson's sense of security and well being. He even developed some enduring friendships with opposing players. One of them was outfielder Joe Phillips of the Mobile Sea Gulls. The proprietor of a vaudeville house in his West Virginia home town during the offseason, Phillips introduced Jackson to the world of show business. The two frequented vaudeville establishments all over New Orleans, and Phillips explained that someday Joe could make good money as a famous baseball star plying his wares on the vaudeville circuit.

When the Southern League season came to a close, a pattern repeated itself for the third straight year. Joe Jackson had amazed everyone with his fielding heroics game after game. He had been selected to another league All Star team. He had batted .354 and won another minor league batting title. And once again, he grudgingly boarded a train for the trip north to a major league team.

Only this time Jackson, along with his wife Katie, was

headed not to Philadelphia but to Cleveland. Connie Mack had traded Jackson to Cleveland for a reported $325 and outfielder Bristol Robotham Lord, better known as Bris Lord, whose nickname was "the Human Eyeball."

CONNIE MACK: "I knew exactly what I was doing. Bristol Lord, of course, helped me at the time. Jackson was a rather difficult man to handle. I knew our players didn't like Jackson, but that isn't why I traded him. I also knew Joe had great possibilities as a hitter. At that time things were going none too well for Charlie Somers in Cleveland, and I was anxious to do him a good turn in appreciation for the way he had helped us out in Philadelphia in the early days of the league. So I let him have Jackson."

3

Cleveland

In mid-September Joe Jackson arrived in Cleveland, a city with a population of almost 600,000, making it the sixth-largest in America. Back in 1890, only about a third of the nation's population lived in a city or town. But driven by the isolation of rural life and the dream of what the city had to offer, more and more people began flocking to urban centers. Immigrants also steamed into metropolitan areas; by 1910, cities accounted for nearly half the nation's population. The growth of the city and the rise of professional baseball were concurrent.

The original 1869 nickname of the Cleveland baseball team was the Forest Citys, because of the city's many trees. Two decades later the name was changed to Spiders. In 1900, the team was called the Cleveland Blues because its players wore bright blue uniforms. By 1903, the nickname once again changed—this time to the Naps, in honor of one of their stars, Larry Napoleon Lajoie.

Lajoie, in 1910, was Cleveland's main man, a thirteen-year American League star. But Ohio newspapers were all agog over the new man who in three years in the minor leagues had won three batting titles. They called him "the Champion Batter of Dixie," the "Southern Star," and the "Carolina Crashsmith."

Joe Jackson reported to manager Deacon McGuire in the home-team clubhouse located beneath the stands on the first-base side of League Park. He was given a loose-fitting white home uniform—with a "C" in blue on the left shirt sleeve and a smaller "C" on the little baseball cap—a pair of blue knee-length heavy woolen socks, and baggy pants that were held up by a black leather belt. Penciled in to bat third in the lineup, Jackson was positioned in center field.

In his first at bat for Cleveland, Jackson crushed the ball—one of his patented, hard, low line drive, "blue darters." The ball shot at the second baseman, who threw up his little glove in self-defense. But the force of the ball ripped the glove off the player and knocked him down.

Newspapers in New Orleans, Savannah, and Greenville kept their readers informed of their local hero's accomplishments:

JACKSON DRIVES BALL TO THE TALL AND UNCUT—LONGEST HIT EVER
RECORDED IN CLEVELAND
GREENVILLE BOY MAKING GOOD

In a game against his former Philadelphia teammates, Jackson put on a show. Eddie Collins, with one out and a runner on third base, hit a deep drive to Jackson. As he gloved the ball, Jackson saw the runner tagging up at third base trying to score. Jackson braced himself and fired the ball home on a line into the catcher's mitt for a double play.

Against Washington on September 17, Jackson came to bat in the eighth inning against right-hander Bob Groom. He got all of the pitch and slugged it to deep center for a home run. It was one of the longest homers hit by anyone that season, and the first of Joe Jackson's 54 major league career home runs.

In twenty games for Cleveland at the tail end of that 1910 season, Joe Jackson batted .387. But one can only wonder what went through his mind as he watched the scrambling intrigue for the batting title play out between teammate Nap Lajoie and Ty Cobb.

It was on April 25, 1901, that Lajoie had played in his first game in the newly formed American League for the Philadelphia Athletics and rapped out three hits on the way to a .422

season batting average and the Triple Crown. Less than a month later, Lajoie came to bat against the White Sox with the bases loaded. He was walked intentionally, in one of the rarest of managerial moves.

Now, with two games left in the 1910 season, Ty Cobb decided to bench himself rather than run the risk of losing the batting title to Lajoie.

The season came down to the last day, October 9. Lajoie needed eight hits to win the batting championship and the Chalmers Award, named for the Chalmers Motor Company. In a doubleheader against St. Louis, he recorded eight hits in eight at bats. Only one of the hits was of the outfield variety—a triple banged over the head of the center fielder. Newspapers called the other seven hits "suspect" bunt singles down the third-base line. They were more than suspect. Red Corriden, the Browns' rookie third baseman, was under explicit orders from his manager, "Peach Pie" Jack O'Connor, to play very deep and encourage the bunt. O'Connor also bribed and bullied the official scorer, offering a forty-dollar new suit of clothes as barter for bunts scored as hits. The scorer followed the suggestion so zealously that he even credited Lajoie with a hit on a play by the St. Louis shortstop that was an obvious throwing error to first base.

The finagling was still not done. Hugh Fullerton was yet to be heard from. "Fair is fair," said the popular and widely respected baseball writer. He announced his reversal of a ruling he had made earlier that season as an official scorer when he had ruled that Ty Cobb had reached base on an error. Now retreating, he said Cobb, after the fact, should be credited with a hit.

When all the fussing and finagling was done, the final averages were Ty Cobb, .3850687; Napoleon Lajoie, .3840947.

A *Chicago Tribune* poem of the time underscored the entire mess and proved to be a harbinger of things to come:

> *When Larry [Lajoie] faced the St. Louis five*
> *He'd eight to go to be secure.*

And what they thought he might require
They slipped it to him, that's pretty sure.

What must a meek outsider think
When tricks like that they put across?
When at one frameup they will wink
How do we know what games they will toss?

The whole episode was investigated by American League president Ban Johnson. Clearing all parties, he decided that Cobb was the batting champion. Then, as balm and whitewash for the whole matter, he exerted his influence and arranged with the Chalmers Motor Company for both Cobb and Lajoie to be awarded brand-new cars.

Despite Ban Johnson's good feelings about the Cobb-Lajoie fiasco, Browns president Hedges did not hedge his. On October 15, just before the World Series between the Chicago Cubs, who had won their fourth National League pennant in five years, and Connie Mack's young Philadelphia Athletics, who had won a league-record 102 games, he fired manager Jack O'Connor for his role in what he termed the "Lajoie travesty."

Lost in the shuffle of what some writers called "the Battle of the Auto Chasers" was the fact that Jackson's batting average was higher than either Cobb's or Lajoie's, higher than anyone's in the American League. Unfortunately, Jackson didn't have nearly enough at bats to qualify for the batting title.

Cleveland owner Charley Somers, along with Ban Johnson and Charles Comiskey, was a key figure in the founding of the American League. Somers developed a fondness for Jackson. He also was very impressed with the young player's accomplishments.

"You're the greatest natural hitter I ever saw," Somers told him. "Some day you're going to be the finest player in all of baseball. But you need more than that. You need an education. Now that the season is over I'll send you to school. It will do a lot for you. Between now and next spring you'll be a different man."

It was the same sort of suggestion proferred by Connie Mack, and Jackson gave the same sort of reply. He agreed with Somers and thanked him for his kind words.

"But I won't be satisfied around a book," Jackson said. "None o' my people ever had schoolin' anyway. I ain't afraid to tell the world that it don't take school stuff to help a fella play ball."

So Jackson returned home to South Carolina after the 1910 season, to the laid-back style of life, to old overalls and home cooking. He ate well but never overate. Throughout his career his playing weight of 186 pounds rarely varied more than a pound.

When neighbors and friends came around to visit with him, they delighted in hearing all the fabulous stories of the big city, the tales of the sounds of the tin lizzies chugging up and down the streets and avenues, the clanging trolleys with their posters featuring baseball personalities like John McGraw, who endorsed Tuxedo tobacco this way: "Tuxedo gives to my pipe smoking a keen enjoyment that I have experienced with no other tobacco."

All of this was fascinating news, but what the neighbors and friends enjoyed hearing about most were the inside stories about their favorite major league players.

Their favorite of favorites, of course, was Joe Jackson. And he brought a flush to the cheeks of many when he told them that after what he had done in 1910, he thought he had a good chance to win the 1911 batting title.

Katie was always there, as childhood sweetheart, wife, contract reader, business manager, and tutor. She spent many hours schooling her husband in signing his paychecks. He painfully practiced copying her writing of his name, but to him it was no more than an abstract design. Now, in the offseason of 1910, she became involved behind the scenes helping her husband in contract negotiations with Somers.

JOE JACKSON: "He wasn't thinking of giving me more than $4,000, and he wouldn't listen to me. But we did some horse trading. I told Mr. Somers that if I hit .400 he should give me the $10,000, and that if I don't you don't give me a cent. We struck a deal."

Spurred by the financial incentive of the "deal," Jackson departed early from his home in Brandon for spring training, which he began with the Pelicans in New Orleans. Newspapers there called him the most popular player in the city's history. Surprisingly, some of the northern newspapers featured negative stories about him. A few claimed that he pulled away from the plate; others revived the old Ty Cobb fiasco from his Philadelphia days and labeled Jackson a coward. Jackson supporters scoffed at these reports. They claimed it was just that newspaper fellows had to find something to write about. Others thought there was a hidden agenda to them—Jackson's illiteracy. Of course Jackson was unable to read any of this, but when Katie and others told him what some reporters had written, he responded, "We'll see about that."

Finishing up with the Pelicans, Jackson joined the Naps in Alexandria, Louisiana, for a continuation of his spring training. When he arrived in camp, he looked very different from the roughly dressed rookie of a year before. Now he sported double-breasted suits and a felt hat of the porkpie style popular at the time. Most writers liked him and his easygoing ways, but there was one journalist who disliked him from the start.

HUGH FULLERTON: "A man who can't read or write simply can't meet the requirements of baseball as it is played today."

On April 12, 1911, President William Howard Taft threw out the first ball at the opening game of the Washington Senators and expressed hopes that the new cork-center baseball to be used in both leagues would stimulate offense. The President got his wish that season as National League offense increased by 500 runs; the American League doubled that figure.

Three days after Taft threw out the first ball, Walter Johnson, signed to a brand-new three-year contract at $7,000 a year, tied a major league record by striking out four batters in the fifth inning as Washington defeated Boston 1–0.

That season E.S. Barnard, the secretary of the Cleveland

team who would go on to be president of the American League, arranged for a sympathetic literate type to room with Joe Jackson. The roommate read letters aloud to him. Sometimes Jackson would pick out one of the letters he had received and make a big deal of reading it silently. Then he would give it to his roommate with the phrase: "Get this, the stuff is rich." The "rich" stuff usually was about the need for new netting wire on the chicken corral on the farm or information that taxes were due on this or that date.

A creature of habit, Jackson was also very superstitious. Black bats and hairpins were two of his fetishes. He would pick up every pin he could find, the rustier the better. There were times his pockets were literally bulging with them. When he got into a batting slump, he would claim the "charm" had worn off, dispose of all his pins, and start his collection again.

The Jacksons rented an apartment on Lexington Avenue close by League Park. Katie would settle in at every home game in her favorite perch, alone in a seat in the last row of the grandstand behind home plate. The Jacksons called it "the hunch," the superstition that her sitting there in that same seat game after game brought her husband good luck out on the playing field. She took her duties as "hunch" guardian, cheerleader, and scorekeeper seriously. However, her best efforts were reserved for the role of the devoted wife.

When the seventh inning came around, no matter the circumstances of the game, Katie left the ballpark and went back to the apartment to begin readying a home-cooked meal for Joe. It was a ritual practiced without interruption. Part of the reason was nutritional, but thrift was also a consideration, for Jackson was never a big spender, especially when he had no reason to be. He made it a practice to sew a $10 or $20 bill in the lining of his coat to be sure he had some cash available when he needed it.

League Park was the home of the Cleveland American League team. Situated at the eastern end of the city at the corner of East 66th Street and Lexington Avenue, it occupied a site selected by Cleveland owner F.D. Robinson. The Payne and Wade streetcars passed close by the main entrance to the park. Thus Robinson, who also owned the streetcar company, delighted in seeing his customers dropped off by one of his business enterprises. He was delighted even more to see them sauntering into the ballpark to patronize another one of his enterprises.

Between the 1909 and 1910 seasons, steel was used to reinforce and enlarge League Park. When Jackson joined Cleveland, the right-field fence had been remodeled with twenty feet of concrete and twenty feet of screen resting on top of that. Batters took aim at the wall just 290 feet from home plate, and there were those who were able to jerk balls over the fence into the street. Some of the baseballs struck nearby buildings, and each season the team was forced to pay out cash to replace at least a score of smashed windows.

For a right fielder playing the wall, it was a game of truth or consequences, an exercise in guessing: would the ball bounce true or in a crazy-quilt pattern off the wall? Would it fall dead to the base of the wall? Would it stick in the screen?

A game in vogue with the youth of Cleveland was "Wall." Using garage doors, brick walls, tin cans—whatever kind of surface they could hit with a ball—the kids would play the game, emulating the efforts of Joe Jackson.

They called him the "outfielding billiardist" because of his unique ability to play fly balls caroming off the right-field wall. He used his powerful arm to hold players to singles on shots that were sure doubles. And, as a hitter, he made his own billiard shots off the oddly constructed walls.

During batting practice, fans would cluster outside the right-field wall. They would wait for Joe Jackson and other outfielders to flip a ball over the fence. Then the scramble would begin. Free admission was given to anyone who brought a retrieved ball into the park. When the game began, a flock of kids and some adults listened for the sound of the bat hitting the ball, the clamor of the crowd, and the sight of the white sphere coming over that right-field fence.

On May 14, more than 15,000 fans came out to see Cleveland play its first Sunday game. They were rewarded as the home team romped 14–3 over New York. Ten days later Nap Lajoie, who was Jackson's best friend on the team, was sidelined by an abdominal ailment. He wound up playing in just ninety games in 1911.

But the man they were calling General Jackson played on, picking up the slack left by Lajoie's absence. In a morning game on the Fourth of July, Jackson came to bat in the sixth inning with one runner on base. The pitcher was Red Nelson of St. Louis. A shot to the outfield, a flubbed shoestring catch, and Jackson recorded his first and only inside-the-park home run.

All over American League ballparks the cries of "Give 'em Black Betsy, Joe. Give 'em Black Betsy!" were heard. And Joe Jackson gave them Black Betsy—in one extended midseason stretch of games he pounded away at a .462 clip.

Such achievement coexisted with ineptitude on major league playing fields that season. Bill Bergen concluded an eleven-year playing career spent with Brooklyn and Cincinnati with a .170 career batting average in 947 games—the lowest ever. With three weeks to go in the 1911 season, the Philadelphia Athletics won eleven of eighteen doubleheaders on their way to a World Series confrontation against the New York Giants, who won the first of three consecutive pennants in 1911.

For a time the great Cy Young was Jackson's teammate that season, but on August 15 he was released and signed by Boston. Young, who had hurled the first perfect game of the twentieth century in 1904 and had 511 career wins, the all-time record, pitched the final game of his career on September 7, 1911. The forty-four-year-old Young lost 1–0 to a rookie named Grover Cleveland Alexander. Young, Alexander, Walter Johnson, Christy Mathewson, Eddie Plank, Kid Nichols—each won more than 300 games in his career.

With just a few weeks left in the 1911 season, Jackson was batting .420, but his Cleveland team had no chance to win the pennant. Somers, who had become one of Jackson's favorite people in baseball, called him in for a talk.

JOE JACKSON: "Mr. Somers called me in to pay off, told me

I could sit it out for the rest of the season. I told him to wait until the season was ended and I wasn't quitting. I wrote my own contract the rest of the time I was in Cleveland."

At season's end Joe Jackson wound up batting .408, with 233 hits, 45 doubles, and 19 triples. Cleveland as a team hit 20 home runs, and Jackson had seven of them. He also had the career rookie year of the century, the only time a rookie ever batted .400.

Yet Jackson's lofty average didn't win him the batting title. Cobb won it using a unique split-hand batting grip that enabled him to move his top hand down if he wanted to pull the ball or push his bottom hand up when he wanted to go to left field. Cobb batted .420 in 1911.

All Jackson could claim was the highest runner-up season batting average of the twentieth century. Cobb, not satisfied with winning the batting title, went out of his way to mythologize the circumstances surrounding the batting race in various articles and in his autobiography. He even tried to change history, claiming that he had trailed Jackson for the batting-title lead. Then, he claimed, with all the resources and cunning at his disposal, cold-shouldering Jackson, taunting him, he was able to pull ahead in the final six games of the season.

JOE JACKSON: "A story that was heard a lot was that Ty Cobb bulldozed me by getting my goat in a conceived plan to ignore me in Cleveland in that important final series. That's just a lot of hooey. Ty was able to beat me out because he got more hits than I did."

The real facts are that after the first month Ty Cobb's batting average in 1911 was never below .400. After 80 games he was batting .450—70 points higher than Jackson. And 130 games into the season Jackson was at .398—18 points behind Cobb.

On October 2, with six games to go in the season, the Tigers and Cleveland met in a three-game series. Both men recorded three hits in the series, but Jackson got his in eight at bats while Cobb had ten official at bats. That tightened up the batting race even more, but Jackson was still about 14 points behind Cobb. In a kind of instant replay of his actions of the previous season against Nap Lajoie, Cobb decided to sit things out. He did not travel with the Tigers to St. Louis for the final three games of the season. His excuse was that for him to pad his batting average against the weak pitching of the lowly Browns was beneath his dignity.

Cleveland took the train to Chicago to finish out the season. Batting against Big Ed Walsh, Joe Jackson stroked three hits and was instrumental in Cleveland's victory, enabling the Naps to clinch third place. He did not play in the final game of the year—a game that had no significance for him or his team. Cleveland had third place; Cobb had another batting title.

TY COBB: "I had to fight all my life to survive. They were all against me . . . but I beat the bastards and left them in the ditch. . . . I was like a steel spring with a growing and dangerous flaw in it. If it is wound too tight or has the slightest weak point, the spring will fly apart and then it is done for."

Except for 1916, when Tris Speaker batted .386, Cobb won the American League batting championship each season from 1907 to 1919.

When Joe Jackson went back home to winter in South Carolina after his rookie season of 1911, he took his beloved bats along. "Bats don't like to freeze no more than me," he said, reflecting the obsessive intimacy with bats that had characterized baseball from the start. Players spent spare hours shaving, honing, heating, fondling, even sleeping with bats. Ty Cobb not only picked the wood for his bats, he also participated in their creation, honing away with a steer bone. Cap Anson allegedly hung bats like hams from the ceiling in the cellar of his house, and there were times the old baseballer had at least 500 pieces of lumber seasoning away. Always on the roam for good wood, Anson would sift through aged logs, shafts from carts, fenceposts, anything he could form into appropriate material for a baseball bat.

One of the more morbid stories about a baseball bat concerned a player named Perring. When the Ohio State Penitentiary was dismantled in 1880, he collected the hickory wood that had formed the prison's scaffolding. Perring fashioned the highly seasoned and strong timber into a bat that lasted nearly two decades.

Joe Jackson had about fifteen or twenty bats, and each one of them had a name. One he called Ol' Ginril, another was Caroliny. But his favorite was Black Betsy, that 48-ounce piece of lumber that he swung as easily as the 32-ounce bats used by some other players.

Jackson claimed that once when he was in a hitting slump, he pushed the end of his bat into some tar. As if by magic, he soon snapped out of his slump. From then on, all the top halves of his bats were black.

It was said that at the beginning of his career a moody and taciturn Jackson communicated more with his bats than he did with people. He would loll about in the dugout with the bat he would use that day, talking to it, telling it what he expected from it, what it had to do.

Sometimes other players were curious about Jackson and his bats. Once a teammate asked:

"Joe, what bats are you working with?"

"Big Jim, mostly."

"That bat's a new one on me."

"He's just a young fella, Big Jim, jes' a busher."

"I guess you're training him."

"Yeah, you're right. He's back in my room talkin' with Black Betsy right now."

The year of 1912 was one of endings and beginnings. The Tinker-Evers-Chance double-play combination played its final game together on April 12. The 1912 season saw brand-new baseball stadiums open—Fenway Park in Boston and Navin Field in Detroit. Both teams had a successful opening day on April 20. The Red Sox defeated the New York Yankees 7–6 in eleven innings, while the Tigers defeated Cleveland 6–5. That season Rube Marquard won a record nineteen straight for the New York Giants and went from "the $11,000 Lemon" to an $11,000 beauty.

On August 11, Joe Jackson became the second American League player to steal home twice in one game. In the first inning he stole home; in the seventh inning he stole second base, third base, and home. But it was the work he did with his bat that had everyone talking.

JACK ONSLOW: "I was a catcher with the Tigers that season of 1912 when Ty and Joe were running neck and neck for the batting championship. Cobb used to bench himself after he made a hit on his first time at bat to preserve his margin over Jackson. One day he told us how to pitch to Jackson and what do you think happened? Joe got three for three and drew closer to the batting lead."

He drew closer but never caught Cobb. Jackson batted .395 and rapped out 26 triples, an American League season record later tied by Sam Crawford. But Cobb hit .410 and again won the batting title. And Jackson gained the distinction of being the only player to bat over .390 for two years in a row yet not win a batting title.

JOE JACKSON: "What a hell of a league this is. I hit .387, .408, and .395 the last three years and I ain't won nothin' yet."

What he did win was the affection of the fans and most of the players on the Naps. As Jackson succeeded more and more on the playing field, his natural reticence began to erode and his sense of humor came to the fore. Those players on Cleveland who were playful or oddballs were enrolled in what was called the "Bug Club." Eddie Plank, Tris Speaker, and "Germany" Schaefer were prominent members. Easygoing Joe Jackson didn't know if it was a compliment or a putdown when he was appointed president.

BOB TARLETON, former baseball general manager: "A year or so after he joined Cleveland he was discouraged—he said they wanted to change his stance. That gave me a chuckle. In the opinion of all of his day, Joe was the most graceful batter in baseball. He stood motionless with both feet together until he was ready to swing. Then he took a stride. Most of the time the ball would be hit as straight as a clothes line."

JOE JACKSON: "I used to draw a line three inches out from the plate, from the front to the back of the plate every time I went to bat. I drew a right-angle line at the end next to the catcher and put my left foot on it exactly three inches from the plate. I kept both feet together and then took a long stride into the ball.

"When I was up there at the plate, my purpose was to get on base any way I could, whether by hitting or by getting hit or by a base on balls. If the hit-and-run was on I'd throw my bat at the ball if necessary to make a connection to keep from messing up a baserunner. I usually made the pitchers bear down and usually they all looked alike to me. I had no special spots where I could hit some pitchers better than others. I was in there swinging and if a pitch looked good enough to hit, I went for the ball, low, high, inside, or out if I had the sign from the manager to hit."

Jack Graney, a teammate of Jackson's in Cleveland who went on to become a popular broadcaster for the team, recalled:

"Jackson never seemed to know whether the pitcher was left-handed or right, or whether he hit a fastball, a curve, a spitter, or any of the trick deliveries. All he'd say, if you asked him, was that the ball was over. 'Over' for Jackson meant anything he could reach."

At bat Jackson was all focus, all business. Rarely did he ever complain about a call from an umpire. There were times, however, when he believed an umpire was mistaken. Then Jackson would simply turn and stare and then go about his business.

On March 4, 1913, the New York Yankees went to Bermuda, becoming the first team to go outside of the United States for spring training. Four days later the Federal League was organized. A six-team structure, the "outlaw loop" was poised to have a tremendous impact on major league baseball in the years ahead.

Baseball boomed that 1913 season; over 300 cities had professional teams. Minor league baseball attendance escalated. There were now forty leagues as opposed to thirteen in 1903.

In 1913, suffragettes attracted headlines marching on Washington. There were over 100,000 "lady typewriters"—

women employed in business offices. Everybody talked about the Gibson Girl: the vision of artist Charles Dana Gibson whose pen-and-ink magazine illustrations symbolized the ideal American girl in fashion and beauty. And at ballparks everywhere, although baseball was still a male-dominated preserve, women were coming out and attending games in larger numbers than ever before.

All over the United States "electrified" scoreboards were mounted outside of newspaper offices, bringing the baseball news to a fact-hungry public. In Times Square in New York City as many as 15,000 assembled at a time to watch the game "play out" on an 18-by-24 board that was suspended from the Times Building. The baseball was a celluloid ball; the players were represented by white lozenges.

Yet baseball in many ways still clung ceremoniously to its nineteenth-century roots. For instance, on June 30 of 1913, the Reds defeated the Cubs 9–6. One baseball was used for the entire game.

That season newspapers all over the country wrote about what Joe Jackson was able to do to a baseball. He led the American League in doubles, hits, and slugging percentage. He led his third-place Cleveland team with a .373 batting average. He finished ahead of all American League batters in hitting except for Ty Cobb. The Georgia Peach recorded a .390 average and another batting championship.

One of Jackson's great accomplishments in 1913 was a home run that he hit on June 4 over the right-field grandstand roof and out of the Polo Grounds. It was the first time anyone had ever done that. Years later, in retirement, Jackson would proudly show off the newspaper clips celebrating that moment—the longest home run ever measured at the Polo Grounds.

JACK GRANEY: "[Russell] Ford broke a low spitter at Jackson, and Joe literally golfed it clear over the top of the upper stand in right center field. It's 400 and something feet to the wall in that part of the Polo Grounds. And remember that the ball was a lump of coal in those days."

BOB TARLETON: "I managed a winter league club in New Orleans that offseason of 1913. We had three great outfielders: Joe Jackson, Detroit's Wahoo Sam Crawford, and Larry Gilbert, Brewer center fielder. We played once a week on Sundays. The clubs split the gate receipts—60 percent for winners and 40 percent for losers. The most Jackson ever collected was $7.20, the least $1.60. We played for fun in those days, not for money. Jackson was a soft-drink salesman on the side."

Working as salesmen on the side, lending their names and image to a product, good, or service—all was part of the scene in baseball right from the start. Tobacco tins like the one that featured Cy Young's likeness proclaimed the wonderful values of imbibing mild Havana tobacco. Tris Speaker and Joe Jackson modeled for ads for Boston Garters priced at 25 and 50 cents. The product was supposed to "hold your sock smooth as your skin." Joe Tinker posed self-consciously in an "Ide Silver" collar ad praising the merits of the product that sold two for 25 cents.

Throughout the era of ragtime, popular songs captured the attention of millions, who played them on pianos or sang them spontaneously at gatherings: "When You Wore a Tulip," "Down Among the Sheltering Palms," "Darktown Strutter's Ball," "I Never Knew I Could Love Anybody," "My Man," "Peg o' My Heart." One of Joe Jackson's favorite songs during his time with Cleveland was "I'm Sorry I Made You Cry." He would come up to the plate smiling, singing the title of the song. He only knew the words of the title; the rest of the song he hummed. Then he would wave his Black Betsy at the pitcher and laugh.

For a while, Jackson teamed up with Napoleon Lajoie, while Ty Cobb and Sam Crawford were a talented tandem for Detroit. Each of the players was something special in his own right. But as one-two batting punches, they rank among the best of all time.

JOE JACKSON: "Lajoie was the greatest hit-and-run batter in history. Batting in front of Nap for five years, I was able to see a master at work hitting behind the runner. And that ball was always hit so hard, it sounded like a bullet whizzing by me."

The Tigers, originally known as the Wolverines because Michigan is the Wolverine State, got their nickname because the black-and-brown stockings they wore reminded Manager George Stallings of tiger stripes. The team also was once known as the Detroit Creams because at one time they had the "cream of California baseball players." Neither Cobb nor Sam Crawford, another Tiger star, hailed from California, but they were the cream of American League baseball players.

Sam Crawford began his major league career with Cincinnati in 1899 and was nicknamed "Wahoo Sam" after his birthplace of Wahoo, Nebraska. While Jackson and Lajoie liked each other, Cobb and Crawford barely tolerated one another. As players, however, they were always in tune.

A familiar scene was Crawford coming to bat with Cobb on third base as the result of a triple or stolen bases. On many occasions Crawford would be walked, and on a signal from Cobb kick it into high gear, round first base, and streak for second while Cobb headed for home.

SAM CRAWFORD: "Sometimes they'd get him. Sometimes they'd get me. And sometimes they wouldn't get either of us."

One of the rare moments of frustration for Cobb and Crawford took place on June 25, 1914. St. Louis catcher Frank Crossin threw out Crawford attempting to steal second base, and the quick return throw to Crossin by Del Pratt nailed Cobb. A double play on an attempted double steal.

A specialty of the left-handed-hitting Crawford was gunning for home runs at League Park in Cleveland. The wire screen over the right-field wall had been placed there to hamper Crawford and others from hitting home runs out onto Lexington Avenue. He looked at the 45-foot barrier as a personal challenge. In the first series he played after the right-field wall had been remodeled at League Park, Crawford homered, placing the ball over the first exit gate.

But there was a Joe Jackson shot that old-timers talked about for years afterwards—a smash over the second exit gate, a distance of 326 feet. The ball left the field finally coming to rest on the other side of the street, a distance of another sixty feet. The 2,606 fans knew the ball was going to be a home run the instant Jackson swung, and if they didn't, a clear signal given by Tiger center fielder Hoffman dispelled any doubts. As the ball jumped off Black Betsy he threw up his hands in disgust.

Line drives against the left-field wall, shots belted to either side of the center fielder, blasts over the right-field wall that roared as they left the park—all were part of the Joe Jackson signature in Cleveland.

Who knows how many home runs Jackson might have recorded had the towering screen not been erected? It was hardly a move aimed against him; it was to please the fans in that era who delighted more in seeing a pitching duel than viewing balls hit out of the park.

While Lajoie and Crawford were mega-stars in their own right, it was the two southerners Jackson and Cobb who shared the American League spotlight. Ty Cobb was the "Georgia Peach" while Joe Jackson was the "Carolina Confection" and the "Candy Kid from Carolina." They were always compared.

"Jackson is Ty Cobb from the neck down," was a phrase always uttered by the Detroit star's supporters.

Manager Joe Birmingham of Cleveland said, "I would not trade Joe Jackson for Ty Cobb. I consider Joe the greater asset to the club of the two."

F.C. Lane, the editor of *Baseball Magazine,* wrote:

Jackson is a better natural hitter by a considerable margin than Cobb who, as everyone knows, beats out many a leading hit. Jackson will be known in after-years as the man who might have been the greatest player the game has ever known. To sum up his talents is merely to describe in another way those qualities which should round out and complete the ideal player. In Jackson, nature has combined the greatest natural gifts any one player has ever possessed, but she denied him the heritage of early advantages and that well balanced judgment so essential to the full development of his extraordinary powers.

Lane's comments were a none-too-thinly disguised reference to Joe Jackson's unpolished behavior and to the fact that he could neither read nor write.

On the road, Jackson would arrive at the hotel dining room for breakfast each morning, engage in an elaborate production of studying the menu with great care, and then in his pleasing Southern drawl say, "I guess I'll have the ham 'n' eggs." At dinnertime he would settle in at a table with a couple of his teammates, wait for them to order, and when hearing something that appealed to him say, "I guess I'll have the same."

Once served, Jackson would go after the food mainly with a knife. He had no need of a fork or spoon. Potatoes, pie, meat, salad—a knife and his fingers were all he used to get at the food. He never spoke when he ate; he would simply hunch over his plate and attack his meal.

For the long train trips, Jackson habitually purchased a lot of magazines. Once comfortably settled in, he would spend much time turning the pages, studying them carefully. Sometimes he would say out loud, "Boy, that was a good story," or, "What a swell idea that was."

A teammate would ask, "What was it all about?"

"Well, it's about a girl," Jackson would respond.

"What kind of girl?"

"Oh, you'll just to have to find out for yourself."

Soon after, he'd hurry off to the smoking car.

His illiteracy was an embarrassment to him and a malicious magnet for opposition fans. One day Jackson hammered out a triple. Standing on third base, he heard the catcalls and the familiar taunts asking him to spell simple words.

"Hey, Professor Jackson," one fan screamed, "can you spell 'cat'?"

Jackson spit out a huge plug of tobacco, stared the fan down, and shouted back, "Hey, big shot, can you spell shit?"

Others taunted him with "Shoeless Joe." He detested the nickname.

JOE WILLIAMS: "As a sportswriter, I knew Jackson, the ballplayer, well. I saw him play in the Southern League, and later as a Cleveland reporter, I traveled with him. He was pure country, a wide-eyed, gullible yokel. It would not have surprised me in those days to learn he had made a down payment on the Brooklyn Bridge."

Ben DeMott, one of the first college players in baseball, played briefly for Cleveland and had a locker right next to Jackson's. He disagreed with the assessment made by Williams.

BEN DeMOTT: "Aside from being a nearly perfect physical machine he had what few of the top-flight performers possessed. As long as I knew him he was never satisfied with his performance, although it seemed ridiculous to the kid who read his letters for him and who was also witness to the most remarkable displays of retentive memory anyone could imagine. Joe was far from stupid. He merely lacked education. I have often wondered if an education would not have taken much from his open-mindedness as well as cluttered up his uncanny memory. He could point to any rule in the book and 'read' it to you, but with enough ad-libbed words to indicate that he was reciting. He could do the same thing with an account of any game that his wife had read to him . . . I marvelled at that."

Wintering in South Carolina that offseason of 1913, Joe Jackson enjoyed the fruits of his growing popularity and business interests. Like other players, he began to engage in a growing and conspicuous consumerism. The automobile became their symbol of opulence; a fancy car was a clear indicator that they had made it. A spate of editorials expressed disapproval. *Baseball Magazine* said:

It is, as a rule, a man's business how he spends his money. But nevertheless we wish to call attention to the fact that many men do so in an unwise manner. A very glaring instance of

this among baseball players is the recent evil tendency to
purchase and maintain automobiles. Put the money away,
boys, where it will be safe. You don't need those
automobiles. The money will look mighty good later on in
life. Think it over boys.

It was not just baseball players who were caught up in the
tin-lizzy automobile craze. More and more, ordinary fans were
driving cars. And many of them drove them to League Park. For
some of those who owned homes close by the ballpark the cars
provided a small source of revenue. Two and three cars could
be parked on a lawn for 25 cents each.

The practice of color-coding tickets began at League Park in
the 1914 season. Box seats were $1.25. Reserved seats were a
dollar. General admission was seventy-five cents. For fifty cents
fans gained admission to the pavilion, the double-decked
grandstand extensions built between the original grandstand
and the foul poles. A season ticket for an eight-seat box cost
$100. Fans coming to the game on weekdays only had access
to the park through the main gate on East 66th Street and
Lexington Avenue. For those times when the park was especially crowded, another gate was made available. Ladies Days
were designated to accommodate and encourage the growing
interest in the sport by women. Anyone who purchased a
grandstand ticket had the opportunity, at no charge, to bring
along a lady.

In 1914, both baseball and United States military might
were showcased for the world. The sixteen battleships of the
United States "Great White Fleet" were sent steaming around
the globe by President Theodore Roosevelt in a show of American power and "big stick" diplomacy.

On July 11, 1914, the Boston Red Sox faced Cleveland at
Fenway Park. A moon-faced rookie named Babe Ruth made his
first major league pitching start. The temperature in Boston
was in the high seventies. Ruth was told not to worry too much
about most of the Cleveland batters but to pay special attention
to their cleanup hitter, Napoleon Lajoie, who crossed his back

leg behind his front leg before he strode into a pitch. The Boston rookie was also told to be mindful of the third batter in the Cleveland lineup: Joe Jackson. Ruth handled Jackson pretty well in their first couple of head-to-head confrontations. Then, in the top of the seventh inning with Boston leading, Jackson came to bat again and ripped into one of the Babe's pitches to send it screaming out on a line. The game was tied 3–3. Ruth exited and was replaced by Dutch Leonard. Boston wound up winning the game 4–3.

The details of that game faded fast from Babe Ruth's memory, but the impression left on him by Joe Jackson lasted a very long time.

BABE RUTH: "I copied Jackson's style because I thought he was the greatest hitter I had ever seen, the greatest natural hitter I ever saw. He's the guy who made me a hitter. I copied his swing. I couldn't copy Ty Cobb's hand action because Ty was looking more for basehits than for power. Jackson stood with his feet fairly wide apart, his right foot shoved forward and the left foot back of the right. This gave him a good turn to start with. I changed this a little. I kept my feet closer together. I could get more leverage that way. But I was more easily caught off-balance by a left-hander. I had more trouble with left-handers than Joe ever had. He never had much trouble with anybody who threw a ball."

The big news in baseball that 1914 season was the play of the "Miracle Braves." In last place on July 19, they came on incredibly to win the National League pennant. But for Cleveland it was the same old story—another losing season. The team lost 102 games and finished dead last, 48½ games behind the pennant-wining Athletics, who won their fourth pennant in five years.

A special moment for Cleveland fans took place on September 27, when Napoleon Lajoie notched his 3,000th career hit in a game against the Yankees. It was a milestone moment in a fabled career winding down. A few months later Lajoie would be gone, picked up on waivers by the Philadelphia Athletics. With Lajoie gone, a local newspaper staged a contest to select a new nickname for the Cleveland team. The winning suggestion was Indians, to honor Cleveland Spider player Louis Francis Sockalexis, who had died in 1913. "The Chief," a Penobscot from Old Town, Maine, performed for Cleveland from 1897 to 1899 and was one of the first Native Americans to play in the majors.

Joe Jackson finished the 1914 season as the only .300 hitter on a team whose collective batting average was .245. His .338 batting average placed him fourth in the league behind Cobb, Eddie Collins, and Tris Speaker. All kinds of aches and pains and injuries that took a little longer to heal nagged at him throughout the season of 1914. And although he was still on the sweet side of thirty, he began to think more and more of life after baseball.

Offseasons once reserved for rest and reverie were now times for moneymaking, to top off the $6,000 or thereabouts of his Cleveland salary. Some of Jackson's funds were invested in business: a poolroom, a farm, a few dollars here and there to back other people's enterprises. He even went on the vaudeville circuit and performed a monologue: "A sob rendition," in the words of a writer of the time, "of his rise in the baseball world . . . from a minor piece in the cotton mill to a major place in the baseball world."

A *Sporting News* item of February 11, 1915, elaborated:

> It used to be the fashion to poke fun at Joe Jackson because he lacks an education, but whether Joseph knows his three Rs or not, he is getting by in this world and after a manner that puts some of his high brow critics to shame. Just now Joe is elevating the stage at a weekly salary that would make many a college professor sigh. He is doing a monologue telling how he plays ball and how he swings on the ball. He made his debut in Atlanta and has been booked for a tour of Southern cities provided he doesn't grow weary of the footlights. One thing Joe tells them is how he turned down $60,000 to play with the Feds for three years.

As the story goes, two agents for the Federal League came to Jackson's Greenville home and offered him a $25,000 cash deal—more than four times his Cleveland salary—to play for their Chicago franchise. They tempted him with promises of luxurious living. Resisting and recoiling at the blandishments, Jackson grabbed his Black Betsy bat and chased the agents away.

JOE JACKSON: "I felt I was duty-bound under contract to stick with Cleveland, and I can truthfully say, in all my playing days there and everywhere, I never shirked a duty to baseball."

Although he was getting worn down by losing, Jackson was comfortable in Cleveland. He and Katie spent many a summer night taking long walks through their residential neighborhood, often being invited in by neighbors for ice tea and rhubarb pie. They felt an affection for the city as well as an affinity for Charles Somers. Jackson especially liked the humane considerations the Cleveland owner exhibited to his players. Whenever the team played against the Senators in a weekend series in Washington where there was no Sunday ball, the Indians would board a train to Cleveland for a Sunday game and go back to Washington on Sunday night.

JOE JACKSON: "There wasn't a time we made that jump that Charlie Somers didn't come down the aisle of the train and give all the players twenty-dollar gold pieces."

Players who made the move to the Federal League received much more than gold pieces. But Jackson's turndown of the Feds further accentuated his farm-boy image. One wit quipped, "The Feds' mistake was in not showing Joe the money in pennies."

The Federal League had more than pennies when it began. Backed by millionaires, it started in 1912 as a minor league (the United States League) but collapsed after five weeks. The following year, with six teams managed by former major league stars, including Cy Young at Cleveland, the league finished a complete schedule of 120 games with teams in Chicago, Cleveland, Covington (Kentucky), Indianapolis, Pittsburgh, and St. Louis. Forty-one games into the season, the Covington franchise switched to Kansas City. In 1914, the Federal League declared itself a major league, added two new teams, and the war was officially on.

Big money men supplied the cash for the Federal League: Robert B. Ward of Brooklyn's Ward banking empire and Tip-Top Bread fortune; Oklahoma oilman Harry Sinclair, later convicted in the Teapot Dome scandal; Charles A Gilmore, wealthy Chicago coal merchant who became president of the Federal League; Philip D.C. Ball, manufacturer of ice machinery in St. Louis; and Otto Stifel, a St. Louis brewer. They along with other wealthy owners enabled their teams to sign up more than eighty major leaguers.

One of the first to jump to the Federal League was Joe Tinker. A shortstop for the Reds in 1913, Tinker wanted a piece of his price of $15,000 when he was sold to Brooklyn. When his demand was denied he jumped, doubling his salary by becoming player-manager of the Chicago Whales. Other stars recruited by the rival league included Eddie Plank, "Three Finger" Brown, Claude Hendrix, Chief Bender, Howie Camnitz, Otto Knabe, Ed Reulbach, Hal Chase, George Mullin, and Jim Delahanty.

The Chicago Whales, who featured outfielder Dutch Zwilling, were one of the more successful teams; they finished in second place in 1914, in first place in 1915, and challenged the major league's pennant winners, only to be rebuffed. Benny Kauff, called "the Ty Cobb of the Federal League," won the batting title both years of the league's existence and was a two-time stolen-base leader. "He has enough money to start a bank," was how his local newspaper in Middletown, Ohio, put it—an allusion to the high salary paid to one of the Federal League's top draws.

The great Walter Johnson was almost a Federal Leaguer, too. Offered a $16,000 salary by the Chicago Whales—$4,000 more than his Washington team was prepared to pay, plus a $10,000 signing bonus—Johnson was set to jump. Senators owner Clark Griffith went to Chicago and spoke with White Sox owner Charles Comiskey. "If Johnson signs with the

Whales," he said, "how would you like to see him pitching on the north side and drawing away all your fans from the south side of Chicago?" Comiskey peeled off $10,000; Walter Johnson remained a Senator. The Federal League offered to double the salaries of Ty Cobb and Sam Crawford if they switched allegiance, but the two Tiger stars declined the lucrative offers.

While the new circuit had some high moments, any real success for the Federal League was doomed from the start. Establishment newspapers condemned it. *The Sporting News* claimed that its players placed "money before honor."

In January of 1915 an antitrust suit filed by what many were calling "the outlaw league" against the major leagues was placed before Judge Kenesaw Mountain Landis's Northern Illinois Federal District Court. In many historical ways the suit set a kind of precedent for the one to be filed seventy years later by the United States Football League against the National Football League.

Since Landis was known as a hardliner against monopolies, Federal League officials and owners thought they would have a responsive ear for their complaint that major league baseball formed a monopoly that controlled the business of interstate baseball.

But strangely, Landis kept procrastinating and delaying his decision. He made a point of declaring how unwilling he was to damage America's national pastime.

JUDGE LANDIS: "Both sides must understand that any blows at the thing called baseball would be regarded by this court as a blow to a national institution."

The Landis delay triggered rising Federal League court costs. The legal footdragging plus dropping attendance sapped the Federal League's treasury. By the end of the first season losses were put at $176,000; the Indianapolis Hoosiers, winners of the 1914 pennant, collapsed.

For 1915, amid much regrouping, there was optimism that the Federal League would make a go of it. The second season began with much fanfare: parades, free tickets, all types of high-powered promotions, more marquee players added to rosters (Chief Bender, who had posted a 17–3 record with the 1914 Philadelphia Athletics, went 4–16 for Baltimore). But the Federal League dream was not to be. Despite teams like Brooklyn opening their gates providing free admission, Federal League baseball couldn't be given away. By the end of the 1915 season, Robert Ward, the league's most powerful supporter, died. The rest of the owners were ready to bail out.

In an out-of-court "peace settlement" on December 22, the major leagues permitted the owners of the Chicago Whales, Charles Weeghman and Harry Sinclair, to purchase controlling interests in the Chicago Cubs. Sinclair was also "paid off" at the rate of $10,000 a year for a decade by the major leagues as balm for the demise of his Federal League holdings. St. Louis businessman Phil Ball was allowed to purchase the St. Louis Browns. Money passed hands as Federal League owners were paid for their players and given hundreds of thousands of dollars for their interests in their franchises. The total settlement paid to the Federal League by the majors was about $5 million. It was truly hush money, enabling major league baseball to skirt the issues of the reserve clause, being a monopoly, and restraint of trade.

Much of the skirting came as a result of Landis's stalling tactics, which went a long way towards enhancing his image with major league owners and put him in their debt. *The Sporting News* ran a two-column photo of the judge captioned, "He's the game's good friend." That was all that had to be said.

Most players went back to their original major league teams. The Giants were able to acquire Benny Kauff, and the Cubs picked up the top Federal League slugger, Dutch Zwilling.

By 1916, the Federal League was a footnote to baseball history, and so were its teams: the Chicago Whales, St. Louis Terriers, Pittsburgh Rebels, Kansas City Packers, Newark Peppers, Buffalo Blues, Brooklyn Tip-Tops, and the Baltimore Terrapins. The league would tarry in memory through a liquor named for it, Federal League Bourbon Whiskey, and a ballpark built for its Chicago franchise: Wrigley Field. And for baseball card collectors, it still survives in two sets of cards issued in 1914 and

1915. These cards were not produced by tobacco companies as was the vogue. Instead they were distributed by Cracker Jacks, an additional wrinkle adding to their uniqueness.

Preseason 1915 gossip about Joe Jackson and his off-the-field activities revealed a different side to his personality. He was so caught up in touring around the south with "Joe Jackson's Baseball Girls," a musical vaudeville farce, that newspapers reported that he was unable and unwilling to report to spring training with Cleveland. It was rumored he was also caught up in an affair with one of his "Girls."

A newspaper reported on April 15, 1915:

> Joe Jackson's admirers have been much put out by that worthy's recent actions. It seems that Joe so misbehaved that his wife threatened to sue for divorce. She sent a deputy sheriff after Joseph, had him brought home and gave him another chance. He has agreed to take it, and the hope is that he will permanently regain his senses. It's the old case of too much prosperity. From a shoeless butcher's boy who didn't know his ABCs to a popular star feted by fans and fawned upon by chorus girls, was too much for Joe's mental makeup and he temporarily lost his balance.

Jackson finally regained his balance and reported very late to spring training with Cleveland. He was soon back in his familiar routine. That spring of 1915 headlines in major league baseball included the Athletics' Herb Pennock coming within one out of an Opening Day no-hitter, the five errors committed by the newly signed Philadelphia baseman, Nap Lajoie, and the first major league home run hit on May 6, 1915, by Red Sox pitcher Babe Ruth in the third inning in a game at the Polo Grounds off New York's Jack Warhop.

As July moved into August, Jackson kept on slashing the ball and making big plays in the outfield for Cleveland, a team whose downward spiral showed no signs of ending. In 1911, the team had finished in third place, 22 games off the pace. The following year it dropped to fifth, 30½ games out. In 1913, it ended up in third place, 9½ games out, and in 1914, it was dead last, a staggering 48½ games out of first. Now in 1915, not only did the Indians have trouble winning games, they faced the problem of drawing fans and paying bills. As one of the weakest teams in the majors, Cleveland was hit especially hard by the challenge of the Federal League.

On August 21, 1915, Charley Somers, desperate to make a move and do something to reverse his negative cash flow, traded Joe Jackson to the Chicago White Sox. In return Cleveland received outfielders Robert "Braggo" Roth and Larry Chappell, pitcher Ed Klepfer, and $31,500. It was one of the highest cash transactions to that time for a major leaguer.

Through years of changing fortune with Cleveland, and through the tenure of five different managers—Deacon McGuire, George Stovall, Harry Davis, Joe Birmingham, and Lee Fohl—Joe Jackson had been the one constant. In 673 games he had batted .374; 400 of his 937 hits were for extra bases. Now he was gone.

Cleveland fans were angry and disappointed. First the legendary Napoleon Lajoie had departed. Now the most popular player on their team, a superstar who was hitting .331, was gone as well.

While gloom pervaded Cleveland, in Chicago there was glee. Charles A. Comiskey bragged that his White Sox "now had the greatest straightaway hitter in all of baseball."

[4]

Chicago

In the 1880s Charles Albert Comiskey, the man they called the Old Roman, was a first baseman-manager who led the St. Louis Browns to four straight pennants in the American Association. When the century turned, Comiskey, a self-made millionaire, returned to his native Chicago and became owner-president of the windy city's American League entry. The Chicago White Stockings, the original name of the franchise, was shortened to White Sox by sportswriters Carl Green and I.E. Sanborn to fit headlines.

In 1901, the White Sox won the American League pennant under Clark Griffith. In 1906, the Sox came up against their crosstown rivals the Chicago Cubs in what was known as the "horseless carriage" World Series. The Cubs under player-manager Frank Chance had won 116 regular-season games, the highest total in baseball history, but they went down to defeat at the hands of the White Sox. In the following seven years, however, the Sox did not win. Defeat prodded Comiskey to make many moves on and off the field in his quest for a championship, hiring and firing five managers in the first eleven years of his team's existence.

On July 1, 1910, the American League Chicago team began play in brand-new White Sox Park, a facility that would last until 1990. The *Reach Baseball Guide* recalled the time: ". . . a gala day in the city of Chicago, and a red-letter day in the eventful life of the white-haired chief of the American League club.

The afternoon witnessed the formal opening and dedication of the White Sox's new ball park, and the evening was devoted to official celebration of the historical event by a great banquet at which a host of notables, including most of the grandees of the baseball world were the guests of Comiskey."

A recordbreaking crowd marveled at the thousands of yards of brilliant bunting that adorned the park for the opening game between the White Sox and the St. Louis Browns. A newspaper of the time called the new stadium ". . . without hesitation and without invidious comparison . . . the finest ball park in the United States."

Located on the south side of Chicago at 35th and Shields and nicknamed the "Baseball Palace of the World," it was a splendid edifice. The steeples of several churches, the facades of brand-new buildings, and the languid leafiness of old trees formed a pleasing backdrop. A symmetrical park with a single-deck grandstand extending from right field to left field, the stadium would be renamed Comiskey Park in 1913 in honor of its powerful owner. The foul lines stretched out 362 feet and the center-field wall was 420 feet away from home plate. The park had been built on the site of a former city dump. Its foul lines were old water hoses that were painted white and flattened out. A green cornerstone was laid on St. Patrick's Day in 1910; it would stay that color until 1960 when Bill Veeck had the entire exterior of the park painted white. Directly east of the stadium stood a small wooden grandstand once used by the Chicago Pirates, the city's entry in the short-lived Players' League, the major league created in 1890 by the Brotherhood of Professional Ball Players. Charles Comiskey had played first base for the Pirates.

Many unusual features were included in the new stadium, which some likened to the ancient Roman Coliseum. Comiskey said the fans were really the ones who built the park, so he had showers installed in the bleachers behind center field to aid them in their efforts to cope with the sweltering Chicago summer. There were picnic areas, including "Bullring" in left and "Bullpen I and II" in right and right-center field. There were

Bavarian and Mexican restaurants and beer halls under the stands behind the plate.

Comiskey showed consideration for the fans by allowing any legitimate Chicago group to use his ballpark for outings, meetings, festivals—free of charge. He extended a lavish hand to the working press, fawning over reporters, cultivating them, providing them with plenty of food and drink at Comiskey Park, and inviting them to his private club in Wisconsin, dubbed Woodland Bards.

On November 13, 1913, the White Sox and Giants began a celebrated world baseball tour that was highlighted by a special exhibition game played before England's King George in London. The teams played fifty-six games in Japan and Egypt, Rome, Sri Lanka, and many other exotic venues. Flushed and buoyed by the receptions he received, Comiskey started making moves to build a White Sox baseball dynasty.

After nearly a month of rumors, on December 8, 1914, the White Sox owner spent $50,000 and obtained second baseman Eddie Collins from the Philadelphia Athletics. Collins was regarded by most experts as the greatest position player of that era. The deal broke up Connie Mack's $100,000 infield. Called "Cocky" because of his confidence, Collins's Ivy League education was a rarity among the players of his time.

With Collins in the fold and signed to a guaranteed five-year contract, Comiskey went about bragging that he was putting together the "best team ever." There would be five new position players on the 1915 team, including promising minor leaguer Happy Felsch, purchased from Milwaukee in the minors. The five would be added to a trio of talented young players—pitcher Red Faber, catcher Ray Schalk, and infielder Buck Weaver.

Nine days after acquiring Collins, Comiskey made more headlines. He reached down to Peoria and hired thirty-three-year-old minor league executive and coach Clarence "Pants" Rowland as White Sox manager. Rowland was young, but so were the Sox.

On August 21, 1915, Joe Jackson became another piece of

the changing team ethos that was the Chicago White Sox, his third major league team in six years. Just about a week before, the White Sox had purchased the contract of minor league pitcher Claude "Lefty" Williams.

The Joe Jackson who joined Chicago was a very different person from the one who had reluctantly reported to the Cleveland American League club more than half a decade before. Although he liked Cleveland as a city and had made many friends there, he had been frustrated by the losing times. He knew the White Sox were loaded with talent and looked forward to the chance to play in a World Series and to garner the fame and financial rewards accompanying that opportunity.

The accents of the South were still with him, and he still looked for rusty pins and stuck them into the back pocket of his uniform pants. He still lavished loving treatment on Black Betsy. He even used his bat to help increase suppleness and strength in his arms and wrists. For more than an hour at a time, Jackson would hold the bat by the handle, his arm outstretched as far as possible. Then he would switch the bat to his other hand and do it all over again. He also kept to his ritual of eye exercises that consisted of his staring with one eye at a lit candle in a dark room until he could barely make out the vision. Then he would go through the same procedure with his other eye. The powerfully built Jackson claimed the procedure not only exercised his eyes but also helped him to pick up a pitched or batted ball better.

In most ways he had stayed the same throughout the years; it was only in his outward appearance that most noticed a change. His teeth had been straightened and cleaned up. For special occasions he now wore thirty-dollar pink silk shirts, and four-dollar Arrow shirts for normal wear. He had a collection of shoes of all types, many of them shiny patent-leather ones. The shoe fetish might have been triggered by self-consciousness over the "Shoeless Joe" label that still clung to him, a label he loathed but could not shed.

That whole time during the 1915 season when the White Sox were at home Jackson did not suit up with the other Chicago players. Instead he came to the park in uniform straight from the hotel where Comiskey had arranged for him to stay.

Jackson found Chicago a lot different from Cleveland. It was a city on the edge, a polygot, ugly, muscular mass of people, places, and plans. Its brick pavements where horse-drawn wagons and cars vied for space symbolized an old century dying and a new one beginning its crest. In Chicago, it all came together: racial tensions, union tensions, the shimmy and the shake, sex and crime and women on the prowl, men and boys looking for trouble, and trouble looking for them. The South Side, where the ballpark of the Chicago American League team was located, was a sprawl of smells, sounds, and sights—a market of goods and services of every kind.

Jackson was pleased to be reunited with Eddie Collins, with whom he had played in Philadelphia. The move elated Collins, always a big booster of Jackson.

EDDIE COLLINS: "I've seen the best players the past twenty years, and no one has been better than Joe Jackson, who instinctively does everything right on the playing field. I can't recall Jackson missing a signal from the bench or coach, when he was at bat or on the bases. And he always threw the ball in from the outfield to the right spot. And how he could throw."

While Collins appreciated Jackson's skills as a player, Jackson was virtually in awe of Collins as player and personality. Always referring to the brilliant second baseman as "Mr. Collins," Jackson was the most attentive listener to the motivational lectures Collins gave on "Inside Baseball."

JOE JACKSON: "Eddie Collins was the smartest man that ever walked on a ball field. He did our thinking for us. He figured out what was going to happen before it happened. Once he told me to play out over on the left-field foul line for Babe Ruth. I asked him why. I could move ten feet, you know, after a ball, and I couldn't figure why. Eddie said Babe was going to hit over third base that day, and he wanted me to be all set. I stood almost on the foul line. Babe hit a smash right into my hands that would have won the ballgame."

With the addition of Collins and Jackson, Comiskey felt he

had a team to bring back the glory days of the White Sox. Comiskey continued to call Jackson "the greatest straightaway hitter in baseball" and bragged to everyone that he was paying him $10,000 a year. Jackson was actually earning $6,000, but what was a $4,000 difference, anyway? The higher figure had a much grander ring.

Comiskey believed in spending money on the working press and on acquiring top talent. But his lavishness ended when it came to paying his players. Those on other teams received four dollars a day for meals; Comiskey, of whom it was said "he threw nickels around for players like they were manhole covers," doled out three dollars a day. He also charged players 50 cents for cleaning their uniforms. Those players who rebelled and played in soiled uniforms had them taken from their lockers and cleaned. For these laundry services Comiskey docked them additional change for each item.

In his first at bat for Chicago at Comiskey Park, in a game against the New York Yankees with a runner at first base, Jackson took a level swing with Black Betsy and rifled a shot against the right-field wall. His personal streak of getting a hit the first time up with every team he ever played for was intact. But despite some heroic moments like this first at bat for Chicago, Jackson hit just .265 for the White Sox in forty-six games and wound up with the lowest season batting average of his career—.308. Difficulty adjusting to new surroundings was part of his personality profile. The schisms and cliques on Chicago also made him feel disoriented.

His high hopes of being in a World Series had not yet been realized, but his new team won 93 games in 1915 and posted a winning percentage of .604—229 points better than Cleveland, who finished in seventh place. The White Sox climbed to third in 1915, a season that saw Ty Cobb steal 96 bases, a record that stood until 1962, when Maury Willis stole 104.

As the 1916 season got under way Jackson was more determined than ever to have a big year. His .308 batting average of the year before was an embarrassment to him. So was an article in *Baseball Magazine* published in March of 1916 entitled

"The Man Who Might Have Been the Greatest Player in the Game."

In the first few games they played that 1916 season, the White Sox showcased the skills and versatility that made it clear that the team was a coming powerhouse. On the first day of the season Jackson gunned down a Red Sox runner at third base with a throw from deep left field. It was a dramatic demonstration of why they referred to his glove as "the place where triples go to die." The throw especially impressed catcher Ray Schalk, who had joined the White Sox in 1912 and was on his way to an eighteen-year Hall of Fame career.

On April 15, Schalk, the man they called "Cracker," impressed Jackson and the rest of the White Sox players. Schalk stole two bases on his way to a season total of thirty, setting a record that would stand for catchers until John Wathan stole thirty-six in 1982. Just 5' 9" and 165 pounds, Schalk was a workhorse behind the plate and one of the reasons the White Sox pitching staff was so successful.

The White Sox faced Cleveland on June 26. Jackson kidded some of his old teammates about the numerals on their uniform sleeves, the first time players ever were identified with numbers corresponding to the scorecard. Then he proceeded to play against some of his old friends with all the verve and vitality he could muster. Playing all out against every team was his way, but the fact that he had been sold by Cleveland gave him additional incentive.

In Chicago, Jackson was a magnet for kids, who flocked around him after a game. They waited for him to emerge from the grounds and fought for the privilege of carrying his bats. Jackson was like a kid himself. His youthful fans would greet him, and he would respond by calling many of them by their names. Sometimes he would stop by a vacant lot near the park, take out a practice ball from his pocket, and toss it to the kids, playing catch with them. Sometimes he would hit a ball far over the railroad tracks. For many days afterward the youth who retrieved the ball would show it off to his friends, a treasured keepsake.

Joe Jackson garnered perhaps the most attention by showing off the throwing power of his arm. Standing with his back to the left-field wall in Comiskey Park, he was able to throw a ball over the grandstand behind home plate. The fans had a name for what Jackson did—"showouts" they were called.

By the time the Fourth of July of 1916 rolled around Jackson was staging a fireworks celebration all his own. Hitting out of that famous pigeon-toed batting stance and going three for five against Philadelphia on Independence Day, he capped an incredible hitting string that saw him rap out 55 hits in 104 at bats in a thirty-game stretch that had begun on May 31. His batting average during that dazzling exhibition of hitting was .524.

Katie, as she had been in Cleveland, was a regular at all the Chicago games and sometimes traveled with the team. With the cliques on the club, it was comforting for Jackson to have her around. Newspapers referred to her as "The White Sox Girl" and the "White Sox Mascot."

On the road Jackson roomed with a fellow southerner, the rookie pitcher Lefty Williams. A part of his milieu and yet apart from it, Joseph Jefferson Jackson attempted to cover up his country ways with city-slicker garb—flashy clothes and always the most expensive shoes. His facade had changed but inside he was still the same. He carried a five-gallon jug of corn liquor with him at all times. And one of his favorite hotel-room activities was getting into bed and eating animal crackers that he washed down with the corn liquor.

JOE WILLIAMS: "In keeping with his growing eminence he demanded and got a drawing room for road trips. He was a drinker but not a heavy one. He carried his own tonic: triple distilled corn. And on occasions he carried a parrot, a multicolored pest who had mastered a few salty dugout phrases. One of these was 'You're out.' Another was 'You're lousy, O'Loughlin.' O'Loughlin was an umpire."

Jackson commented on the parrot: "The kid's got more brains than the old man."

New York, Philadelphia, Washington, Cleveland, Boston, Detroit, and St. Louis—Jackson traveled around the American

League circuit. The brass spitoons in the hotel foyers and lobbies, the beds welded from brass that he slept on—it was all becoming a ceremony to him.

The 1916 Sox were described by *Chicago Tribune* columnist "Si" Sanborn as neither "fish, fowl, nor good red herring." The team had a lot of talent but inconsistent play dogged it all season. Under .500 until the end of June, they reached first place on August 3, stayed there a week and then were overtaken by the Red Sox, powered by the pitching of Babe Ruth, league ERA leader and winner of twenty-three games.

Norman Rockwell did his first *Saturday Evening Post* cover in 1916. It was little noticed compared with all the exciting things happening in baseball. Fans were caught up in the New York Giants' record twenty-six game winning streak from September 7 to September 30 and the last hurrahs of Christy Mathewson and Mordecai "Three Finger" Brown. Both baseball immortals pitched the final game of their careers on September 4—against each other in the second game of a doubleheader in Chicago. Before the game the old adversaries were each presented with a bouquet of American Beauty roses. Mathewson's Cincinnati team outlasted Brown's Chicago club, 10–8.

The once-mighty Philadelphia Athletics lost twenty straight games in one stretch that 1916 season on their way to a last-place finish. The now-mighty White Sox finished in second place, just two games behind Boston. Jackson's hitting heroics were a major reason for his team's excellent season. He had a banner year—third in the league with a batting average of .341, first in total bases and triples, second in slugging percentage and hits, third in doubles, fifth in RBIs.

There was a hunger in Joe Jackson to succeed on the baseball field; there was also a powerful drive in him to acquire and indulge himself in the good things in life. The early years of doing without, the clothing patched and repatched and worn year after year, the grinding sounds of the mill that he sometimes heard in his sleep—all of these had shaped Joe Jackson. Contrary to the "stupid hick" label that he somehow could never shed, he had a lot of business acumen and common sense.

Joe Jackson had become so enmeshed in commercial enterprises that he was virtually a mini-conglomerate. He was the owner of part of a poolroom in Greenville, a farm, and the best house in West Greenville, which he had purchased as a gift for his parents. The poolroom and the farm would fail, but he told people that "you had to lose some to make some."

He owned the "Baseball Girls," which toured the Southern vaudeville loop. He also organized a barnstorming team featuring his five brothers and two first cousins. Money also came in from endorsements like the one that depicted him fashionably dressed behind the wheel of an automobile in a newspaper advertisement with the slogan: "The Oldsmobile Eight for me every time."

When the 1916 season ended, he purchased a house for $10,000 on the Savannah waterfront. From the time Jackson had played in Savannah, he had always harbored an affection for that lovely city. That, coupled with the fact that his sister Lula had married and moved there, clinched his decision to take up residence in Savannah.

There were those who wondered why Jackson did not reside in Chicago year-round and capitalize on his growing popularity there.

JOE JACKSON: "If all my business interests were not down South, I reckon I'd live up here in the north all the time."

His response was diplomatic but evasive. He was a man of the South, comfortable there, accepted there.

Five days before the opening of the 1917 season, the final season of future Hall of Famers Honus Wagner, Eddie Plank, Johnny Evers, and Sam Crawford, the United States declared war on Germany. Hank Gowdy, a catcher for the Boston Braves, was the first major leaguer to enlist in the United States Armed Forces.

War fever was everywhere. It made players like Heinie Zimmerman and Heinie Groh change their first names to Henry. Resolutions were passed by the National and American Leagues mandating an hour a day of military drill for players. Teams balked at the idea but went along; only iconoclastic Brooklyn refused to cooperate. Beginning in spring training and continuing throughout the season, the close-order drills consisted of players—their bats mounted on their shoulders instead of rifles—supervised by Army sergeants. Ban Johnson put up $500 as a prize in a competition for the best-drilled team, which turned out to be the hapless St. Louis Browns.

Spring training sites for most teams were closer to home to economize on railroad travel. As the season moved through its ritual of April, May, June, and summer into fall, games were interrupted for the selling of war bonds and baseball would be exported to Germany, England, Belgium, Italy, France, and even Guam. Each major league team sported on its uniform some type of badge or shield that reflected patriotism; red, white, and blue shields and American flags sewn onto uniform shirt fronts were most common.

A wet and cold spring impacted dramatically on the new season, causing the National League to postpone forty-eight games the first month of the season. American participation in World War I, however, had a more profound effect than the bad weather. The government ordered all horse racing suspended until the end of the war; baseball was allowed to continue. With racetracks closed down, gamblers seeking another outlet to ply their trade turned their attention to the national pastime. The lobbies of hotels where major league teams stayed became conspicuous congregating places for gamblers and their assorted retinue. And they vied with each other for the bragging rights to which games and which players they had been able to fix.

That 1917 season White Sox manager Pants Rowland and owner Charles A. Comiskey bragged about the prospects of their team. The catching position was solid with fiery Ray Schalk, who would catch a major league record four no-hitters in his career. Schalk's career batting average would be only .253, the lowest of any nonpitcher in the Hall of Fame. But he was a player who revolutionized the catcher's position, inno-

vating the now routine procedure of backing up plays behind
first and third to protect against a wild throw.

Swede Risberg and veteran first baseman Charles Arnold
Gandil, better known as "Chick," were newcomers to the 1917
Chicago roster. Acquired from Cleveland for $3,500 on Febru-
ary 25, 1917, Gandil actually was a member of the White Sox
in 1910, but only lasted part of the year and was sold to the
Washington Senators. His circle of friends included Sport
Sullivan, a bookie and gambler with mob connections. Gandil
had run away from home at age seventeen to compete in baseball in the rough towns along the Mexican border. He picked up
$150 a fight by boxing in the local heavyweight division to sup-
plement his baseball wages. He was a big man, 6'2" and a well-
built 200 pounds. Paid just $4,000 in 1917, Gandil and the
truculent Swede Risberg, who earned $2,500 that year, were at
the low end socioeconomically on the Sox.

The rough and rangy man they called "Swede" had a flashy
style, a powerful arm, and a quick temper. In the minors he had
once kayoed an umpire with just one punch after a dispute over
a called third strike. The arrival of Risberg at shortstop for the
White Sox in 1917 allowed Buck Weaver to move back to third
base, his natural position.

Hawk-faced Buck Weaver was born George Daniel Weaver
on August 19, 1890, in Pottstown, Pennsylvania. A switch-
hitter, he was such a nimble fielder that it was said that even Ty
Cobb would not bunt against him. Weaver's hallmarks were his
smiling face and his mincing steps closer and closer to the batter—body language daring the bunt.

Second baseman Eddie Collins may have been the best ever
at his position. In 1917, he was at the midpoint and prime of
his twenty-five-year career in the majors. A left-handed batter,
Collins could bunt, slash away at the ball, or hit and run. It was
his intelligence and poise, however, that set him above virtually
all the players of his time and enabled him to make plays in the
field that many thought were impossible.

Center fielder Happy Felsch possessed almost as much
range as the great Tris Speaker. A native of Milwaukee, Felsch

had a passion for baseball, silly riddles, off-color jokes, and any kind of whiskey. Felsch attracted attention for his range in the outfield and powerful throwing arm. His given names were Oscar Emil, but "Happy" characterized his personality—always smiling and ready for a good time. It was this nature that compelled him to throw in with the more earthy members of the White Sox.

Right field was capably manned by right-handed batting Shano Collins, who was in his seventh season with the White Sox in 1917. A defensive specialist and fine all-around athlete, he hit against left-handed pitching while Nemo Leibold, a southpaw swinger, batted against right-handers. Leibold's given names were Harry Loran. But his small size—5' 7" and 157 pounds—earned him the Nemo nickname that derived from the comic-strip character "Little Nemo."

On the mound, Chicago had three of the best in the game. Catcher Ray Schalk bragged about how much fun it was to catch pitchers Ed Cicotte, Red Faber, and Lefty Williams.

A native of Detroit, Eddie Cicotte began his major league career in 1905 with his home-town team. The following year he moved on to the Red Sox. On July 22, 1912, he was sold to the White Sox. Deception on the mound was his game, as was pinpoint control and the ability to change speeds. The St. Louis Browns saw Cicotte's whole bag of tricks on April 14, 1917, when he no-hit them 11–0.

Spitballer Red Faber was born in Cascade, Iowa, in 1886 and joined the White Sox in 1914. There he would remain for twenty years, winning 254 games and winding up as a member of the Baseball Hall of Fame in 1964.

Claud "Lefty" Williams was born in Aurora, Missouri, but lived in the South. In 1916, his first year with the White Sox, he had won 13 of 20 decisions. He was a moody and inarticulate type.

On the sixth of June this all-star cast moved into first place in the American League standings. They would trade places at the top with the Boston Red Sox through the rest of that month. On June 23, the Red Sox were involved in one of the most unusual games ever played. Ernie Shore of Boston relieved Babe Ruth, who was tossed out of the game after he walked the first batter and got into an argument with umpire Clarence "Brick" Owen. The baserunner was caught stealing, and Shore retired the next twenty-six batters, pitching a perfect game. Shore was one of the most successful pitchers of the era. Like many of his contemporaries, he marveled at Joe Jackson's skill with a bat.

ERNIE SHORE: "Everything he hit was really kissed. He could break bones with his shots. Blindfold me and I could still tell you when Joe Jackson hit the ball. It had a special crack."

JOE WOOD: "You tried your best and hoped it wasn't his day."

CHIEF BENDER: "Pitching to him made me feel like an ass."

ED WALSH: "Jackson hit the ball harder than any man that ever played in the big leagues and I don't mean except Babe Ruth."

Pitchers strained for adjectives to describe what it was like going head to head against Joe Jackson and his Black Betsy. Holding his hands down at the bottom of his bat, the little finger of his right hand curled around the knob, taking a full cut, Jackson rarely struck out. His flawless, whiplash left-handed swing was the envy of all the hitters of his time, including Babe Ruth and Ty Cobb.

TY COBB: "Joe's swing was purely natural, he was the perfect hitter. He batted against spitballs, shineballs, emeryballs and all the other trick deliveries. He never figured anything out or studied anything with the same scientific approach I gave it. He just swung. If he'd ever had any knowledge of batting, his average would have been phenomenal. Chances are Joe could've learned to bunt and beat out slow bounders to the infield because he was fast enough, the same as I did, but he seemed content to just punch the ball, and I can still see those line drives whistling to the far precincts. Joe Jackson hit the ball harder than any man ever to play baseball. What's more, he would have gone down as the greatest batter of all time had he made a study of the scientific side of the batting art."

Cobb's statement was not exactly on target; Jackson did adjust to some pitchers and circumstances when he was up there at the plate. Against the flamethrowing Walter Johnson, Jackson never took a full cut. He moved his bat forward in more of a half-swing, seeking to neutralize the Big Train's fast stuff. It worked. There were some estimates that in his career Jackson batted close to .500 against Johnson.

JOE JACKSON: "No doubt in my mind, Walter Johnson was the fastest pitcher of all time . . . but my career batting average against him was .475. How did I manage to connect against his fastball? Why, I just pecked at him. . . . The only way you could hit him was to poke the ball. I used to wait for his curves. Used to kid him by standing up straight with the bat leaning against my hip. Walter wouldn't hit a batter if he could possibly keep the ball away from him.

"I recall one game that I broke up against Johnson and Washington with a home run. As I jogged around the bases I said to Johnson in all sincerity: 'Tough luck, Walter, I guess it just had to happen.' And the big fellow replied: 'Ain't nothing tough about it. You just know how to hit.'

"Yep, I guess I used to hit Johnson pretty good. . . . But I had to smarten up on him. He's the only pitcher who ever made me choke up on my bat, and I never tried to poke him for anything more than a single."

WALTER JOHNSON: "Jackson didn't seem to have a weakness. I was always glad when he had been disposed of without having him break up the game. . . . He gave me more trouble than anyone else. I always figured I was in a hole whenever Jackson came up there. He was always looking down your throat ready to hit the ball. Cobb made himself a good hitter. Jackson was born a good hitter."

Jackson had some curious encounters against Hubert "Dutch" Leonard, a left-hander who began in the majors with the Red Sox in 1913 and ended his career with the Tigers in 1925. But his opportunities to come up against Leonard were limited. At the start of his career the pitcher was so frustrated pitching to Jackson that he once entered a game declaring that he would knock him down each time he came to bat. In Jackson's first at bat, Leonard fired a pitch that cracked Jackson behind the neck. The next time a Leonard pitch slammed into Jackson's ribs. Coming to bat for the third time in the game, Jackson was hit in the head by a Leonard pitch. The ball caromed off his baseball cap and bounced into the stands. Jackson staggered down to first base.

"I caught that game," recalled Larry Woodall, former Detroit backstop. "Jackson was so innocent and free from guile that he said to Leonard while going down to first: 'I never knew you to be so wild before.' Joe just didn't realize that Dutch was throwing at him."

The wild ones, the wily ones, the control artists, the legends, all were fair game for Joe Jackson and his whiplash swing.

JOE JACKSON: "All the left-handers I ever saw were suckers. I never could understand why left-handed batters complained that they couldn't hit left-handed pitchers. You needed just nerve out there. . . . I used to laugh at the pitchers and it would make them mad. Once Huggins told Waite Hoyt to walk me and I kidded Hoyt. He lost his temper and threw one that just grazed my ankles. I hit it into the stands. I used to get Coveleski crazy. I said 'Just throw that ball anywhere near me, Polack, and they will have to pick it out of your throat!' "

TRIS SPEAKER: "Jackson was not only a natural hitter, but he had a set style, a grooved swing. I can't remember that he was ever in a batting slump. His swing was so perfect there was little chance of it ever getting disorganized. He was the greatest natural hitter who ever lived."

As a fielder, there were also very few better than Jackson. It was said that he could throw a ball 350 feet with speed and accuracy. After catching the third out in left field he would sometimes trot to the wall, turn, and throw the ball over the home-plate backdrop—more than 400 feet.

In 1917, a charity All Star Game in Boston, the Tim Murane benefit exhibition, was staged. The game was preceded by a field meet and a throwing contest.

JOE JACKSON: "I didn't even know I was in it. Cobb and Speaker slipped around and entered me. I was sittin' out by the flagpole and when they called my name, I just picked up a ball and throwed it to home plate and that was the winning throw."

The throw was 396 feet, eight inches. The next-best throw was a tie—Duffy Lewis of Boston and Clarence (Tillie) Walker of the Philadelphia Athletics both reached 384 feet, six inches.

For the effort Jackson received a big silver bowl inscribed "Won by Joe Jackson of the White Sox, the World's Greatest Slugger, for throwing a baseball farther than any of the stars . . ."

JOE JACKSON: "When the All Star Game started, it was a 10-to-1 shot we'd beat 'em to death. I thought we had the prettiest ball club I ever did see stacked together."

The American League outfield was Tris Speaker, Ty Cobb, and Jackson, Stuffy Mcinnis and George Sisler at first base, and Eddie Collins at second. Buck Weaver played third base and Boston's Everett Scott was at shortstop. Walter Johnson was the American League's starting pitcher. But the Nationals, on a double by Rabbit Maranville, won the game.

On August 19, 1917, the first Sunday baseball game was played in the Polo Grounds in New York City. Managers John McGraw of the Giants and his former star pitcher, Christy Mathewson of the Reds, who had never performed on a Sunday when he was an active player, were arrested for violating a New York City law that banned baseball on Sunday.

On September 2 and 3, Chicago won a pair of back-to-back doubleheaders from the Tigers. Later charges would surface that Detroit "lay down" and that a pool was collected among the White Sox players to reward the Tigers for their non-efforts. The charges were never proven. But the twin doubleheader sweep triggered a Chicago breakaway to the pennant. On September 21 in Boston, Red Faber was tabbed to pitch the pennant clincher. He faced Babe Ruth with the bases loaded and got him to hit into a game-ending double play. Faber had his sixteenth win, and the White Sox wound up finishing the season nine games ahead of Boston.

Before a game that September Jackson shared a few quiet moments with an old adversary: thirty-seven-year-old Sam Crawford, in his nineteenth and final major league season. Crawford retired from the majors with a record 312 career triples and 50 inside-the-park home runs. He would play on for a couple of more seasons in the Pacific Coast League.

Nagging injuries that 1917 season saw Jackson bat .301, his career low. But the White Sox won the pennant, recording the best winning percentage in the club's history by winning 100 of the 154 games they played. They were virtually unbeatable at Comiskey Park: 57 wins and just 20 losses gave them a .740 percentage. They led the league in stolen bases, triples, and runs scored. "Pants" Rowland became the first manager with no major league playing experience to win a pennant.

Ambivalent work ethics, factionalism, divided loyalties, cliques, and outright hostility between teammates, characterized some of the major league teams of that time. There were cliques of college players that included Christy Mathewson, Harry Hooper, Eddie Collins, Jack Coombs, Frank Chance, Chief Meyers, Ed Reulbach, Eddie Plank, and Art Devlin. There were factions based on sectionalism—city slickers versus farm boys like Joe Jackson. There were schisms springing from ethnic background. There were problems stemming from disproportionate salaries. Nowhere was this more evident than on the Chicago White Sox.

Debonair Eddie Collins was so disliked by many of the players on the White Sox that none of the other infielders threw the ball to him during warmups; Collins had to settle for Ray Schalk to play catch with. Risberg harbored a special dislike for Collins, begrudging him his high salary, talent, education, good character, and gentlemanliness. Buck Weaver was even more hostile, often criticizing Collins for never sharpening his spikes.

BUCK WEAVER: "He figures they might come back at him and he'd get hurt playing there in the infield. He was a great guy to look out for himself. If there was a tough gent coming down to second, he'd yell for the shortstop to take the ball."

Yet, despite their interpersonal problems, their prejudices against one another, their private vanities and petty jealousies, the 1917 White Sox of Chicago were a solid team, a group of men that played an exciting brand of baseball, a team appreciated by the fans.

Charles A. Comiskey appreciated them, too. Hungering for the first White Sox pennant in the dozen years since the time of the "Hitless Wonders," he had promised all of his players a bonus if they won the flag. And he kept his word. A case of cheap champagne was their bonus.

RING LARDNER: "It tasted like stale piss."

The New York Giants and their feisty manager John J. McGraw were the competition for the White Sox in the World Series. The man they called "Mugsy" had a notorious past. In 1902, McGraw had arrived in New York on July 7. He had been released or relieved—depending on who is telling the story—as manager by the Baltimore Orioles, who owed him $7,000, a loan he had made to cover club debts. McGraw brought along some help with him to the Giants in the battery of "Iron Man" Joe McGinnity and catcher Roger Bresnahan. Stripped of these three and others, the Orioles were unable to field a team for a game against St. Louis on July 17. An infuriated Ban Johnson restocked Baltimore and kept that team and his league alive.

For John McGraw, the World Series against the White Sox was a holy war between the National League and the American League.

Prior to the series Charles Comiskey garnered headlines by announcing that he would donate one percent of Chicago's World Series shares to Clark Griffith's Bat and Ball Fund for American soldiers in France.

During the 1917 season the White Sox had attracted special attention all around the American League when they were on the road. The team had given up its gray road uniforms and worn a kind of reverse pinstripe—white stripes on a dark blue fabric with matching caps. For the World Series Comiskey ordered up a uniform that was even more unique. The Sox wore a specially created spangled red-white-and-blue uniform. Even the white stockings were given red-and-blue designer stripes. "Gaudy" was the word most fans used to describe the uniform that had a one-time use in the 1917 Series and was then retired.

A seven-hitter by Eddie Cicotte, who that season at the age of thirty-three had won twenty-eight games and posted a 1.53 ERA, gave Chicago a 2–1 home victory in Game One on October 6. A home run by Felsch in the fourth inning off Slim Sallee was the game's decisive hit.

In Game Two a five-run fourth inning on six singles gave the Sox a 7–2 win. Red Faber outdueled four New York pitchers to notch the win for Chicago. He also revealed the lack of communication on the White Sox when he attempted to steal third base in the fifth inning. Buck Weaver was on third at the time.

The series shifted to the Polo Grounds for the next two games. Rube Benton became the first left-hander to pitch a World Series shutout, beating Cicotte 2–0 in Game Three. Then Ferdie Schupp, 21–7 during the regular season with a 1.95 ERA, fanned seven and shut out Chicago, 5–0, to tie the series. In that game Benny Kauff smacked two home runs, one an inside-the-park drive to deep center field.

The fifth game back in Chicago saw the teams combine for a total of 26 hits and nine errors as the White Sox won 8–5. The good news for the White Sox in that game was the gutsy relief pitching of Cicotte, who came in for Reb Russell in the first inning and pitched six strong innings, giving up just two runs. Eddie Collins singled in the go-ahead run in a three-run eighth.

Game Six took place in New York on October 15 before 33,969, the biggest crowd of the Series. Red Faber and Rube Benton hurled three scoreless innings each. Then, in the fourth, Eddie Collins wound up on second base after hitting a ground ball to third that Heinie Zimmerman threw past first baseman Walter Holke. Jackson lofted a fly ball to right. The ball was dropped by Dave Robertson. Collins moved to third base. Felsch then tapped one back to Benton. Collins headed home. Benton threw to Zimmerman at third, and Collins kept running. Catcher Rariden came up to help get Collins in the rundown, but he came up too close. Collins spun past him before Zimmerman could throw the ball. All the frustrated Zimmerman could do was chase Collins all the way across home plate. Later, when he was criticized, Zimmerman snapped, "Who the hell was I going to throw the ball to—umpire Bill Klem?" A single by Gandil then scored Jackson and Felsch.

JOE JACKSON: "That game gave me one of my biggest thrills, I guess, in baseball. That was the game when Heinie Zimmerman chased Eddie Collins across the plate with the tying run and then, with me and Felsch on base, Gandil hit for two bases scoring us and we win the ballgame 4–2 and the Series."

The 1917 World Series performance of Joe Jackson was good but not sensational. He collected 7 hits in 23 tries, a .304 clip, scored four runs, drove in two runs, and stole a base.

On October 16, a day after the World Series, in Garden City, Long Island, the Giants and the White Sox met in an exhibition game before 600 soldiers. Chicago won the game, 6–4.

That offseason of 1917 the main news was the death and destruction in Europe, the ravages of World War I. The nation's music reflected the time with such titles as "I Didn't Raise My Son to be a Soldier," "Over There," "Smiles," "Goodbye Broadway, Hello France," and "I'm Always Chasing Rainbows." And so did sporting goods catalogs. The Partridge Company issued a catalog depicting Rube Marquard in Uncle Sam's uniform at bat with the headline: BATTER UP—UNCLE SAM IS AT THE PLATE.

By the end of the Great War 550 men who had or would play major league baseball had served in the Armed Forces. That figure included 124 players from the American League and 103 from the National League. Several, like A.T. Burr and Eddie Grant (who was killed in action in the Argonne Forest) were just a part of the 50,000 American dead and 200,000 wounded.

The Sox began 1918 in a snakebitten mode, and they continued that way. The train carrying the team to spring training derailed near Weatherford, Texas, on March 18. Miraculously no one was injured. A couple of days later Jackson was in a friend's touring car along with Schalk, Cicotte, and Gandil.

They were returning from a golf course. Another car plowed into them. Again, all the players escaped injury. The only problem was whiplash sustained by Cicotte.

CHARLES COMISKEY: "Their place was on the ball field, not out experimenting with golf sticks and looking at scenery."

At first there were fears that the 1918 season would not be allowed to get under way. But a compromise was worked out that cut the schedule to 140 games and mandated that the World Series would start on September 5. Roster player limits were abolished to accommodate losses to the draft. Most teams also cut players' salaries because of what the owners claimed were the demands of war. Connie Mack told his players that they should trust him and take a chance on their salaries. Profit sharing, he called it. "If we make ten thousand," Mack said, "we will gladly share it with them."

The federal government created a special 10 percent entertainment tax on admission that was applicable to any "rented space." Even those who watched games from rooftops adjoining ballparks were not immune from the tax, which impacted on ticket prices at Comiskey Park. In 1918, a bleacher seat was priced at thirty cents, grandstand admission was raised to fifty-five cents, and box seats were $1.10.

The season got under way. Then, on May 23, a government order deemed baseball nonessential to the war effort, and a "work or fight" edict was issued, giving eligible major league draftees the choice of entering the service or working for wartime industries. The New York Giants were hit hard by losses as Kauff, Benton, and Jeff Tesreau were lost to the draft-or-defense work.

Schisms on the White Sox widened. Some players, like Eddie Collins and Red Faber, went off to the Armed Forces. Others, like Lefty Williams, who only pitched in fifteen games for the Sox and Joe Jackson, who played in just seventeen games and was slugging the ball at a .354 pace for the 1918 White Sox, opted for wartime industry. Jackson made his decision after his draft board in Greenville reversed its Class-4 designation and advanced him to Class-1—eligible for military service.

Jackson was, at age thirty, the sole support for his wife Katie, his mother, and a brother. He felt he had been treated unfairly by the political power structure. But he said nothing and just did what many other players did—accepted the choice offered by the government order—employment in wartime industry.

Jackson worked in the shipyards and played in a "patriotic baseball league" for the Harlan and Hollingsworth Shipbuilding Company, a subsidiary of Bethlehem Steel located in Wilmington, Delaware. Players who followed Jackson's course and others who managed to play in the majors while the war raged were scorned as slackers.

Curiously, however, it was Joe Jackson who was most on the cutting edge, the one major leaguer who received the bulk of the bad press. A newspaper account of May 16 reported:

> Either the fighting blood of the Jacksons is not as red
> as it used to be in the days of Old Stonewall and Old
> Hickory or 'General Joe' of the Chicago White Sox
> concluded there was enough of the family in the war
> already . . .with four brothers in service, he has indicated
> that he will flee to the refuge of a shipyard hoping thus to
> escape service. Probably Mrs. Jackson who is the boss of
> the family has had some influences also in her husband's
> determination to take up ship building in preference to
> trench work.

The *New York Herald* reported that he had "conscientious objections to getting hurt in defense of his country and to associating with patriots."

A *Chicago Tribune* editorial particularly took him to task, characterizing Jackson as a person of "unusual physical development, and presumably [he] would make an excellent fighting man, but it appears that Mr. Jackson would prefer not to fight." The diatribe ended with the words: "Good Americans will not be very enthusiastic over seeing him play baseball after the war is over."

Even American League president Ban Johnson got into the act: "I hope that the provost marshall yanks Jackson and these other evaders from the shipyards and the steel works by the coat collar. I hope they are sent to cantonments to prepare for future events on the western front."

Major league club owners were especially piqued by the movement of their players into industrial league baseball. They viewed the moves as a not-too-subtle skirting of the reserve clause, their legal tool that gave them total power over players. Comiskey, one of the owners so angered by the state of affairs, snapped that when the war was concluded there would be "no room for the jumpers" on his team.

CHARLES COMISKEY: "I don't consider them fit to play for my club. I hate to see any players, particularly my own, go to the shipyards to escape service."

In 1918, Mississippi became the last state to pass a compulsory education law. That summer United States soldiers and sailors played exhibition baseball games before King George of Great Britain. The Somme, Armentieres, Trading with the Enemy Act, Doughboys—new terms like these evoked images of war.

Boston manager Jack Barry was drafted, and executive Ed Barrow took over the Red Sox. He decided to have Babe Ruth play the outfield between starts. It was a decision that would have a profound effect on baseball history. The Babe won thirteen games as a pitcher; as a batter he hit .300 and led the league with eleven home runs, the first of his dozen home run titles.

Without Jackson, Faber, Collins, Risberg, Felsch, and Williams, all gone for most of the year in the service or wartime industry, the White Sox hovered around the .500 level until about the middle of June. Then the team fell apart.

The abbreviated baseball schedule created some statistical oddities. Sherry Magee led the National League in RBIs with just 76, and no senior-circuit pitcher worked more than 300 innings. The only bit of normalcy was Ty Cobb's performance. He won another batting title, this time with a .382 average.

The negative publicity about able-bodied athletes avoiding military service and a shortened schedule of 128 games made the 1918 season the biggest financial flop of the ragtime era. The White Sox drew just 195,081 fans, down from 684,521 the year before. Their record dropped to 57–67 from the 100–54 of 1917. They finished in sixth place, seventeen games behind the Boston Red Sox, who faced off on September 5 against the other Chicago team, the Cubs, in the World Series. Ironically, the home park for the postseason event for the Cubs was Comiskey Park. The Cubs abandoned their North Side ballpark and agreed to play at Comiskey Park, a much larger facility, with hopes of bigger gate receipts.

The owners were criticized for even scheduling a World Series in wartime, when so many players had gone off to France. With wartime travel restraints in operation, the World Series had just one scheduled shift for travel after the third game.

With Boston leading in the series three games to one, players feared that they would not receive their World Series shares. The rules of the Series payout had been changed, with payments made instead to the top four finishers in each league. Harry Hooper led a delegation of four players to meet with the National Commission, the ruling body of baseball, before the game the next day. Hooper, the right fielder on Boston's fabled George "Duffy" Lewis-Tris Speaker-Hooper outfield, was one of the more respected players of the era. But even he could not obtain satisfaction from the power structure that the players would be rightfully compensated.

Game Five was about to begin that afternoon in Boston. There was a restlessness in the crowd of nearly 30,000. No players had taken the field. It was the second "strike" in baseball history. The first one was in 1912, a one-game walkout by the Detroit Tigers.

American League President Ban Johnson, a drinking man, was in high spirits when he met with Cubs spokesmen Harry Hooper and Leslie Mann just before the game. Ignoring Mann,

Johnson turned his attention to Hooper. "Harry, do you realize you are a member of one of the greatest organizations in the world, the American League? And do you realize what you will do to its good name if you do not play? Go out there, Harry, the crowd is waiting for you." Then Boston Mayor Fitzgerald also intervened, using the war effort as a goad to convince the men to play.

Taking the field almost an hour late, the Red Sox and Cubs played the game. Boston lost that day but clinched the title a day later on a three-hitter by Carl Mays, his second win of the Series. Babe Ruth posted the other two wins as a pitcher for the Sox.

The expected winner's share of $2,000 became $890 per player, and the loser's expected share of $1,400 was $535. War taxes, it was said, and other deductions were factored in. It was just another case of owners shortchanging players—a practice most of the moguls had a lot of experience in and at which they were quite proficient. And it was said that no one did it better than Charles Albert Comiskey.

5

1919

In 1919, the "war to end all wars" was over. More than 50,000 young American soldiers had died in action and more than 200,000 were wounded. There were new heroes with names like Sergeant Alvin York, Black Jack Pershing, and Captain Eddie Rickenbacker. And a war-weary nation returned to peaceful pursuits.

Grover Cleveland Alexander had come back from France, deaf in one ear because of exposure to severe shelling. In 1919 he would win sixteen games—nine of them shutouts—and lead the National League in ERA. But epilepsy and alcoholism were ready to seize control and haunt him the rest of his days. It was a season when Ty Cobb would bat .384 and win his final batting title, when Babe Ruth would set a new slugging percentage record of .657 and a new home run record with 29, breaking the major league record of 27 set in 1884 by Ned Williamson.

In New York City, Sunday baseball was legalized. National League rosters were cut from twenty-five to twenty-three players. American League rosters were reduced to twenty-one players. Both leagues moved to save money. Owners reduced scheduled games to 140 from the usual 154. Their reasoning was that there would be lessened interest in baseball. But the very opposite was the case, as fans sickened by the war sought escape through baseball.

Many experts felt the White Sox of Chicago were the best

team in baseball, and one of the best of all time. Although the *Chicago Tribune* had picked them to finish third, a sense of high optimism pervaded their ranks as they readied themselves for the long season. The team was essentially the same one that had won it all in 1917.

CHARLES COMISKEY: "It's the best bunch of fighters I ever saw. It's a wonderful combo, the greatest team I ever had."

On the road, the White Sox were an attractive aggregation. They drew the largest crowds in baseball during that era, even larger than McGraw's New York Giants. At home their loyal and knowledgeable fans came out in record numbers to watch them play ball. Even late-summer race riots in Chicago would not diminish the enthusiasm of their supporters.

Charles Comiskey continued to glory in his nickname, "the Noblest Roman of Them All," a reference to his aquiline nose and the public perception of his alleged generosity. In truth, his image and nickname belied reality. He alone decided how much each player on his team was paid. The amount was subject neither to discussion nor appeal. A classic example of Comiskey's niggardliness concerned Hall of Famer Ed Walsh, a forty-game-winner one season. Walsh was rewarded with a salary of $3,200.

The White Sox salaries were among the lowest in the sport. The 1919 White Sox payroll topped out at $85,000. A few years later Babe Ruth would earn that much by himself. Except for Eddie Collins, who earned $15,000—a little more than the combined salaries of Felsch, Gandil, and Jackson—all the White Sox players were grossly underpaid.

Joe Jackson earned only $6,000. Eddie Cicotte, thirty-five, the ace of the pitching staff, a player who was 28–12 in 1917, earned $500 less than Jackson. Perhaps the best pitcher in the league next to Walter Johnson, Cicotte was called the master of the shineball.

EDDIE CICOTTE: "Oh, heck that wasn't any shine-ball. One day in New York the Yankees asked, 'What is that froggie going to throw us today?' And our guys said, 'Wait until you see this one, this shine-ball.' But I didn't put paraffin on it like the newspapers said. I used to rub it on my pants but it was shiny already. I didn't have anything on my pants but sweat. But Ban Johnson, he called me in five times and he said, 'You better cut that out.' I would say, "Cut what out?' He would say, "Never mind what. Just cut it out.' One day in Cleveland when I got through, two detectives grabbed my pants and Johnson sent them to a laboratory looking for paraffin. I pitched with a curve and a riser—I could throw the ball through a curtain ring all afternoon."

Pitcher Lefty Williams was referred to as "the biggest and littlest man in baseball" because he had a burly neck and shoulders but a small body. His salary was just $2,600. Newly acquired pitcher Dickie Kerr, a soft-spoken Texan, earned under $3,000. Swede Risberg, who said he quit school in the third grade in San Francisco because he "refused to shave," was paid $3,250.

Clarence "Pants" Rowland was no longer the manager of the White Sox. The scapegoat for Chicago's failure in 1918, Rowland was fired by Comiskey and replaced by William "Kid" Gleason. A former pitcher and second baseman, the fifty-two-year-old Gleason's nickname derived from his enthusiasm for the game and his small physical stature. He was barely over 5'6".

JOHN McGRAW: "He was, without doubt, the gamest and most spirited ballplayer I ever saw and that doesn't except Ty Cobb. He was a great influence for good on any ball club, making up for his lack of stature by his spirit and fight."

One of Gleason's first managerial decisions was to appoint Eddie Collins team captain. Gleason harbored no special affection for Collins, but he knew that class and intelligence won out in crucial situations on the playing field. Collins would run the team out on the field.

Gleason had been a coach for the White Sox for a half a dozen seasons, and Joe Jackson respected him.

CONNIE MACK: "I guess that Kid Gleason knew how to handle him. The Kid was a rough, tough fellow who would fight his weight in wildcats and a man like Jackson couldn't help but toe the mark when Kid said the word. The Kid thought the world of the big fellow, too."

Spring training in 1919 did not begin until late March. The owners delayed its start as an additional cost-saving device. Joe Jackson had hit very well in the shipyard leagues in 1918 and reported in good condition to spring training. There he used his time wisely to further condition his already lean body. As spring training neared its conclusion Jackson felt fully primed to have a big year. But he was very concerned about the reception he would receive when the season opened. Though there were many ballplayers in the Armed Forces in World War I, lots of them had been placed in Special Services. There they did nothing but play ball, but they escaped the degree of criticism Jackson suffered. Fearing he would be a magnet for abuse and because of the charges of being a slacker, he readied himself for Opening Day of the 1919 season in Chicago.

Jackson was ready for anything, but he was quite unprepared for what happened. When he came to the plate for his first at bat, the game was halted for a moment while a delegation of his most loyal fans presented him with a glistening gold pocket watch. In later years he would carefully finger the watch and remember that moment. All through the game about four hundred fans, "Jackson Rooters" they called themselves, milled about and marched behind a booming big brass band.

Each time Joe Jackson stepped up to the plate, "Give 'em Black Betsy, Joe! Give 'em Black Betsy!" rang out. In the fifth inning a big bedsheet was draped along the railing of the right-field boxes. Printed in big black letters were the words JACKSON ROOTERS.

That season, Joe Jackson honed in on his game and himself. At age thirty, a ten-year veteran, he had already borne his share of ragging—the charges early on that he was a coward, the ribbing about his illiteracy, and the slacker charges that he still heard from time to time. He was content to swing Black Betsy, to hit the blue darters, to keep his batting average well above .300. Of course, he heard his teammates whining and complaining in the clubhouse. He listened to the cursing on the trains. He shied away from it all. There was also the midseason aborted plan for a strike aimed at getting salary increases. He would have no part of that, either.

Through that long season he found serenity in quiet moments with Katie. They had no children and would have none, but they had a good marriage, a strong bond to each other. He would tell her about the common types on the team, the hostility, and the fact that the White Sox were split into factions, in Jackson's words "split up into two gangs."

One side was led by aristocratic Eddie Collins. The other was headed up by coarse Chick Gandil. The Collins faction included Schalk, Shano Collins, Red Faber, Dickie Kerr, and Nemo Leibold. Gandil's group was an aggregation of the less educated, more earthy players: Swede Risberg, Lefty Williams, Buck Weaver, Happy Felsch, Eddie Cicotte, and Fred McMullin, a reserve infielder. Education and geography placed Jackson in this camp. Off the field there was little cooperation or communication between the two camps. Some players didn't talk to others; very few spoke to Gandil or Felsch. Yet, somehow on the field they worked together like a fine-tuned machine.

On May 30, the White Sox were in first place with a four-game lead. But the lead didn't last for long. Through the blazing days of summer they traded places up at the top of the American League with Cleveland and the emerging powerhouse New York Yankees.

On June 14 workhorse Eddie Cicotte defeated the Athletics for the twelfth straight time. On June 23 Happy Felsch tied a record with twelve chances in a nine-inning game. On August 14, his four assists in the outfield would tie another major league record.

Around the circuit through the dog days of summer the White Sox of Chicago played their games. The heart of their batting order—Buck Weaver, third; Joe Jackson, cleanup; and Happy Felsch, fifth—pounded the ball steadily, a nightmare trio for opposing pitchers. But despite the collective skills of the Chicago players, the pennant race was a tough one.

On September 10, the American League's only no-hitter

that season was pitched by Cleveland southpaw Ray Coveleski. He baffled the Yankees, 3–0. Just a couple of weeks before, Coveleski had been struck by lightning and knocked unconscious. There were those who said his no-hitter was charged with high voltage. Coveleski's no-hitter triggered a ten-game Cleveland winning streak. The Indians wound up winning thirteen of their final seventeen games, but their final spurt saw them fall short.

On September 24 a 6–5 Chicago win over St. Louis clinched the pennant for the White Sox. Joe Jackson's ninth-inning blue darter drove in the winning run. The White Sox finished the season 3½ games ahead of Cleveland.

It had been a great season for major league baseball. Overall attendance for 1919 was 6.5 million, up dramatically from the 3 million of the year before. Some teams tripled their attendance figures of 1918, and even the weakest of teams like the Phillies, Cardinals, Braves, and Senators finished in the black.

On paper the White Sox of Chicago were hands down baseball's best team. Their team batting average of .287 and their 668 runs scored were tops in the majors. The siege gun for their attack was Joe Jackson, who missed just one game in 1919 and batted .351, fourth in the league behind Cobb, Bobby Veach, and George Sisler. He was also third in hits and RBIs, fourth in total bases and triples, fifth in slugging percentage, and the club leader in home runs.

The Sox had tremendous defense from catcher Ray Schalk, shortstop Swede Risberg, center fielder Happy Felsch, who led all American League outfielders in assists, second baseman Eddie Collins, who batted .319, and third baseman Buck Weaver. Twenty-nine-year-old Fred McMullin batted .294 and was a valued reserve.

The pitching staff lacked quantity but made up for it in quality starters. Workhorse Eddie Cicotte led the league in wins (29), complete games (30), and innings pitched (307). Control pitcher Lefty Williams posted a 23–11 record and led the American League in games started with 40. Rookie Dickie Kerr won 13 games, and Red Faber won 11 but would see no action in the World Series because of injuries. Comiskey knew his team would need Dickie Kerr at the top of his form in the World Series against Cincinnati.

The Reds were managed by Pat Moran, known affectionately to the Cincinnati fans as "Dot Irisher" and not so affectionately to National League bench jockeys as "Old Whiskey Face." A native of Fitchburg, Massachusetts, Moran had been hired on January 30, 1919, when there was no word about the whereabouts of manager Christy Mathewson, still in France.

The Reds were a solid but not a sensational team. On July 6, they swept a doubleheader from the Pirates and took over first place. They were in and out of the National League's top spot throughout July. In August, they clamped down on their hold on first and finally pulled away from the pack. They wound up winning the National League pennant by nine games. The pennant victory now had fans referring to Moran as "Miracle Man." The one legitimate star on the Reds was center fielder Edd Roush, whose .321 batting average led the National League.

EDD ROUSH: "One of my chores was to milk the cows, which meant getting up before dawn and going out to that cold dark barn. I didn't expect to make it all the way to the big leagues. I just had to get away from those damn cows."

Cincinnati also had Jake Daubert, a solid performer at first base, and third baseman Heinie Groh, who batted .310 in 1919. They had a lot of good pitching: left-handers Slim Sallee (21–7), and Dutch Ruether (19–6), and right-handers Hod Eller (20–9), Jimmy Ring, Ray Fisher, and Havana-born Dolf Luque.

It was with a great sense of anticipation that baseball fans, especially those in the Midwest, looked forward to the 1919 World Series—a matchup of the underdog Cincinnati Reds and the powerful Chicago White Sox.

The ten-cent World Series preview issue of *The Sporting News* featured a team picture of the Reds with a seven-column headline: JOY IF REDS WIN—BUT A SHOCK IF THEY DO. Lesser headlines proclaimed SENTIMENT PICKS MORANMEN, BUT JUDGMENT PICKS SOX. And THOROUGH OPINIONS OF MOST CRITICS IS NOTED

THREAD OF CONVICTION THAT GLEASON HEADS TEAM THAT CARRIES A
CLASS NOT POSSESSED BY NATIONAL LEAGUE RIVAL.

As if knowing that the 1919 World Series would be of special and supreme importance to him, Joe Jackson intensified his
fetish of collecting hairpins. He looked everywhere for them.
He also extended the time he spent sitting alone in a dark room
staring with one eye closed at a lit candle. Not really able to put
how he felt into words, Joe nevertheless sensed there was
something magical and mystical about the process. The one
closed eye, the other open wide and burning into the luminous
light—the ritual was for Jackson not only a means of strength-
ening his vision but a conduit toward better mental focus, a passage for relief from the stress of the moment. He also felt the
eye exercises made his vision keener and were a reason why he
was such a tough strikeout. Jackson struck out just once every
twenty-five at bats throughout his career.

The first two games of the World Series were scheduled for
Cincinnati. Redland Field was the home of the Reds. When it
had been formally dedicated on May 18, 1912, Ban Johnson,
previously a Cincinnati sportswriter, and Charles Comiskey,
who managed the Reds in the 1890s, were present. Now they
were on hand in vastly different roles.

The Cincinnati ballpark, unlike some others, had club-
houses for visiting and home players. That was a relief for the
visiting White Sox who, throughout most of their travels,
steeled themselves for the rides on public transportation while
dressed in full uniform. At least performing at Redland Field
they would not have to worry about how they would dodge
mudballs thrown at them on their way to the park by some of
the more brazen youth.

The park's dimensions were spacious—360 feet down the
lines and 420 feet to dead center field. Single-deck pavilions
stretched along the outfield foul lines. Right field contained a
bleacher section. There was a wooden scoreboard and a primitive public address system created from more than a dozen
loudspeaker horns. A flagpole rose eighty-two feet above the
playing surface, although any ball striking it remained in play.

The Redland Field flagpole was actually the third tallest "in play" structure in baseball history. Only the flagpole in Tiger Stadium in Detroit and the left-field light tower in Grayson Stadium in Savannah were taller. Joe Jackson, interestingly enough, was one of the few players in history able to take aim at all three of them.

A few days before the start of the best-of-nine series the White Sox were a 3–1 betting favorite. To everyone the odds were on target. The American League had won eight of the last nine series; position for position the vaunted White Sox had the edge on the Reds.

But suddenly huge amounts of money began to appear, put up by bettors who favored Cincinnati. Big time New York gambler Arnold Rothstein allegedly was behind a lot of the money swing to the Reds. Actually, it was more than a swing—it was closer to a hurricane.

Sportswriter Hugh Fullerton, who had obtained his first job in journalism through the efforts of Charles Comiskey and was friendly with the Chicago owner, told some of his sportswriter friends, "Every dog in the streets knows it smells. Keep your eyes open. A lot of strange things may happen before this series ends."

A lot of strange things had already happened in baseball throughout its rather brief history. In the National League's initial season of 1876, the Brooklyn Mutuals and the Philadelphia Athletics had dropped out before the season ended. They were unable to make the final western swing because of financial problems. That spared baseball from a lot of messy headlines, because league president Morgan G. Bulkeley was set to expel both teams for throwing a game.

In 1877, four Louisville players sent telegrams to gamblers that contained the code word "SASH," which meant "sure as shit" the fix was on. Those four players were banned for life.

Through baseball pools thousands of dollars changed hands weekly during the ragtime era. A fan could purchase a pool ticket for as little as ten cents and then win by selecting the team that won the most games, scored the most runs, and so on, in a specific week. The managers of the pools had the cooperation of the newspapers, who published the betting line on games and ran weekly statistics on hits, runs, etc. The climate for gambling was always sunny.

At one time there was a ban on any public announcement of who the starting pitchers would be for a given game for fear hurlers would be approached by gamblers. There were instances where outfielders poised to catch a ball would have rocks thrown at them by fans. The rocks were not thrown in anger, but as a distraction to the play by those who had something to gain financially if the catch were not made. More extreme instances also took place. Once a gambler charged onto the field and tackled a player to prevent a play. Another time a sharpshooter with a gun pelted the ground around a player who was chasing down a long line drive.

Players placed bets on themselves and their teams. Even the legendary Walter Johnson and the great Ty Cobb were involved in this practice. Various owners, managers, and players had intimate links with underworld figures. New York Giants manager John J. McGraw spent a lot of his time with gamblers, owned a part interest in two race tracks, and had a passion for playing the horses.

In the first World Series, in 1903, catcher Lou Criger allegedly walked away from a $12,000 bribe. In the second World Series, gamblers offered Rube Waddell $17,000 not to show up. He didn't, but he couldn't, injured as he was from tripping over a suitcase.

In 1908, some highly irate Phillies players threw a gambler down a flight of stairs from the clubhouse at the Polo Grounds. In a series in 1916, the New York Giants reportedly played with little verve to enable the Dodgers to beat out the Phillies for the pennant.

Hal Chase was a skilled first baseman with a great deal of style. Fans loved to see him charge in on the batter, scoop up the ball, and make plays at any base. But those inside the world of baseball spoke about his "corkscrew mind." New York manager George Stallings accused Chase of throwing a game in

1910. Using that "corkscrew mind" to his advantage, Chase survived the charge and even wound up taking Stallings' job. In 1918, then with Cincinnati, Chase was accused in several court affidavits of tampering with games. One affidavit presented by manager Christy Mathewson and owner Garry Hermann of the Cincinnati Reds contained a letter from pitcher Mike Regan. It told of an offer made to him by Chase in Boston in 1918 that carried a $200 price tag. It was tied to Regan pitching to win or lose as Chase instructed. Regan refused the offer. Another affidavit by Reds right fielder Greasy Neale claimed that Chase had bragged that he had won $500 after the Reds were swept in a doubleheader in Philadelphia. Neale also described how Chase told him at another time to bet $200 on the Reds because "this is the day for the Reds to win."

William D. (Pol) Perritt, a pitcher on the New York Giants, swore in an affidavit that Chase approached him before the Giants' final visit to Cincinnati in 1918 and inquired as to which game Perritt was going to work. "You needn't be afraid of me," Chase told Perritt. The pitcher told John McGraw what had happened and the Giants manager said, "The players ought to drive Chase from baseball." McGraw corroborated that conversation in an affidavit, noting that he had observed Perritt engaged in lengthy conversation with Chase.

It was a customary practice during the ragtime era and even before for a contender to offer a suit of clothes as a reward to a pitcher on a non-contending team who defeated a contending team. In 1917 the appreciative White Sox, presented new suits to Detroit players who lost two doubleheaders.

There was a lot of damnable evidence against players and managers throughout the ragtime era. But no action was ever taken in response to any charges of gambling by the National Commission, the ruling body of baseball. A cover-up of all reports was the order of the day.

Despite the fact that baseball, since its inception had been tied to gambling, with constant rumors of fixed games and other irregularities, what Fullerton was intimating seemed pure balderdash. And most of those who heard his remarks dismissed them as the words of an iconoclast, the bluster and boasting of a man who liked to startle others.

A World Series being fixed? How can you fix eighteen men? The World Series was America's premier sporting event, the glamorous, the crowning culmination of a long season. It was ceremony and ritual intertwined—the best versus the best. The World Series being fixed? The thought boggled the imagination, defied the odds, conjured up fantasies. . . .

On the final road trip of the 1919 season, the White Sox were in Boston. Joe Jackson was out enjoying the New England air in Kenmore Square, in the shadow of Fenway Park. Chick Gandil approached him. After a few pleasantries were passed, Gandil snapped out, "Seven of us have gotten together to frame up the World Series. You'll get $10,000 if you help us out."

Jackson was taken aback. But he recovered and said, "No, I want no part of that." Gandil persisted. Jackson turned down the offer again and walked away.

A few days later in Chicago, Gandil again approached him. This time the ante was raised to $20,000. "Joe," Gandil said, "it's going to happen with you or without you. You don't have to do much." Again Jackson refused, but the two offers had upset him. And though he had declined to be part of any plot, he felt a bit like an apple poised to be thrown into a barrel of rotten ones.

JOE JACKSON: "I never said anything about it until the night before the Series started. I went to Mr. Comiskey and begged him to take me out of the lineup. . . . If there was something going on I knew the bench would be the safest place, but he wouldn't listen to me. . . ."

6

World Series

On October 1, 1919, an unseasonably hot fall day, both teams came out under blue skies to take batting practice at oddly shaped Redland Field in Cincinnati. Unbelievably, the betting odds were now even money. Outside the park, scalpers were elated. They were asking for and getting as much as twenty-five dollars a ticket—a previously unheard of price.

Jack Doyle, owner of the Billiard Academy in New York City, a famed betting center of the time, said, "You couldn't miss it . . . The thing had an odor. I saw smart guys take even money on the Sox who should have been asking 5 to 1."

Ed Bang was one of a hundred members of an expanded press corps who covered the World Series.

ED BANG: "I recall vividly the late [sportswriter] Ed P. Strong phoned me at the LaSalle Hotel before the first game and told me he had a great story for me. He couldn't discuss the matter over the phone but came to my hotel room and gave me the information about the scandal. He named eight players and concluded with 'and they are taking poor Joe Jackson for a ride.' In other words Ed conveyed to me the easygoing Jackson didn't know what it was all about. I have always believed that because I never knew Joe to have even an off-color thought . . . of conniving to blacken the name of baseball which had been good to him."

In the stands, vendors were hawking the Cincinnati Golden Jubilee World Series program for twenty-five cents each. The sixteenth World Series was about to begin—the underdog Reds from the Queen City against the high and mighty White Sox from the Windy City.

The high and mighty of baseball were on hand for the annual gathering of the clans. The new owners of the Yankees, Colonel T.L. Huston and Colonel Jake Ruppert, were there; Harry Frazee, Broadway producer and owner of the Red Sox; Branch Rickey, who dreamed big dreams for St. Louis; Yankee manager Miller Huggins; Wilbert Robinson; John J. McGraw; Connie Mack; Clark Griffith; and Detroit manager Hughie Jennings. Tris Speaker, manager of the Indians, headed a Cleveland delegation of more than 500. And George M. Cohan of "Give My Regards to Broadway" fame was on hand, a passionate rooter. Many of the most prominent political figures of the Midwest and South were there, among them half a dozen governors, including James M. Cox of Ohio, honored guest for that first game.

The Reds were dressed in white home uniforms with red trim and piping. Their left sleeve fronts displayed a horseshoe "C" that curled around the words "Reds." Stirrup-type outer red stockings accentuated the team's image. Chicago players were clad in gray pin-striped road uniforms; their stockings were solid white. The left side of their uniform shirt sported a large blue "S." An "O" was inside the top curve of the "S" while an "X" was printed inside the lower curve.

The scheduled pitching matchup was Chicago's Eddie Cicotte against Cincinnati's Walter "Dutch" Ruether, 1919 National League leader in winning percentage with a 19–6 record.

DUTCH RUETHER: "All our players paid strict attention to Joe Jackson in batting practice. Up to that time no batter had ever hit a ball on the fly into the right-field bleachers. Joe poled three halfway into the bleachers."

Every seat in Redland Field was taken, and the overflow crowd congregated behind the temporary stands in front of the bleachers in right and left field. The game was played before 30,511 fans. All across America before radio broadcasts of this and every game of the Series would be followed by crowds of people who stood around for hours near newspaper shops and other stores observing the progress of the action through the movement of little figures on green boards. As far away as Cuba and Canada, each pitch, each ball, each strike, each swing, each run, hit, and error would be re-created by Western Union for waiting millions who paid for the privilege of listening to the recreation in halls and candy stores, in poolrooms and movie theaters.

Baseball writers of the time, covering those games played on grassy fields through languid days, had until three the next morning to file their stories for afternoon editions, plenty of time for full narratives and embellishments.

Up in the press box a who's who of the journalistic fraternity readied themselves: Taylor Spink of *The Sporting News,* Damon Runyon, Ring Lardner, a young Westbrook Pegler, Fred Lieb, and Hugh Fullerton in rimless glasses. Dubbed the game's greatest dopester, Fullerton's track record proved again and again that he was indeed the most accurate forecaster of his day. He had unhesitatingly predicted that the White Sox would easily win the Series.

Seated alongside Fullerton was the great Christy Mathewson, who had thrown his first major league pitch for the New York Giants on the afternoon of July 18, 1900, and had astonished the baseball world in 1905 with three World Series shutouts against Philadelphia. The image of "Matty" in the ragtime years leading the Giants out onto the field from the center field clubhouse at the Polo Grounds had been a familiar one to fans. At the end of the 1918 season Mathewson had enlisted in the Army. In Europe, the pitching immortal had been exposed to mustard gas at Flanders Field. Now returned from the war, Mathewson was at the Series as a correspondent for the Pulitzer chain of newspapers. Throughout the series he would sit close by Fullerton, circling in red questionable plays on a wirebound scorebook about the size of a sketchpad.

The anticipation level picked up in Redland Field as netted ropes were dragged across the diamond by turf levelers. Then the man known as the "March King," John Philip Sousa, stepped up on the band podium and began conducting the National Anthem. Fans, players, and the large press corps snapped to attention.

Game One

The White Sox did not score in the top of the first inning. The Reds came to bat against Eddie Cicotte, still ruffled a bit by an incident he had just experienced: on his way to the park a man on the street had told him that someone was looking for him with a rifle.

Cincinnati's leadoff batter was second baseman Maurice Rath, the same journeyman infielder who was sent along with Jackson in 1910 by Philadelphia to Cleveland for Brisco Lord. Cicotte's first pitch was a letter-high fastball. Rath took it for a strike. The next pitch hit Rath right between the shoulder blades. The plunking of Rath by Cicotte would later be reported as the signal that the Series was fixed. Jake Daubert singled Rath over to third base. Heinie Groh came to the plate with his distinctive bottle-shaped bat, fashioned to allow him to slide his hands upward to bunt or execute the hit and run. Close pitches twice sent Groh bailing out to the dirt. On the next pitch he gripped the bat a little firmer and made contact, slugging the ball to deep left field. Jackson caught up with it, but Rath tagged up and scored.

The game moved to the bottom of the fourth. The score was tied, 1–1. Pitching out of his big windup, Cicotte seemed to have things under control. With two outs and Larry Kopf the runner at second base, it seemed Cicotte might get through the inning. But Greasy Neale singled. Then Ivy Wingo singled. Kopf scored. Dutch Ruether, a notoriously weak-hitting pitcher, came to the plate. He gave a half smile to his teammates leading off second and third. Cicotte's first pitch to Ruether was a ball, low and off the plate. Ruether jumped on the next pitch. The ball headed to the fence in left center field. Neither Jackson nor Felsch could catch up with it. As they chased it down, the roar of the crowd seemed to triple in volume. Neale scored. Wingo scored. Ruether huffed and puffed his way into third base. Three runs for the Reds, and the inning wasn't over yet.

Gleason started up rookie right-hander Roy Wilkinson in the Chicago bullpen. Cicotte fidgeted around on the mound getting set to pitch to Rath. With the count 2–0, Rath ripped the ball past Weaver and down the line for a double. Then Jake Daubert shot the ball through the infield to right field for a single. Five straight hits. Five runs. An infuriated Kid Gleason would not even go out to the mound. He just stood on the baseline. "Cicotte," he screamed, "You're finished!" Wilkinson came in and retired Heinie Groh on a fly ball to center, and the inning was finally finished.

Jackson batted fourth in the Chicago lineup behind Buck Weaver and went 0 for 4. His final at bat of the game in the ninth inning came with the Sox losing, 9–1. He flew out to deep right field.

Greasy Neale, the only man to ever play in a World Series, coach a Rose Bowl football team, and be admitted to the Pro Football Hall of Fame as a coach, ripped out three hits for the Reds in the Series opener. Neale's good hitting never abated; he would bat .357 to lead all Cincinnati hitters in the series. Game One was also a showcase for Cincinnati pitcher Dutch Ruether, who held Chicago to six hits while pounding out two triples.

In the hotel lobbies around the American League, the White Sox of Chicago were often an elegant blur of diamond rings, pearl stickpins, silk shirts, and white cuffs adorned with elegant cufflinks extending two inches out from their expensive suit sleeves. But in the locker room after losing the first game of the World Series, they were anything but elegant. Eddie Cicotte was somber and silent along with the other White Sox. Only catcher Ray Schalk was animated, wondering out loud why Cicotte kept crossing him up on his signals.

Hugh Fullerton went around telling people, "I don't like what I saw out there today. There is something smelly. Cicotte doesn't usually pitch like that."

Cincinnati owner Garry Herrmann was elated over what he

had seen. Filled with pride after the game, he presided over a lavish party at the exclusive Peruvian Club. Each guest was presented with a barrel of pickels to be taken home as a gift.

The page-one story the next day in *The New York Times* read:

> The fondest dreams of Cincinnati's overjoyed baseball fans came true this afternoon when the Reds put the White Sox to rout. . . . Never before in the history of America's biggest baseball spectacle has a pennant-winning club received such a disastrous drubbing in an opening game as the far-famed White Sox got this afternoon. . . . The heralded White Sox looked like bush leaguers.

The banner headline in *The Chicago Daily Tribune* on Thursday, October 2, read WHITE SOX LOSE IN OPENER, 9–1. Three front-page stories headlined: ALL CINCINNATI HAILS RUETHER, MORAN'S BIG GUNS WHO CRIPPLED CICOTTE, ACE OF THE SOX HURLING CORPS, and REDS DRIVE CICOTTE TO DUGOUT; RUETHER HOLDS FOE HELPLESS."

The White Sox had problems; however, the multitude that attended the Series had problems of its own. Cincinnati was a city where no hotel rooms could be had. Thousands were put up in private homes, with some even sleeping in Turkish baths.

A *New York Times* article reported:

> The great crowds surged through the lobbies, and into the public parlors. Head waiters at the various hotel cafes were at their wits' ends when 9 o'clock arrived and the last of the diners had departed. Never were they faced with such a serious problem. . . . Hundreds of guests swarmed into the hotel dining rooms and demanded service. With every table filled and hundreds clamoring for entrance to the cafes, the head waiters' dilemma was complete. But the crowd was in a holiday mood and joked about the delay, despite the fact that everyone was hungry, after early luncheons.

Westbrook Pegler was one of the members of the press corps providing extensive coverage of the Series. He, along with the visiting White Sox and most of those covering the Series, was quartered at the Hotel Sinton, the best hotel in Cincinnati. Pegler reported that he "never saw as much loose money in a crap game. For three nights running they shot for hundred-dollar bills and they had sheaves of them."

With gamblers brazenly strutting their stuff, the rumors of a fixed Series were now intensifying. They reached Kid Gleason in the form of telegrams from concerned White Sox fans from several different states. Something crooked, the telegrams claimed, was going on in the World Series.

Gleason had been around baseball for a long time. He was fond of telling people that he had seen everything. Fixing a World Series, he thought, was an impossibility. The White Sox manager knew that too many players would have to cooperate for games to be dumped. But he was getting a bit suspicious.

Late that night after the first game, he met with Comiskey in his room in the Hotel Sinton, showed him the telegrams, and told his employer how he felt. Comiskey was noncommittal. He thanked Gleason for the information and said he would follow up. Then, though the hour was late, Comiskey went to John A. Heydler's room. Heydler in 1918 had succeeded John K. Tener as National League President. Comiskey told Heydler what Gleason had said.

JOHN A. HEYDLER: "You're wrought up too much, Commy. You're just being a bum loser. Your team was too confident and the Reds rushed them off their feet. They were taken unawares. You can't fix a World Series."

Some might have called Comiskey's heart-to-heart chat with Heydler "sleeping with the enemy," inasmuch as he was the president of the other league. But Comiskey had no alternative. He had not been on speaking terms with American League president Byron Bancroft "Ban" Johnson since 1917.

JOE JACKSON: "Mr. Comiskey had caught two big trout and they were such beauties he sent them to Mr. Johnson. He packed the fish in ice and expressed them, but by the time the fish got to Chicago the ice had melted and the fish had spoiled. They smelled awful."

Johnson always thought that Comiskey had insulted him, and that was why the two never spoke again and why the Chicago owner approached Heydler.

But now the two of them were outside Johnson's suite. It was about three A.M. The rooms and lobbies of the Hotel Sinton and Congress Hotel in Chicago that night and throughout the series resembled Hamlet's Elsinore Castle. There was much excitement and intrigue, secret meetings, loose women, and even looser men.

Upset and ruffled after being awakened by the knocking on his door, the heavyset Johnson was taken aback by the sight of Heydler and Comiskey on his doorstep. When Heydler explained their mission, an irritated Johnson snapped, "What he [Comiskey] says is like the crying of a whipped cur." And he closed the door.

Game Two

There were 29,698 in the stands on October 2, another warm day of what was being called the "first vestless series." The Reds were now favored by oddsmakers at 7–10. Lefty Williams was matched up for the White Sox against Cincinnati's thirty-five-year-old Harry "Slim" Sallee. It was the same Sallee who had lost two games to the White Sox in the 1917 World Series when he was a member of the New York Giants. "Watch Williams closely," Kid Gleason told Ray Schalk. The little catcher watched.

Black Betsy was smoking for Jackson in the second game. He led off the second inning and lined a double to center field, the first of his three hits in the game. Sacrificed to third by Felsch, he was stranded there as Gandil grounded out to short and Risberg flew out to right field.

Schalk kept watching Williams, who breezed through three innings. Then in the bottom of the fourth inning he walked Rath. Daubert sacrificed him to second. Groh walked. The noise level at Redland Field was picking up. Edd Roush singled to center, scoring Rath. Then Roush took off for second base. All the pent-up frustration in Schalk went into a powerful throw that gunned down the Cincinnati center fielder. Then Williams walked Duncan, his third free pass of the inning. Die-hard Chicago fans could never remember seeing the southpaw that wild. Williams had walked just 58 batters in 297 innings during the regular season. Larry Kopf, the Cincinnati shortstop and the sixth man in the batting order, came up to hit. He smashed a two-run triple. That was all the hitting and scoring the Reds needed. They won the game 4–2.

In the locker room, sweaty and disgusted, Schalk's fury was up a few notches after Chicago's second straight loss. "Three fucking times, three times," he told Kid Gleason, "Williams shook off my signals for curve balls."

Gleason tried to placate Schalk. It was baseball, he said, things like that could happen. But the little catcher would not agree. Then Gleason noticed a smug Gandil sitting around smiling.

"You sure had a good day today," Gleason snapped sarcastically.

"So did you, Kid!" was Gandil's wisecrack reply.

The comment so enraged Gleason that he rushed Gandil. It took the efforts of two players to pry his hands loose from Gandil's throat.

A shower and a change of clothes did not do much to soothe Ray Schalk's seething anger. His juices were flowing as he waited for Williams under the grandstand. When Williams came out, Schalk jumped the pitcher and pummeled him repeatedly with both fists until he, like Gleason, was pulled away by a couple of the other players.

Despite all the talk that was being bandied about of fixed games, there were still many who were not surprised that Cincinnati had won the first two games. Ruether and Sallee had won forty games between them during the regular season.

The Series shifted to Chicago for the third, fourth, and fifth games. A contingent of New York City sportswriters plus Col. T.L. Huston, half-owner of the Yankees, and John Orr, a stockholder in the Reds, were quartered in a private railroad car all during the Series. Their talk centered on the home-field advantage, the differences between the two leagues, and how gamblers played around with odds for their own special reasons.

One who shied away from most of that talk was thirty-four-year-old sportswriter Ring Lardner, a Chicagoan. He was also a fan of the White Sox. Two of his favorites on the team were Eddie Cicotte and Joe Jackson. Through the years Lardner had spent a lot of time on the road reading Katie Jackson's letters to her husband. He had also enjoyed drinking away the hours with Cicotte. After Game One was concluded, Lardner had a private chat with Cicotte and asked whether there was any truth to all the rumors going around.

"Bullshit," Cicotte said. "That's all it is."

Saying it was "bullshit," Lardner knew, did not make it so. Although he never put his fears into writing, Lardner was uncomfortable and agitated about the atmosphere that surrounded Cicotte, Jackson, the other White Sox players, and the Series. In the railroad car of the sleeper that carried players and press to Chicago for Game Three, he had more than his fill of alcohol. And then he lurched about singing, humming and, whistling a parody of "I'm Forever Blowing Bubbles":

> *I'm forever throwing ball games,*
> *Pretty ball games in the air.*
> *I come from Chi*
> *I hardly try*
> *Just to go to bat and fade and die:*
> *Fortune's coming my way:*
> *That's why I don't care.*
> *I'm forever blowing ball games,*
> *. And the gamblers treat us fair.*

Once again Joseph Jefferson Jackson was part and apart from the scene as the White Sox and Reds, the press contingent, fans, gamblers, and assorted hangers-on made the all-night trek from Cincinnati to Chicago. For Joe Jackson the clickety-clack of train wheels, the hooting whistles in the night, the taste of whiskey and Pullman food, the smell of cigarette and cigar smoke, the sound of dirty jokes, laughter, confessions, the feel of rumpled clothes, the packing and unpacking and packing again—this had all long ago become ritual. Joe Jackson was a much different person after a decade in the majors with three different teams than when he made that first train ride up north to Philadelphia from Greenville. He had already played in one World Series, but this one was far different. The 1917 competition was between two major cities. This one was, he thought, the small guy, Cincinnati, against the giant, Chicago. The White Sox fans adored and loved their team, knew their baseball, were used to winning teams. From what he had seen of the Cincinnati fans, baseball to them was merely a carnival.

Special trains transported rabid Cincinnati rooters into Chicago. They turned it into their own personal parade grounds, singing and shouting all over the length and breadth of Michigan Boulevard. Thousands camped out all night, waiting outside festively decorated Comiskey Park to buy bleacher seats. By midmorning there were more than five thousand there.

And vivid red was everywhere—red dresses, shirts, flags, pennants, banners. The vast Congress Hotel in Chicago was swept up in a sea of red. Reds fans by the thousands were there, and ready.

Game Three

On October 3, rookie southpaw "Wee Dickie" Kerr took the mound for the White Sox in Comiskey Park before 29,126, most of whom were there to cheer on the team in white. They were ready with streamers of blue and white, noisemakers to accentuate the moment, and sweaters and coats to stave off the cutting edge of the chill that blew in off the lake.

Joe Jackson led off the second inning singling to left field. A hurried throw to second by Reds pitcher Ray Fisher on Felsch's bunt went into the outfield. Jackson took third; Felsch wound up on second base. Then Gandil slapped the ball up the middle through the drawn-in infield for a single and two RBIs.

That was all the scoring the White Sox needed. Kerr, constantly encouraged by the shouts of his infielders, was a master on the mound, allowing only three Reds to get as far as second base. He hurled a three-hit shutout as the White Sox won, 3–0, in a game that took just ninety minutes to play. Adolfo Luque hurled one inning in relief for the Reds, becoming the first Latin American player to appear in a World Series.

Afterwards, *The New York Times* had this to say about Kerr's glittering moment:

> Not so long ago Dicky Kerr was a professional boxer out in Milwaukee. He was a bantam and could take a beating and give one. Instead of a wild lefthander shaking with stage fright in the face of the Redland troupe, Kerr looked them over with nerves of chilled steel.

There were those on the inside who also noted that the offensive power that won for Kerr and the White Sox was supplied by Jackson, Risberg, Gandil, and Felsch—all members of the faction on the team that the little Texan did not belong to. They were those who also noted how Jackson's stroke had come alive. His two singles in three at bats in that third game gave him five hits in his last seven at bats. He was batting .435 for the series.

Game Four

Cicotte was slated to pitch the fourth game against Cincinnati's Jimmy Ring. Kid Gleason had his doubts. But "Chubby Eddie Cicotte," *The New York Times* reported, ". . . begged manager Kid Gleason to let him go in. Eddie wanted to vindicate himself for his failure in the opening clash in Redland."

Game-time temperature was about 70 degrees, and Cicotte seemed to thrive in it. His pitching was back on track. But his fielding was atrocious.

What many saw as a pivotal play or non-play in the game took place in the fifth inning. Cicotte awkwardly attempted to field an infield tapper by Pat Duncan but wound up throwing the ball into the outfield. Duncan made it all the way to second base. Larry Kopf hit the ball into left field, and Jackson uncorked one of his patented throws to the plate in an attempt to cut down Duncan. But Cicotte waved at Jackson's throw to the plate. It seemed he was trying to stop the ball. He only managed to deflect it, and Duncan scored easily. To most observers it was obvious that Jackson's throw would have nailed Duncan had it not been cut off. A double by Neale then scored Kopf.

The twenty-four-year-old Jimmy Ring, who had his curve ball snapping, pitched one of the best games of his career. He allowed just three hits, by Jackson, Gandil, and Felsch. The Reds won, 2–0. Cicotte had made just three errors during the regular season, but his two fielding errors in the fifth inning allowed the only two runs to score. And the talk again started up about the White Sox. A team that had always found ways to win was now finding ways to lose.

That night Chicago's Loop was a swarm of red. Cincinnati fans, boosted by the ragtime strains of a band, drank and sang and stumbled their way through the streets. Some of them were still there as morning dawned.

Sunday, October 5, was the date for the scheduled fifth game of the World Series. But there would be no game that day. After four consecutive Indian summer sunny days, rain fell. It became a day for the White Sox to lick their wounds, and for the Reds to collect their thoughts. The Chicago players sat in their clubhouse at Comiskey Park fingering gloves and picking imaginary splinters out of their bats. There was an edginess and a silence that was broken from time to time with recriminations. Several players taunted each other about pitches that should have been better, throws that could have been more accurate, balls that could have been fielded more crisply.

Kid Gleason was doing most of the talking to the raft of reporters hovering about him. Luck, he told them, was something that could swing from team to team, and up to now the White Sox had been out of luck. He made the point that he still believed his team was the best one to ever go into a World Series. Sure, he said, his club was down three games to one, but he still was certain that his crowd would come back.

Joe Jackson half-listened to all the talking; he had very little to say. Working on his glove with a little bit of sweet oil, stretching out his long legs before his locker, and chewing tobacco, he kept himself busy. His dark eyes avoided contact with anyone. In his mind he was playing at the top of his game—flawless in the field, hitting better than anyone on the White Sox. He did not like the atmosphere in the clubhouse.

Game Five

Although Gleason had said he would not use Lefty Williams when his pitching turn came up again—"I think I'll go in myself," he'd said—Williams took the mound for the White Sox against Hod Eller, a specialist in trick deliveries.

Umpire Cy Rigler, a hulk of a man who had started the tradition in the minors in 1905 of umpires raising their right hand to signify strikes, watched the battle play out from behind home plate. Williams was in all-star form; Eller was in Hall of Fame form. In the second and third innings, the Indiana native struck out six White Sox in a row: Gandil, Risberg, Schalk, then Williams, Leibold, and Collins. In the fourth inning Eller retired Weaver and Jackson on infield grounders and struck out Felsch. Williams did not give up a hit until Kopf singled with two outs in the fifth inning.

Through five innings the game played out—a double shutout. This was the kind of baseball the 34,379 fans had come to see, tight, taut, and heads-up all the way.

But in the sixth inning it all came apart for Williams. Eller doubled to left center, the ball falling in between Jackson and Felsch. The moment was described in *Reach's 1920 Official Guide:* "Jackson seemed to be day-dreaming when Eller's fly was hit in his direction." Then a single by Rath to right scored Eller. Daubert laid down a sacrifice bunt to Weaver. Rath took third. Heinie Groh worked the count full. The he walked on what many thought was a questionable call. Schalk was in a fury and screamed and spit at Rigler, who avoided confrontation. Edd Roush was next. He caught a pitch on the fat part of his bat for a booming blast to deep center, Happy Felsch's territory. The White Sox center fielder raced for the ball, seemed to lose it for a moment, and caught up with it. Then a two-handed lunge and the ball was in his glove for an instant. It fell out, and Felsch was all arms and legs scurrying about to pick it up. Rath scored. Groh headed for home, and there were those who swore later they heard Edd Roush screaming, "Get running, you crooked son of a bitch." Felsch cut loose a powerful throw to Eddie Collins, who relayed the ball to Schalk. The ball and Groh seemed to arrive at the same time. Schalk put the tag on, but Rigler screamed "Safe! Safe!" Livid, Schalk cursed and bumped the umpire. He was thrown out of the game and replaced by second-string catcher Bird Lynn.

That was the least of it. The Reds wound up with a four-run sixth inning. They won the game, 5–0. Eller hurled a three-hitter and struck out nine. An interesting postscript to Eller's performance was that before the series started he had told Cincinnati manager Moran that he had turned down a $5,000 bribe from gamblers. Moran permitted Eller to pitch but told him, "I'm gonna watch your every twitch out on the field."

Every twitch of the White Sox players was watched out on the field by Kid Gleason. Through the five games his offense had failed to score a run in 41 of the 45 innings played. They had been shut out in their last 22 innings. They had scored but six runs in the entire five games. He knew it was a batting slump, a terrible batting slump. Joe Jackson, he thought, was caught knee-deep in it, not even getting the ball out of the infield in that fifth game: three popups and a ground out.

Newspapers announced after the fifth game that the players' World Series shares would be $5,000 each for the winners and $3,254 for the losers. Baseball's National Commission would pocket the proceeds for the remaining games.

Game Six

On October 7, Game Six was about to get under way in Cincinnati, a city burning with World Series fever. More than 32,000 were in the stands at Redland Field. More than 10,000 had been turned away. With Chicago down four games to one, most conceded victory in the Series to the Reds. After four innings, with the home team leading 4–0, it certainly looked that way. The White Sox had now gone twenty-six innings without scoring. Then they suddenly woke up, scoring a run in the top of the fifth—their first run since Game Three. In the sixth, after a Weaver double, an RBI single to center by Jackson, a double by Felsch that scored Jackson, and a single by Schalk that scored Felsch, the score was tied.

The game and starter Dickie Kerr labored on into extra innings. In the top of the tenth, Weaver doubled, and advanced to second on a bunt beat out by Jackson. Gandil singled in Weaver, and the White Sox had a 5–4 triumph.

Joe Jackson, not one to suffer mood swings or show that much emotion, admitted later, "I got a mighty big kick out of the two games Dickie Kerr pitched and won for us. That was something."

Like the boxer that he once was, Dickie Kerr was on the ropes throughout the game. He gave up eleven hits, but he stayed the distance. And like a prizefighter coming off the ropes, the White Sox seemed to have awakened. Their bats, Kid Gleason thought, were popping at last. The batting slump was over. They could still pull this thing off.

Game Seven
On October 8 only 13,923 fans showed up, less than half the capacity of the Redland ballpark. The thinking was the fans were disappointed at Cincinnati's defeat in Game Six. The mood around the White Sox and their supporters was up; the four hits pounded out in the sixth inning the day before showed what Chicago was capable of doing. Today, with Cicotte on the mound, the talk in the dugout was that there was hope for another win. Gleason was going around telling everyone that his top pitcher would prevail.

As if they believed this, the Reds were especially vituperative, some would say vulgar, in the pregame bench jockeying.

They tried their best to distract Cicotte as he threw his warmup pitches. But he would have no part of such distraction. Honed in, looking at Schalk's glove and home plate, throwing the ball—that was Cicotte's entire world.

It carried over through the game. After five innings the White Sox led 4–0. Cicotte was a master, spacing seven hits and throttling the Reds, 4–1. Joe Jackson's first-inning single to left scored Shano Collins. His two-out single to left in the third inning again drove in Collins.

It seemed that the Sox were finally back on track.

Game Eight

On October 9, the teams took the field at Comiskey park for the eighth game. There were 32,930 in the stands, pushing the total Series attendance to 236,928, a record for that period. Many of the fans believed the White Sox, trailing four games to three, would win and deadlock the series. But a gambler, as the story goes, told Hugh Fullerton, "All the betting's on Cincinnati! It's going to be the biggest first inning you ever saw."

The game matched up Lefty Williams in his third start for the Sox against Hod Eller of Cincinnati. Williams, who would later say he received a death threat on the telephone the night before the game, walked Rath, the Reds leadoff batter. Then Daubert, Groh, and Roush singled. Duncan doubled. After throwing just fourteen pitches, Williams was finished. So were the White Sox. The Cincinnati lead stretched to 10–1 by the eighth inning, when Chicago scored four runs. It was too little and much too late. The final out of the 1919 World Series was made by Joe Jackson when he grounded out to second baseman Maurice Rath with two men on.

The Reds were World Champions.

The White Sox were in disgrace.

In that eighth game Joe Jackson had a two-for-five day, came in all the way from first base on a single, hit the only homer in the Series, and drove in three runs to cap off a .375 batting average and a .563 slugging percentage. His batting average in the 1919 Series led all hitters and was 71 points higher than what he had managed in 1917. He played flawlessly in the field throughout the series, handling thirty balls in the outfield; he made no errors. His twelve hits were a new World Series record. It was originally thirteen. But a hot grounder that Rath at second was unable to make a play on was changed to an error for Rath rather than a hit for Jackson.

By any stretch of the imagination it would have seemed that the 1919 World Series performance of Joe Jackson was indeed that of a player beyond reproach.

On the other hand, Eddie Collins batted just .226 with two errors while Nemo Leibold hit .056 in eighteen at bats. Roush, the National League batting champ, hit but .214, and his fellow batting star Heinie Groh finished with a .172 average.

That night, after the final game of the World Series, Lefty Williams came into Jackson's suite at the Lexington Hotel. He had been drinking, and he held two dirty envelopes in his hand. "One of these is for you, Joe. Some of us players sold the Series to a gambling clique. We told the clique that you would play crooked ball, too. There's $5,000 in the envelope. It's not all what we were promised, but it's better than getting nothin'."

JOE JACKSON: "I told Williams I didn't want the money and that he had a hell of a lot of nerve using my name in the affair. Also I told him that I was going to tell Comiskey just what had happened."

Williams, reeling about the room, threw the envelope down on the floor and left. Katie was in the bathroom, and when she came out, Joe told her what had happened. "What an awful thing to do," she said.

The following day with $5,000 in his pocket, Joe Jackson went to see Comiskey at his office in the ballpark. In a kind of symbolic show of arrogance and power, Comiskey always kept the door to his office locked. Anyone seeking entrance had to knock on the drawn wooden shutters. Jackson knocked. Harry Grabiner, the quasi-general manager and secretary to Comiskey came to the door. "The old man isn't feeling well," Grabiner said. "Go home, Joe. We know what you want."

Jackson and his black bats. When he went back home to winter in South Carolina, he took his beloved bats along: "Bats don't like to freeze no more than me." *(Chicago Historical Society)*

Knuckleballer Eddie Cicotte possessed pinpoint control and an expert ability to change speeds. *(Library of Congress)*

Center fielder Happy Felsch owned nearly as much range as the great Tris Speaker and had a powerful throwing arm. *(National Baseball Library)*

Buck Weaver was the only third baseman Ty Cobb would not bunt against. *(NBL)*

Second baseman Eddie Collins: "The smartest man that ever walked on a ball field." *(NBL)*

Shortstop Swede Risberg had a flashy style, a powerful arm, and a quick temper.
In the minors he had once kayoed an umpire with just one punch after a dispute
over a called third strike. *(NBL)*

Lefty Williams was a master of the sweeping curve, and he had a lofty .652 winning percentage in his four full major league seasons. *(NBL)*

Ty Cobb and Jackson. The "Georgia Peach" and the "Caroline Confection" were constantly compared. The fellow southerners shared the American League spotlight for a decade. *(NBL)*

Manager Kid Gleason: "A rough, tough fellow who would fight his weight in wildcats." *(NBL)*

White Sox owner Charles Comiskey and Cubs president Bill Veeck at the 1923 Cook County Grand Jury hearings. *(NBL)*

Judge Kenesaw Mountain Landis: "He typified the heights to which dramatic talent may carry a man in America if only he has the foresight not to go on stage." *(NBL)*

Jackson, Risberg, Collins, Gandil, right fielder Shano Collins, catcher Ray Schalk, and Buck Weaver relax before a 1917 World Series game. *(CHS)*

During the 1917 season, major league teams held close order drill for an hour each day; even the mighty White Sox, shown here, went through their paces before a game. Weaver and Felsch are on the left and Jackson is third from the right. *(CHS)*

The second game of the 1919 World Series: Chick Gandil is called out attempting to steal second base. (*CHS*)

The Black Sox in court with their attorneys: (seated from left) attorney William Fallon, Jackson, Weaver, Cicotte, Risberg, Williams, Gandil. (Felsch must have stepped out, and the case against McMullin had been dropped due to insufficient evidence.) *(CHS)*

Jackson played with mill teams, outlaw barnstormers, and the semipros for almost twenty more years. Although he often changed his name to avoid detection, his unmistakable swing always gave him away. *(NBL)*

DATE DUE

OCT 07 1993	SEP 20 2007	
OCT 31 1995	JUN 17 2010	
FEB 24 1996		
	JUN 27 2013	
MAY 16 1996		
NOV 9 1996		
JUN 30 1997		
SEP 24 1997		
NOV 22 1997		
JAN 26 1999		
JUL 13 2000		
SEP 17 2003		
JUN 01 2005		
NOV 09 2006		

JUNIPER

Also by Monica Furlong
WISE CHILD

JUNIPER

Monica Furlong

ALFRED A. KNOPF
New York

Copyright © 1990 by Monica Furlong
Jacket illustration copyright © 1991 by Leo and Diane Dillon
All rights reserved under International and Pan-American
Copyright Conventions. Published in the United States by
Alfred A. Knopf, Inc., New York. Distributed by Random
House, Inc., New York. Published in Great Britain by
Victor Gollancz Ltd. in 1990.
First American edition 1991
Book designed by Mina Greenstein
Manufactured in the United States of America
1 3 5 7 9 10 8 6 4 2

Library of Congress Cataloging-in-Publication Data
Furlong, Monica.
Juniper / by Monica Furlong.
p.   cm. Summary: While apprenticed to the witch
woman Euny, a young girl struggles to save her family from
the evil machinations of her power-hungry aunt Meroot.
Prequel to "Wise Child."
ISBN 0–394–83220–5 (trade)
ISBN 0-394-93220-X (lib. bdg.)
[1. Witchcraft—Fiction.]   I. Title.
PZ7.F96638Ju   1991   [Fic]—dc20   90–39800

ONE

1

THE NIGHT I was born, according to my nurse, Erith, was a night of black frost and dense darkness in a bitter January. White owls who lived in some nearby trees never stopped hooting and flying around the palace, or so the story goes. No one slept a wink. Erith thought it was a sign that I was a remarkable child, and by the time I was old enough to hear the story, I liked to believe her. Remarkable or not, I was bathed and oiled and bandaged, as all babies are, and then they dressed me in a little shift and wrapped me in a rabbit skin to keep me warm. My mother and father showed their first baby to the ealdors, the elder statesmen, as was the custom, and then Erith cuddled me all night so that, as she said, I would not feel strange in this new country I had come to.

IN MY EARLIEST MEMORY I was toddling around on the big grassy enclosure at the center of the palace. Many grownups were walking about, men mostly, holding strange forked twigs in their hands. They moved slowly, eyes fixed on the ground, and they did not notice me or talk to me as they usually did. Because I was bored and wanted to copy them, I picked up a forked twig that someone had dropped and began to move toward the middle of the grass. Suddenly I screamed and screamed, so wildly and in such terror that everyone stopped and looked at me. What had happened was that the twig in my hand had turned into a snake. Well, it hadn't really. It was just an old twig, but while I had held it, all of a sudden it had started moving and wriggling in the most horrible way. My father came over to me.

"What happened?" he asked.

"It turned into a snake," I said, knowing that they would all laugh at me because there it was, just being a stick.

"It's all right," he said. "It wasn't really a snake. Would you do it again to show us?"

So rather nervously, but wanting to please, I picked up the twig again by its two handles, and almost at once it began to jerk downward as if it had a life of its own, and once again I dropped it with a yell. I thought my father would be cross with me, but he picked me up in his arms with a laugh.

"Well done, little girl. You've found us another supply of water. We thought there was one here somewhere, but no one could ever find it."

I SUPPOSE I should mention that my father was *regulus*, that is, a small chieftain or king, in Cornwall, and we lived at Castle Dore in the Wooden Palace that he had built on a high grassy place—the site of an ancient fort. There was a house around a courtyard where my mother and father and I lived, a house for the astrologers and another for the bards, an armory, a bakery, quarters for the knights and ealdors, and a big hall where my father dined with them every evening. The house stood in the hills with a long view of farms and other hills, and the air sparkled with that special radiance of Cornish light.

My mother, Erlain, was a tall, graceful woman who was very clever. She could read and write and had learned mathematics and poetry. She could sing beautifully to the harp, and it was she, I heard tell, who brought the bards to our house and with them a very different atmosphere from the days when my father had lived alone with his knights. She taught him to read and write, and gradually, warrior though he was, he began to enjoy learning as much as she did. Later on, as a result, he wanted me to have the sort of good education that girls often do not have even now.

I should tell you that whenever a child was born to a knight or ealdor among my people, the astrologers studied the heavens and its charts to work out the portents for the child's life. Then they wrote some words, almost a sort of poem, to help the child remember the main points, and this was inscribed in tiny writing on parchment and put into a little horn case that was worn on a leather thong around the neck. Later on, when I was older and had learned to read, I liked to take the parchment out and read the words through, just to remind myself. They went like this:

Named for the strong and twisting tree
Of medicine, when she finds the way
By earth, air, water, fire
Then will she mend what is broken.
The dark teacher will correct her,
The fair one will protect her,
The strong man will love her,
And all may be well.

IT DIDN'T make much sense to me because after all, I
was *not* named after a tree but was called by the good
Cornish name of Ninnoc. The rest of the words seemed
just as puzzling.

Other early memories are of a huge chamber at the
Wooden Palace with a fire leaping and flickering in the
hearth. I had a big bed and Erith had a little one in
the corner, but because I felt lonely in my big bed I
often jumped out of it and climbed in with Erith. Erith
was young and pretty, with red hair and lots of freck-
les. I used to count them to tease her. Sometimes I
woke her to make her tell me a story or sing me one
of her Irish songs. I was quite bossy with Erith—I be-
haved like a little princess who expects the servants to
do as she tells them—refusing to get dressed or have a
bath or eat my dinner or whatever it was she had to
get me to do. Once or twice she threatened to tell my
father about my bad behavior, but she never did.

Sometimes my father would appear in my rooms in
the evening, just at the time I should have been going
to bed, and tell Erith to dress me in my prettiest gown.
(I had some beautiful clothes made from pieces of gold

and silver material like liquid flame left over from my mother's gowns. I was very proud of myself in them.) I had earrings and bracelets made of silver or set with gems, and on special occasions Erith hung jewels in my long black hair. Erith would put my little squirrel-skin slippers on me and comb my hair, and then I would walk with my father in the procession to the Great Hall. He would sit me on his lap and feed me tidbits from his plate. After dinner I would be passed around on the knees of the knights and they all would tease me and play with me. Once or twice I stood on the table and sang one of the songs my mother or Erith had taught me.

I enjoyed being spoiled, but I was disappointed that my mother did not have another baby who could have been a playmate for me. Only much later did I realize that my parents also wanted more children. But soon I acquired a new playmate whom I will tell you about later, and also Erith let me play with the children of some of the knights and ealdors. We played marvelous games. The old fort on which the palace had been built was surrounded by enormous ditches and ramparts constructed in a maze to make it hard for enemies to find the way in. We raced one another around the ditches, slid down the ramparts on wooden sleds, learned the mazes by heart, and had wonderful games of hide-and-seek there.

Once when we were playing a thin dark-skinned woman approached the entrance to the maze that led to the palace. She had strange black eyes, high color in her cheeks, and a strong, determined gait. She was dressed in worn black clothes, not much better than rags, really, and she did not wear the head covering that all the grown women except beggars wore. Her black hair hung straight down her back, as if she were a child. She wore boots so old that part of her foot showed through one of them. Her whole appearance offended me.

"What do you want here?" I asked bossily.

"I have business with Marcus Cunomorus," she said, sweeping me aside and moving into the maze.

"He won't see you!" I shouted scornfully to her back. After which we children climbed onto the ramparts for the pleasure of seeing her lose her way in the maze. (We had often enjoyed seeing strangers turn repeatedly up the blind alleys until they were forced to ask our help and even to bribe us with a coin.) The thin woman did not lose her way but moved skillfully toward the entrance. The guard must have let her through because a few moments later we could see her making her way toward my father's rooms.

"Who was that woman who came to see you?" I asked him that evening. "The one in dreadful clothes."

"That was Euny," he said, and was silent, although he and my mother exchanged glances. I wanted to ask who she was and what she had come for, but he always discouraged me from asking about things that were not my business, so that I did not quite dare. And that was the last I was to hear of Euny for some time.

IT WAS SOON after this that I found a tiny baby owl out in the fields, and since he appeared to have lost his mother and was in a sad, bedraggled condition, I insisted on taking him home. Erith kept saying that my parents would not allow me to keep him, but I hid him in a small room off my sleeping chamber and only she ever knew. Erith was sure that I would not bother to feed him, but I used to beg mice that the cook had caught in her traps, and other little pieces of meat, and the baby owl seemed quite content. His white feathers looked clean now, especially when he fluffed himself out. I loved to take him on my hand and stare into his blank amber eyes. Sometimes he sat on my shoulder, but often he liked to perch for hours on a shelf over the hearth, dozing in the dim winter light. Later he took little flights around the room, moving beautifully with his wide wings. I called him Moon.

As I grew older, I am sorry to say that I became ruder to Erith. She was often quite worn out from the effort of getting me to rise, wash, and dress, even though it was she who did the work of washing and dressing me. I could never do anything to look after myself in those days. When we went out I was always wanting to go farther than was permitted or to do things that Erith thought were dangerous—walking on the ice of ponds when it was still too thin, jumping over the autumn bonfires that the farm people built at harvest time, climbing high into trees, swinging from one branch to another and refusing to come down. Erith would stand imploring me to do as I was told, torn between her love and care for me and her fear of heights or water or fire. In those days I seemed to be afraid of nothing.

I was tormenting Erith like this one day. I had gone

into the stable where my father's stallion was kept, a great black animal who had lamed a groom and whose kick could probably have killed me. I moved closer and closer to it, determined to stroke it and give it an apple, while Erith, half crying, beseeched me to return to her. I think I knew that I was being stupid, but somehow Erith's pleas drove me on to misbehave.

Suddenly, to my amazement, I felt myself seized by the neck and shoulders and marched out of the stable by someone behind me whom I could not see. As soon as I was able, I turned furiously around and was astonished to see that it was the woman Euny, still as shabby as ever, gazing at me with blazing eyes.

"Juniper!" she said. We stood and stared at each other for a few moments, both of us angry, and then, annoyed that she was rebuking me for distressing Erith, I mumbled, "It's not your business anyway."

Euny did not reply to this but gave me a little push in the direction away from the stable and herself turned and walked off. Glancing at Erith, I saw that she looked sickeningly smug.

"There!" she said. "You've annoyed your god-mother."

I was so surprised at this that I forgot about her smug look.

"My godmother! Euny my godmother! Why would someone like Euny be my godmother?"

"That was your mother's choice," she said. "Not that your father disagreed." And she closed her lips very firmly in a way she had when I talked about things that made her uneasy.

So naturally I asked my mother, Erlain, at the first opportunity.

"Is Euny my godmother?"

"Yes."

"Why?"

"Because she is wise. And we needed her."

"Why?"

"I can't tell you now."

"I don't like her. She looks like a beggar woman."

My mother did not answer.

"And she called me Juniper. Why was that?"

My mother laughed with pleasure.

"It was a special name she had for you, your secret name. She whispered it in your ear when you were a baby. Later she told me and said that the secret name was who you really are."

All this seemed very peculiar to me, although not so peculiar as my parents asking this strange woman to be my godmother in the first place. I went out and walked in the ditch between the ramparts to think—a place I often walked when I wanted peace and quiet. There between the grassy walls under a gray spring sky I tried out the name for sound and meaning.

"Juniper. Juniper. Juniper!"

As I spoke it, an extraordinary sense of conviction seized me, as if I had moved and saw the world more clearly and freshly from this new place.

"Juniper!" I said it more loudly, and finally I shouted it as hard as I could.

A sentry's face looked reproachfully over the top of the ramparts.

"Now then!" he said kindly, meaning that making loud noises was worrying to a man whose job was to look out for sudden attacks by our enemies. But I had finished. I knew that Euny, however odd, was right, and that Juniper was my proper name. Later on I had another question for my mother.

"Where does Euny live?"

"She's an Outlander." That meant she lived in the country beyond the farms that were under my father's special protection, in a place where she was always in danger of marauders and brigands.

"Doesn't that frighten her?"

"Not Euny. I don't believe she's ever afraid."

2

THERE WAS only one person at the court whom I disliked, and who I felt disliked me in return—my aunt Meroot. She was my father's older sister. All his life he had loved and admired her, so that when I said I did not like her he would sharply tell me not to be silly. When I was about four, Meroot's husband died in mysterious circumstances. My father had a house built for her in the Wooden Palace, and she and her son, Gamal, who was about my age, came to live with us. Unlike my father, who had wonderful ruddy hair and powerful blue eyes, Meroot had sandy hair and eyes like cold, pale sapphires that I felt watched me critically from behind the curtain of her white lashes. Gamal, on the other hand, was a handsome, blond-haired little boy, not at all like his mother. At once he became a brother to me—we played, slept, and ate together a lot of the time—but as far as we possibly could, we kept out of Meroot's way. Meroot, who my father used to say jokingly would have made a wonderful soldier, was determined that Gamal should grow up strong and fearless, and almost from his infancy she had little suits of armor and small swords made for him and had him trained in fighting and wrestling and archery at an age when most little boys were playing marbles or looking for birds' eggs. She made him wear very few clothes in the winter so that he would become tough (it had the effect of giving him endless colds), and she forced him to sleep on the hard floor with few blankets and to eat the sort of diet soldiers ate. It was a hard life.

Gamal was very loyal to his mother and hardly ever complained, but as a result of these hardships, he spent a lot of time getting warm at the fire in my apartment, wearing a rough coat Erith stitched for him out of a blanket, eating any spare food we had, and occasionally dozing off to sleep in corners. In spite of his mother's treatment he was a cheerful, uncomplaining boy who worked hard at all the strenuous training Meroot prepared for him, but he secretly learned to read. He was very musical—a gift Meroot thought wasted on a future soldier. It was lucky she did not know the hours he spent in our house playing any instrument he could lay his hands on. He composed tunes too and put words to them. There was one very special song he used to sing, a lullaby, the rhythm of which haunts me still.

"Where did you learn that?" I asked him. A slightly puzzled look came over his face.

"A woman taught it to me," he said. "A woman with fair hair like mine."

"Was she your nurse?"

Gamal hesitated. "I don't know," he said.

I knew by his air of embarrassment that there was something mysterious about the song that he himself could not explain.

Even apart from her treatment of Gamal, I never liked Meroot. She always *seemed* to be kind to me, drawing me to her and kissing me, stroking my hair, using flattering words, bringing me presents from her frequent travels, but there was something about her that made me uneasy. Her words sounded false, and I felt that though she claimed to love me, actually she didn't really like me at all. Once, when Gamal and I were about five, we were alone with her in her apartment having a quarrel over a toy, a wooden bird with moving wings. We shouted at each other and grabbed the bird back and forth between us. Suddenly Meroot leaned over, smacked me, snatched the toy from my grasp, and gave it to Gamal. The look she gave me was one of pure hatred, and I shrank back from her. I never trusted her after that.

Soon I realized that my mother's lips tightened whenever Meroot's name was mentioned and that she never entertained Meroot except on official occasions when her absence would have been noticed. Once when Aunt Meroot was away on one of her journeys and Gamal was happily living in our house, I said to my mother, "Wouldn't it be nice if Aunt Meroot never came back?" My mother laughed in a slightly rebuking way, as grownups do when they agree with you but don't want you to know it, and I could see that she felt just as I did, and that like me and Erith, she enjoyed spoiling Gamal as if to counteract Meroot's influence.

I spent a lot of time with my mother just then. Usually she was a woman who liked her own company, and she would sit contentedly for hours in her chamber reading or sewing. Yet when I wandered in from playing or riding my pony she seemed pleased to see me and we had long conversations together.

In one of these conversations I was surprised to discover that Meroot, just like Euny, was my godmother. I tried to get Erlain to discuss it, but she would say nothing except, "She is your father's sister." But her face was cold and her lips disapproving, and I guessed that the choice had not pleased her.

"Why is Meroot so nasty to Gamal?" I asked. "She makes him sleep in that cold room without proper blankets."

"She wants to make him a great warrior," Erlain replied.

"I can't be a great warrior," I said.

"No," she said, her eyes meeting mine, "you will need other powers."

"What other powers?"

"It is too soon to say."

"If I had a brother, would he rule the kingdom after Father?"

"Yes," said my mother, expressionless.

"But if I don't have a brother?"

"That would depend," she said. "On your power. The strength of the warrior is not the only kind."

I went out to the ditch to think things over, and

crouching against the grassy rampart, I wondered whether I had any power. I didn't feel as if I did, although I *had* used special powers to find water. I had not set out to use them, however. It had simply happened when I wasn't thinking about it. I couldn't see how that would be much use in running a kingdom, and I could well imagine that if my mother did not bear a son, a powerful knight or a distant cousin might take the kingdom over or . . . Gamal . . . !

Just as his name occurred to me, a pebble struck me lightly on the head, a shout came from above, and Gamal slithered down the bank beside me and landed with a bump at the bottom. It was as if thinking about him had brought him there.

"Gamal!"

"Mother's away and I've got the afternoon free from swordplay. Let's go somewhere."

The two of us saddled our ponies and rode away, galloping over the moorland toward the distant sea. We made for a little valley, quite deserted, where the horses moved down trails between the trees toward a stream that led to the sea. When we reached the sandy beach, we threw off our clothes and plunged into the waves. Afterward, sunning ourselves on the rocks, we played a game of seeing how long we could sit on one rock before the incoming tide engulfed us. We had the sense to know that if we waited too long it would be really dangerous, but it was fascinating to see how long the sea took, making occasional bold sallies farther up the beach and then, as if preparing to trick us, not moving in our direction for a long, long time.

"Will *you* become *regulus* of Cornwall when my father dies?" I asked Gamal bluntly. "Is that what Meroot wants?"

Gamal reddened. "It's what she wants. It doesn't mean it will happen." Then he added, "Your mother may have a son."

"And if she doesn't?"

Gamal shrugged. I considered for a bit, then remembered my mother's words.

"The strength of the warrior is not the only kind," I repeated. "There are other kinds of power. I intend to learn what they are and, as my father's daughter, rule after him."

Gamal gave me a long, thoughtful glance.

"I hope you do," he said. "As you know, I want to be a musician, not a ruler, though Mother would never let me." He stood up as if the game with the tide no longer interested him. "If you have the power to rule and do it rightly, you will have my allegiance and my fealty," he said. "I would be glad to serve you." He pretended to take an imaginary cap off his head and swept a low bow to me. Then he climbed on his horse and rode away.

I was surprised and touched by his response, by the love and faithfulness in his gray eyes, and by the fact that he had not mocked my claims to power. But I suddenly felt very weak and frightened.

IT WAS AROUND that period that I began to dream—a dream that always had the same ingredients, except that each time the action proceeded a little further, and each time I woke up with a worrying sense that there was something I should do about the dream, only I could not imagine what it was. This feeling was slight at first but grew stronger and stronger.

The first part of the dream was tranquil and beautiful. There was a hazel tree with a full moon hanging in the sky beyond it which lit its leaves and branches until they shone like jewels. This passed into a sense of flying in a night sky rich with stars. Up to this point the dream was delightful, but then suddenly I was in a dark tunnel. I was not alone—I was running, terror-stricken, with some other people, and there was a deafening sound in our ears that I could not identify—was it thunder? As if the noise were not bad enough, there was a most peculiar smell, as of a wild beast, which inspired a sense of fear. At my mother's suggestion I discussed this dream with one of our astrologers, but though my people thought dreams were very important, he seemed unwilling to ponder what it might mean. I think he was afraid that he might have to prophesy a terrible accident—or even worse—and he preferred not to think about it. So I struggled to think about it all by myself, but apart from remembering that hazel was the wood we had used to find water on the day the twig turned into a snake, I could make nothing of it.

As I grew older, I spent less time with Erith and more with my tutors and my mother. I liked learning most of the time, and I had the best of teachers. I had long outstripped Gamal, who spent most of his day in mock battles on the green enclosure where the men shot their arrows and wrestled and practiced with their weapons. Only in music, even though his fingers were tired and wrenched from his day's exercise, could he outshine me. He played beautifully upon the harp and flute, and he could sing well too, in a pure angelic treble. Most afternoons, sweaty, tired, hungry, he would come to see me after a day of wrestling or riding or swordplay. I too had finished my day's work—writing, translating, listening to my father giving judgment on a difficult case. Erith would bring both of us scented water in which to wash, and we would change our clothes. Then we ate some fruit or sweetmeats and settled down to play. Even Meroot did not forbid this. On wet days we played finchnell or made music. On fine days we walked or rode, coming home in the twilight to share a stew or roasted bird in front of the fire.

Together too we played with Moon, who liked to walk up our arms and sit on our shoulders. He had a way of apparently listening to our conversations, his head on one side, a thoughtful, judicial expression on his face that was irresistibly funny. Gamal often addressed questions to him, then replied in a pretend owl voice.

"*Isn't* Ninnoc in a bad temper today, Moon?" Gamal would ask, and then reply owlishly to himself, "I don't know what you're complaining about. I have to put up with her all the time."

Gamal and I had begun to share a secret. When, day by day, he returned from his labors as an apprentice soldier, he was often cut or bruised. He would have a long scratch down his face, a nasty graze on his leg, a pulled shoulder, a twisted ankle. To begin with I would bathe these injuries for him, put ointment on them, bandage them, until we began to notice something strange. The injuries began to grow better as soon as I looked at them or touched them, and often before I had reached for the bandage.

"Don't tell anyone!" I begged him, suddenly shy at this discovery.

"What is it that you do?" he asked me. That was the embarrassing part. I didn't *do* anything. I just looked at the sore place and touched it and did whatever was necessary to make it feel better.

"I wonder what you *couldn't* heal," Gamal went on. A week later we had the chance to find out. He came in with his arm broken after a bout of wrestling in which he had slipped and fallen. His tutor stood at the door waiting to take him to the bonesetter, but Gamal insisted on coming to me first. Seeing his face twisted with pain and the protective way he held his arm, I put out a hand and touched him with the utmost gentleness. This time, because it was so important to make him better, I concentrated really hard on healing his broken arm. Nothing happened. We had discovered the limit of my power. I could manage cuts, scratches, and bruises, but anything else was beyond me.

3

SINCE THE DAY when she had found me in the stable Euny had not spoken to me, which I thought was odd behavior for a godmother. Perhaps twice a year I would see her at Castle Dore, marching purposefully through the palace on her way to my father's apartments. I noticed that she would spend hours with him, but then scorn the feasting and the presents with which we regaled most of our visitors and leave as simply as she came, setting off on the long walk to the mysterious place where she lived in the Outland. I had no idea what she and my father could talk about.

One day, however, a change came. Erith entered the room where I was practicing my calligraphy—I remember that I was gilding a letter *A* that had a tiny blue man sitting sideways on the crossbar and swinging his leg—and said, "King Mark wants to see you. Right away." She turned sharply and went out. I sighed—I had been enjoying my work and was annoyed at being interrupted, but no one kept my father waiting. I suppose because that day changed my life I can still remember the look of the writing, the brilliant autumn sky, and even the gown I wore—blue, with a belt worked in precious stones and silk.

My father sat in the great chair that he used when he was meeting people officially. On a smaller chair beside him, very upright, sat Euny, who did not greet or notice me. I sat on an even smaller chair, suddenly feeling insignificant and shy.

"We have been talking," said my father, "Euny and I, about your future. As you know, it is the custom of this country to send a noble child away from home for a year or two to stay in another house as part of that child's education. It is usually boys who are sent, but in this case the circumstances are unusual. Euny, as your godmother, has proposed that in, say, a year's time, we should send you to live with her for a while. She believes, and I agree with her, that she will have valuable lessons to teach you."

The expression on my face must have betrayed my horror at the idea of living with Euny, because my father frowned sternly at me. I had forgotten that however startled I was, he expected me to show good manners.

"Go away from here!" I said. "From Erith and you and Mother and Gamal and everyone? To go and live *in the Outland?*"

"You will come to no harm."

I was so upset that I felt my lower lip begin to droop

with the threat of tears. Euny spoke, but she was not in the least reassuring.

"It is necessary," she said. "There are things you need to learn—things only I can teach you. I am your godmother, and I claim the right to instruct you."

"I don't want to go," I said sullenly, half under my breath.

"For a year and a day," Euny went on as if I had not spoken. "That should do it. You will come to me in about a year. I shall not send for you—you will know when the moment comes. Come alone, on foot, with a few clothes. That should suffice."

"Very well, then," said my father. "It's settled." I knew that this was the signal for me to leave, and unwillingly I got up to go. Euny followed me, and when we were outside the door, she turned to me with a rather wolfish smile, hissing through her teeth the one word, "Juniper!" almost as if she were making a joke. Then she turned and walked away.

I was deeply shaken by this encounter. I discussed it with Erith, who was indignant at the suggestion that I should go anywhere without her, and I mentioned it to my mother, Erlain, who was sympathetic but who, predictably, sided with my father. However, she shed a new light on the idea.

"We have spoken of the power you may need one day," she said. "I think it is too soon to say whether you will have that, or should use it, but Euny is one who has power. That is why we chose her for you as a godmother. She is quite right—you could learn from her."

This made the whole idea seem a little better, but at

the same time I dreaded leaving all the places and people I knew and going to live in the Outland.

"What is Euny's house like?" I asked sulkily.

"I don't know. I have never been there. I've heard that it is beside a great hill—a tor—near the sea, and I think she appoints herself a sort of guardian of the hill."

This was comforting in a way—I liked the idea of living by the sea—but I was still puzzled. And hurt.

"You will send me to the Outland to stay at a house you have never seen? The Outland is *dangerous*— everybody knows that. I might easily be killed by brigands or by our enemies. None of you seems to care. And Euny is so dirty and horrible."

Quite apart from the dangers of the Outland, I could not understand why my parents trusted Euny so much. I did not like Euny, nor trust her, and I was afraid of her rags and poverty.

My mother hesitated.

"The Christians say that there is no magic—that the world is ruled by love. I cannot decide whether they are right. Our forebear Arthur was a Christian yet believed in magic," she said. *"This* kingdom seems to be controlled by magic, good magic and bad magic. For those who choose the good magic it is important to have strong allies who choose good magic too. Euny is your father's strongest ally. If you let her, she will become your ally, and that may be important."

Erlain said all this very gravely, and though the words she used were simple, it was as if she were talking to a grownup. Somehow, without really understanding, I knew that I would have to go to be Euny's pupil.

I wondered when. Euny had said in about a year and

that I would know when the time came, but I could not imagine how. In any case, a year seemed a comfortably long time away.

AUTUMN SLIPPED into a snowy winter, and little seemed to have changed in my life. Except one thing. The dream of the hazel tree was coming more and more often. Always I was delighted by its beauty—it filled me with a sort of hunger that was also a kind of joy, the feeling that if I could find it I would be supremely happy. Occasionally I woke up at this point and there were tears of happiness on my cheeks. But far more often I was back again in the tunnel, running in terror from the dreadful fate that pursued me and my companions and which was heralded by the intolerable noise and smell.

I told Gamal about the conversation with Euny. He was so fascinated that he went right home and told Meroot. Later he said that she was "very angry" about it. I could not understand why it would make Meroot angry, but I was not in the least sorry that it did.

I grew a lot in that year and felt as if I came to understand many more things. I played the harp every day, I learned and sang many of the famous songs of my people, I studied the stars and learned astrological law, I read Latin and wrote what I believed was a beautiful script. More often my father took me into his council chamber when he was listening to a dispute and afterward would ask me what I thought of his decision. I usually got bored in the middle of all the explanations, though, and went off into a daydream. I daydreamed a lot at that time. Sometimes I daydreamed that I was a beautiful woman whom everybody adored, sometimes that I was a brave soldier who was afraid of nothing.

One day something odd happened, as odd as the day when I had felt the twig move in my hands. It was a bright spring morning and Gamal and I had run away, in my case from lessons and in Gamal's from the perpetual wearisome drilling of his life as a boy-soldier. We were riding a long way from Castle Dore in the Outland territory, which my father had forbidden to us. We were cantering in a wide grassy space with trees on one side of it. I knew from previous experience that a bit farther the ground rose steeply, passed into a narrow gully by a stream with cliffs on both sides, swung toward a narrow place where you could pass only one at a time, and then opened toward an estuary and the sea.

I suppose I was thinking about the place, anticipating it, when suddenly, with total clarity, I saw it in my mind's eye. On the far side of the narrow gorge was a camp with ragged women and children and skinny horses grazing. But in the narrow place between the rocks several men were crouched holding weapons, clearly with the intention of killing or holding for ransom anyone who attempted to pass. So vivid was this picture that I had to look around me to make sure that I was not actually at the gorge. No, there was the spacious stretch of grass, the trees, and the lithe movement of our horses beneath us. But there we were, it seemed to me, heading fast toward danger.

At once I told myself I was making up a story and

that I must order my thoughts, but then, as if from beside me, came a voice, very like the owlish voice in which Gamal imitated Moon. "Don't go . . . don't go." On that day, as on many others, I was carrying Moon asleep in my pocket. I slowed my horse, and though I knew the owl hated bright daylight I pulled him out. He fluffed his feathers, blinked crossly, and said again (I could see his beak moving), "Don't go . . . don't go."

"You can talk, Moon!" I said.

"Of course," he replied wearily. "But now I want to go back to sleep."

I shouted to Gamal to stop, reined in my horse, and slipped to the ground. Gamal rode back to me, puzzled. He was even more puzzled when I told him.

"You just made that up!" he said.

"Perhaps I did. I'm not sure. But I am quite certain that if we ride through the gorge we will be in danger."

Gamal chewed thoughtfully on a piece of grass.

"In that case, how about climbing that path up above the gorge—you remember the one—and looking down on the camp? Just to see."

I did not want to appear cowardly, so I swallowed my longing to turn and go home and set off with him on foot along a path through the trees. There was something very reassuring about having an adventure with Gamal. He had such a sensible, cheerful air as he stalked along in front of me, once or twice stopping to listen carefully. As we approached the head of the gorge, we became very quiet indeed—I knew that Gamal must really have believed what I had told him. Then we were in sight of the place where the gorge, that huge split in the surface of the earth, began. We stole lightly across to the rock that overlooked the gorge and stared down. All was just as I had seen it! I was about to gloat over this when I glanced to one side. A hundred paces away two robber scouts were staring intently at us and beginning to move in our direction!

"Gamal!" I hissed. "Run. Run!" Both of us turned back to the woods and ran, fleet of foot, driven by the sound of the robbers crashing through the undergrowth behind us. Our only hope was the two horses tethered where we had left them. In spite of our start the robbers were not very far behind when we leaped into our saddles and urged our horses away. Catching our panic, they took off at full speed, manes and tails flowing in the wind. I looked around once and saw one of the robbers about to fit an arrow into his bow. I did not look again.

After that, Gamal was inclined to be respectful of my gifts but to wonder why I had foreseen the robbers in the gorge but did not know about the robber scouts. I could not tell him.

"Can all women do magic?" he asked me.

"I don't think so," I replied.

"Meroot can, you know," he said.

"What kind?"

"I'm not sure. She won't talk about it. It's just that I see her books and parchments. There's a terrifying picture in one of them . . . And sometimes she mixes potions." He sounded unhappy.

"What sort of picture?" I was intrigued.

"There was someone drinking something and falling asleep . . ." Gamal spoke unwillingly. "Then they were in a coffin buried in the ground, but alive, awake, fighting to get out. It gave me nightmares for weeks."

"You think people . . . you think *Meroot* would do a thing like that to her enemies?" I asked, frightened.

"I don't know," Gamal said wretchedly.

"I don't really understand magic," I said. "That's why I'm going to Euny's, I suppose."

"Do you want to go?"

"I don't know."

Somehow that day made me feel that I needed to be taught whatever it was Euny knew. Perhaps, I thought, she could teach me really effective magic and I would be able to use it to make people do anything I wanted them to do. That was a pleasing thought. In any case, I felt myself moving inevitably toward her—even though I didn't like her much. It was very odd.

"So how is it," Gamal persisted, "that if you can see into the future you cannot beat me at finchnell? You should be able to see my moves several turns ahead."

"I do beat you sometimes," I said indignantly, but I saw his point. There was something that didn't make sense.

Now that I had discovered that Moon could speak I spent a lot of time talking to him, but to my disappointment he did not utter another sound. He would gaze at me very intelligently with his head to one side or sit blinking his amber eyes, but that was all.

"Please say something, Moon," I would beg. "I know

you can." But he simply ruffled his feathers and blinked at me with those astonishing eyes.

One night I dreamed again of the hazel tree and the tunnel. This time whatever was pursuing me was close at hand. I woke up after the dream, and the feeling of fear was very great, though it was gradually succeeded by a longing for the hazel tree. I knew that something had to change, but I could not imagine what it might be.

4

THE NEXT MORNING I woke at dawn, shivering and sweating from my dreams, and for the first time I knew what I must do. I got straight out of bed and began to prepare a bundle for myself. I put in two of my simplest smocks and chose another to wear, with a large pocket that could accommodate my owl. I included a bone comb that had been a present from my mother, sandals, and a cloak. I wrapped a shawl around my shoulders and put on the boots I wore in wet weather. I was very tempted to leave without saying good-bye to my parents or Erith, but I feared that if I did, there would be a hue and cry in search of me. So I sat down to wait until the rest of the household was awake.

My parents were breakfasting when I entered their apartments. Erlain looked distressed when I told her that the day of my departure had come, yet all the same I believe she thought that I was right to go.

"We shall miss you," she said, "but I shall think of you every day. Be my brave girl and learn whatever Euny can teach you. And remember, it is only for a year and a day. Not *such* a long time." It seemed a very long time to me. My father kissed me warmly but said little. I felt that he did not like the parting, yet trusted Euny and her conviction that I needed to learn from her.

The person who made the greatest fuss was Erith, who wept and hugged me and wrung her hands in a truly heartbreaking way.

"I'm coming *back*, Erith," I kept explaining, but she did not seem to think that helped at all. In the end I gave up trying to comfort her—it only made *me* want to cry. I picked up my bundle and simply walked out the door. Once safely away from the Wooden Palace, I felt much more cheerful; it was very pleasant walking along in the morning's coolness. There was an autumn bite in the air that made me move quickly, but I felt full of energy, as if I could walk forever. After about an hour I heard the sound of hoofs behind me on the path, and looking back, I saw Gamal following me. When he got closer I could see that he was angry but trying to hide it.

"You went away without saying good-bye to me."

"I am sorry, but I only decided to go this morning, and by then I knew you would be out on the field practicing. I asked Erlain to say good-bye for me."

"She did, so I just left the field. Old Talan's in a rage."

I thought Gamal was rather brave. Meroot had punished him severely the last time he had run away from his tutors to ride with me.

"I'll have to go back, but I was determined to say good-bye." He slid off his horse and gave me an awkward, boyish kiss. "I hope you'll be happy with Euny. She looks like a bit of an ogress to me."

"I'll miss you."

Unable to think of anything else to say, Gamal mounted his horse and soon disappeared toward home. I missed him the moment he was out of sight; now, instead of feeling light and exhilarated, as I had when I set out, I felt sad and lonely. I continued my journey more slowly.

As the day wore on, it became hot—a dazzling September day. After I had walked for several hours my feet became sore, and I took off my boots and walked in the dust, which felt silky and comforting. Foolishly, I had not thought to bring any water with me, so I drank out of the wayside streams. Later, however, I became very hungry and wondered why I had forgotten to bring bread. I found a few berries.

I was not very sure of the way, but I had a sort of landmark. Once on a trip I had made with my father, he had pointed out to me an odd-shaped hill in the distance. "That's where Euny lives," he had said. I could see the hill, purple-black, away in the distance, a hill that rose sheer out of a flat landscape. Sometimes I lost sight of it as I passed through woods or along deep leafy tracks, but then it would reappear and I would know that I was not lost. For a long time, though, it did not seem to get any closer.

In the late afternoon I came to a great forest that lay between me and the hill. I knew that forests were dangerous for unarmed travelers—that there might be boars or wolves or outlaws who lived there, and I feared being eaten or robbed and killed. I sat down in despair on the edge of the forest and wondered what to do. It would be a sad end to my journey to die in the forest—I was much too young to die, I thought.

Despite my fears I found it very beautiful in the forest, with the tawny autumn colors glowing like fires, and away in the distance the dim blue light of the dying day. I had discovered one of the broad roads that ran through the forest, and it seemed to me that if I stuck to the road (and it was going in the right direction), I might be safe, though once when I heard someone approaching I hid in the bushes. It was a party of monks, and I thought of coming out and asking for their protection, but then it occurred to me that they might disapprove of Euny, so I stayed in my hiding place. It was growing cold in the forest and I shivered in my shawl. I knew that it would be dark before long, and I fervently wanted to be out of the forest before nightfall.

Just as if I were being taken care of, I stepped out of the forest as the first stars were coming out. I was on a path that led straight toward the mysterious hill. I walked on, very tired now, the hill slowly looming larger between me and the sky yet still a long way off. I thought I could hear the distant grumble of the sea. I was cold and stiff from the walk, my legs were scratched and bleeding, and my bundle felt heavy, yet I kept going, one foot after the other. I sang to myself to keep up my spirits and looked at the great stars above me. Suddenly, as if time had compressed itself, I stood at the foot of the great hill. Now, I thought, if I walked around it, I would find Euny's house.

This was not as easy as it sounds. There were deep ditches and streams, little coppices, and high walls of bushes. Although I could dimly see the stepping stones over the stream, I was so tired that I stumbled right into it and fell full-length into the water. I gasped at the bitter cold and then staggered out, my clothes dripping and my flesh shivering in the night wind. I was past crying; I was simply trying to endure in order to reach Euny. When I drew poor little Moon out of my pocket he was ruffling his wet feathers indignantly. I thought it might make him cross enough to say something, but he did not speak. Nor did he speak when a bit later I fell heavily down a bank, hurting my ankle and scraping my arm.

"Euny! Euny!" I had begun to say out loud. It was just then that a crescent moon swung into view over a clearing, and in its gentle light, black against the sky and the curve of the hill, I saw a little hut with firelight showing under the door. I did not know whether it was the house I sought, but I knew that I could go no farther. I stumbled toward it and pressed the latch. The door swung open on a small square room. Between me and the fire was a rocking chair with someone sitting in it who did not turn around.

"So Juniper decided to come after all, did she?" said Euny's voice. "Shut the door behind you—there's a terrible draft."

TWO

5

SHIVERING and exhausted, I crept toward the fire as an animal would have done and sank down before it. I must have looked a terrible sight—my hair and clothes sopping wet, my limbs covered in blood and mud, my ankle beginning to swell. If Euny had uttered one word of sympathy I would have burst into a flood of tears. Instead she sat in silence, perfectly still. After a bit she said, "There's a blanket on the bed," and eventually it occurred to me that she meant me to strip off my damp clothes and wrap myself in it. I looked around the room. There was a box bed in one corner, and I went over and took out the ragged blanket and put it around my cold shoulders. Meanwhile Euny had filled a bowl with soup from the fire and set it in the hearth for me.

I put a hand out of my blanket, grasped the battered spoon she gave me, and ate the soup. It had odd bits of gristle in it and the strange flavor that I was to discover Euny's soup often had, but it sent a shiver of delight through me. It was hot and spicy, and I could feel some faint flicker of energy return to my exhausted body.

"There won't be much food to eat here," Euny said, "so you needn't expect it."

What I was wondering at that moment was where I was going to sleep. I had always slept in a bed with down pillows and linen sheets. I could see that there would be no room for me in Euny's tiny bed.

"Please, where shall I sleep?" I asked at last.

"On the hearth, of course," said Euny. "This isn't a palace, you know." She managed to inject a lot of scorn into that remark. She got up, went across the room, and fetched a furry skin. It had an odd smell that I didn't like at all.

"This will keep you warm," she said.

Now I had another problem. Every night of my life Erith had helped me take off my clothes, brushed my hair, and tucked me into bed. Every morning she had bathed me, dressed me, and braided my hair for me. I had no idea how to do any of it for myself. It had not occurred to me that anyone dressed and undressed without help.

"Please, will you help me undress?" I asked.

Euny laughed, a bark of a laugh, not altogether unkind, and without a word went back to her rocking chair. I realized with astonishment that she had no intention of giving me any help. With humiliating difficulty I managed to get my clothes off and comb my hair. I remembered that the little owl was still in my pocket, so I took him out, stood him on a beam, and fed him a tidbit of mouse I had brought from home. I was nervous that this would provoke further rudeness from Euny, but to my surprise a broad smile spread across her face.

"How just like you!" she said as if she were laughing at a private joke. Since she scarcely knew me, I could not see how she knew whether it was like me or not.

Later I lay curled up in Euny's fur rug, half of it beneath me, protecting me from the cold of the flagstones, half of it above me. Now that I was inside it the smell was overpowering. My head lolled uncomfortably on one of the creature's paws. There was warmth from the fire, though the shifting of the ashes disturbed me at first. Tired as I was, I went quickly to sleep but woke long before dawn, cold and miserable and hating the sound of Euny's snores from across the room. It seemed to me that I might have made a terrible mistake—that although Euny had told me to come, she was not glad, as I had expected her to be. In any case, I would never survive the discomfort and squalor of life there, with no one to dress me and take care of me. Great tears of self-pity ran down my cheeks.

I sat up, my body cramped and frozen. It was not light yet, but I could leave as soon as it was dawn. My torn smock, hanging over the rocking chair near the fire, had dried in the night. I had simply to dress and leave before Euny woke. Just then, however, my ankle jarred with pain as I moved. I could see that badly swollen as it was, I would never manage the long walk home. I groaned and curled back again into the strong-smelling skin.

I must have dozed, because the next thing I knew, it was light, and I could hear Euny moving around and smell ham frying.

"Thought you'd be hungry this morning," said Euny. "This is the last of the old pig—it's a bit high, but it'll do you good. We'll kill the next pig before winter." She handed me a plate—it didn't look like a very clean plate to me—with a bit of fried ham and a hunk of black bread on it. She was quite right, I *was* very hungry, and although the ham had a rancid taste I gulped it down together with the black bread and some lumpy porridge she was stirring over the fire.

"I can see you'll eat me out of house and home," Euny said in her cross voice. "Get dressed, wash yourself, comb your hair, try to look like a human being even if you can't look like a princess."

Obediently, though very slowly and awkwardly, I washed myself clean in the freezing water, combed my tangly hair, put on another of the smocks in my bundle, and tied on my sandals. I was surprised to find that I could do it all by myself.

"Now sit down," said Euny. "We need to talk."

Stiff and tired from my long walk and my night among the ashes, and still rather hungry, I sat miserably down, my swollen ankle in front of me.

Before we talked, Euny selected some herbs and tied them around my ankle.

"Walk on it," she said, "but not too much." My ankle hurt badly with each step I took.

"Now," she said, "I expect you feel very hard done by this morning, living in this miserable hole after the splendors of the palace." She sounded as if she were gloating, and I was too angry to trust myself to speak. Children in my country are trained to be very polite to grownups.

"But I am a poor person—not rich like your father—and this is the way poor people live."

I knew, because Erlain had told me, that Euny had been offered a house at the Wooden Palace and all kinds of presents by my father, but that she had always refused.

As if she guessed my thoughts, Euny went on. "I find life easier this way. Let me tell you why I think you are here. I won't talk much about it after today, so listen carefully. What I know about is power. Not the sort of power your father has with soldiers and armies and weapons, but a power that comes from knowing—"

"I know a lot," I said, eager to please. "I know Latin, and about the stars, and mathematics, and poems . . ."

"Not that sort of knowing," she said, interrupting me rather contemptuously. "That sort just gets in the way—makes you think you are clever, like weapons make men think they are strong. My sort of power is about *seeing*—seeing into the future, seeing into someone's heart and mind. Sometimes it is about knowing what a tribe or people must do to escape danger. Sometimes it is just about understanding yourself or one other person. Seeing and knowing—and being very truthful about what you see and know—they make things begin to happen, maybe more things than battles and armies. Sometimes they prevent bad things." I thought of the moment with Gamal on the hillside but did not feel like mentioning it.

"So could I have power?" I asked.

"It is too soon to say. It is possible. But you may spoil it."

"How?" I asked anxiously.

"By wanting it too much. Or by using it badly."

"And if I don't spoil it?"

"Then you will become what the powerful ones call a *doran*. And that might be very important for your father and his kingdom. But it is a long, difficult path and it may be too much for you."

"It won't," I said, determined not to miss my chance.

"Or you may decide you don't like the idea when you know more about it."

I thought that was very unlikely. I remembered Gamal's question.

"Is it only women who become *doran*s?" I asked her.

"No. But there are more women who take that path. Men prefer to put their trust in weapons and fighting. They don't know it, but it makes them weaker."

Asking Gamal's question had reminded me of something else.

"Is Meroot a *doran?*" I asked Euny. Her face darkened and her lip curled with scorn.

"Meroot only uses magic to make other people do what she wants."

I remembered my own fantasies of doing just that.

"Is that bad?" I asked timidly.

"It is *wicked*," Euny replied with a terrifying emphasis. Then, with the air of one who has had more conversation than she is used to, Euny stood up and packed some bread into a basket before hoisting it onto her back.

"I have work to do today," she said, "so you'll just have to stay here. Light the fire and make some soup for supper. I'm not sure if I'll be back by nightfall."

6

WHEN EUNY had gone I spent a little while sitting glumly in her rocking chair, my sore ankle propped up in front of me. Now that I was alone I examined the room in more detail. There were the ashes of the fire and hanging above it the chain, which held a griddle and a kettle. There also hung a large piece of mutton, left to blacken in the peat smoke. That, and no doubt the tallow lamp made from mutton fat, gave the hut an unpleasant smell. Beside the fire was a basket of peats, a little brush for cleaning the hearth, the lamp on a shelf, and a small stool. In addition to the rocking chair, the skin rug, and the bed, the room contained a rickety table and an upright chair, a rather dirty woven rug, a bowl and jug, some cups and plates on a simple dresser, a hand mill with meal spilling out of the top, and a jug with some milk. In a corner stood a woodpile with some sticks lying on top and a tinderbox on the floor beside it.

There were dried plants hanging from the ceiling and
the remains of the pig's carcass. Euny owned nothing,
it occurred to me, that was not absolutely necessary to
keep her warm or fed, and I thought with wonder of
the way she had refused my father's offer of money
and possessions. The books, the musical instruments,
the goblets, the jewels, and the fine clothes to which I
had been accustomed at home seemed unimaginable
here.

What was I to do with myself all day? Euny had gone
and might not be back till the morrow and there was
I, all alone with nothing at all to do and only able to
walk with difficulty.

As so often since the day out with Gamal, I tried to
talk to Moon, but he did not stir from his daytime sleep.
I had never before lit a fire or attempted to cook, but
because I was cold and would soon be hungry again, I
thought I had better learn how. I thought it might be
easier to light a fire of wood than of peat. I placed
some big pieces of wood in the hearth and set some
moss on top of them. Then I struck at the flint. Even
when the sparks fell on the dry moss, the little fire-
seeds gradually faded. I tried time after time, feeling
more and more irritated. After a bit it occurred to me
that the twigs might light more easily than the wood.
This time I transferred the moss to the twigs; the twigs
sizzled a little, and I thought that maybe the fire would
light, but still I did not succeed.

I sat back on the rocking chair and looked despair-
ingly at the cold hearth. Other people could light fires.
Why was I so stupid? Then I remembered seeing ser-

vants at home sweeping up the ashes and carrying them away. Without much hope of it making a difference, I took down my pyramid of wood, cleared away the ashes with a shovel that lay beside the hearth, relaid the fire, and repeated the procedure with the tinderbox. This time, to my delight, the twigs flared up, making a generous blaze, and soon the logs were aflame. I felt very proud of myself.

There was still some soup left in the cauldron, and although it was only midmorning, I heated it up and ate it with some black bread that I had found on the dresser. I noticed the same odd taste that I had noted the night before. I later discovered that Euny had a way of throwing whatever food she had into her soup, not just bread and cheese but meat or even offal together with any herbs that came to hand. It did not always taste nice. But I would have to devise another soup for our evening meal.

My hunger appeased, I went out to look at the pig and the chickens Euny kept. The pig was a huge black beast that lived in a sty behind the hut; its grunts and snufflings had disturbed me more than once during the night. The chickens' white feathers looked dirty and bedraggled, but I was glad to notice that several eggs were already lying inside the henhouse, and I carefully collected them. I saw that Euny was growing some beans and flax and some bere corn. There were two stunted apple trees with a few apples left on the boughs.

Time hung very heavily on my hands for the rest of that day. I talked a bit to Moon, hoping as always that he would reply or even give me some advice, but he

merely blinked and went back to sleep. Limping painfully, I drew some water from Euny's well, washed out
the smock I had worn the day before, and hung it over
the chair to dry. I washed my hair too and let it dry in
the bright, warm noontime sunshine. I carefully arranged blocks of peat on the fire and loved the smell
as the fire reached them. Mindful of the charge to make
some soup, I managed to persuade a little more meat
from the pig's carcass and added some water and herbs
and a little meal, but it was a poor, thin broth. When
darkness fell I ate the soup with a couple of the eggs
and the rest of the black bread and some milk, reluctantly saving what was left of the milk for the next
morning. Before going to bed I built up the fire as
much as possible, and wrapping myself once more in
the strange-smelling animal skin, I lay down before the
hearth.

The fire threw alarming shadows onto the walls of
the hut. The silence outside felt ominous to me. Except for the occasional scream of a rabbit caught by a
stoat or a fox, I could hear nothing at all, but I imag-
ined outlaws surrounding the hut, preparing to break
into it. Because of my fears and the discomfort of the
floor, I slept very badly—the shifting and sighing of
the fire disturbed me. There was a growing feeling of
cold as the night drew on. "I don't like this at all," I
thought, "no matter how much power I get out of it,
nor how important it is to be a *doran*. I'd rather marry
the son of a neighboring prince, or even the son of one
of the knights, as all the other girls do. That would be
much better than spending my life cold and hungry in

a place like this. As soon as Euny returns I will tell her, and then when my ankle is better I will go back home." Feeling that I had settled something, I rearranged the skin and sank into a sound sleep. I was woken several hours later by Euny lifting the latch and entering the hut.

7

ALTHOUGH I HAD decided so firmly to leave Euny, I found it difficult to get around to telling her about it, perhaps because I was a little afraid of her. Maybe too, I thought that some marvelous thing might still happen that would make it worthwhile to live there.

On the second morning, when I woke up cold and stiff, Euny decided promptly that my ankle was better, though it felt far from better to me, and sent me out before breakfast to collect two buckets of water from her well, to gather sticks and relight the fire, and to wash my face in the cold water and comb my hair. All this before our very meager breakfast of porridge.

"Please, what I am going to give Moon?" I asked her anxiously. At the Wooden Palace, I had always begged the contents of the mousetraps from the cook, or she had given me other scraps left over from our meals.

"There are plenty of field mice around here. Let him

go and hunt for himself," said Euny. I looked up anxiously at Moon. Suppose he starved because it did not occur to him to seek his own food?

Actually I was still fairly hungry myself, though trying hard not to notice it. I thought that we would now settle down to lessons as I would have done at home, only in something much more interesting, like spells, but it didn't turn out that way. After a brisk tidying up of the hut (that is, *I* tidied it while Euny looked on and made sarcastic comments), we went out for an interminable walk in which Euny sought roots for some medicine she wanted to make. It was a chill, windy day and we marched for hours over meadows and through woods. Every now and then, for no reason that I could see, Euny would point to a plant that looked like all the others and order me to dig it up. Some of them had deep, tough roots, which she insisted I must dig up intact. I had no tool apart from a stick and my fingers, and in no time my pretty nails were full of earth, and my hands and smock were filthy. The only time she spoke was to give me long explanations of what the roots were and what they might be used for, which I promptly forgot.

In contrast to Euny, who walked lightly and quickly, looking about her as if everything were interesting and must be noticed, I shuffled along, sullen and miserable, until I began to take refuge in comforting daydreams.

"How many birds?" Euny asked suddenly.

"How do you mean?"

"There was a row of birds sitting on a branch. How many?"

Of course I had no idea. I had not even seen the birds.

This unpleasant trick, I was soon to discover, was a favorite one of Euny's. She was given to precise, detailed questions. What color was the roof? What color *exactly* had the sky been? What direction was the wind blowing from? What animals had I noticed? Where were they? What flowers had I seen? She would ask, but I never knew the answers. It made me feel very silly.

What I was thinking about was not the number of birds nor the direction of the wind but the bliss of returning to the comforts of Castle Dore. I reflected that as the winter came on, life, which was already hard at Euny's, would become intolerable, with the cold, hard floor feeling even colder at night and the hunger becoming even more painful. It would be lonely too. I had been with Euny only a day and a half, and already I was missing Erith and my parents and other children to talk to. It was at this point I remembered that, after all, it was Euny who had asked me to come, and I thought that perhaps, as I was her godchild, she held some affection for me that she found difficult to show.

"Did you . . . sort of . . . want me to come?" I asked her timidly in the middle of a dark forest. I hoped for some sort of declaration from her that she loved me and was pleased that I was coming to live with her.

"It's all one to me," she said disappointingly.

But there was something even more fundamental that I needed to know, only I scarcely knew how to ask the question.

"I know what you said yesterday, but I still don't see

how I . . . what you . . . what I am here for," I got
out at last. Euny gave a heavy sigh as if this were an
unreasonable bit of curiosity on my part.

"Earth, air, fire, water," she said, and stopped.

"Like my rhyme," I said with interest, remembering
my neck charm.

"Well, there you are."

I didn't seem to be anywhere.

"There are . . . things I can do," I said. "I can find
water hidden underground, I can heal people—sometimes. I can see into the future, and once I thought I
heard Moon speak."

"Don't boast!" she said sharply.

"But what does it *mean?*"

"It means that you must do exactly what I tell you!"

To make it all worse it began to rain during the
afternoon, but in spite of that we did not make for
home. Cold and wet, with the rain plastering my hair
to my head, carrying the full basket of roots, hungry
because we had not eaten since that meager plate of
porridge at breakfast, I stumbled along behind Euny,
now with my mind fully made up. Tomorrow I would
get up early, while Euny was still asleep, grab my things,
and set off for home. I might even leave my things
behind, I reflected, in case collecting them would wake
Euny. After all, there were plenty more clothes at home.
I pictured Erith's rapturous welcome and all the sympathy I would get as I told my story, though I also felt
a spasm of shame that I did not quite understand.

I was very tired now, and the long day's walk had
caused my ankle to swell again. It was dark by the time

we got to our own forest, but Euny entered it without hesitation and kept up a steady pace that, exhausted as I was, I found hard to match. I could think of nothing but sleep—my former raging appetite had died down now. When we came out of the forest there was a moon that showed the stepping stones across the stream as bright as day. It swam huge and golden over the shoulder of the tor and outlined the roof of Euny's hut. This was magical enough—a scene so beautiful that in spite of my exhaustion I felt transfixed by it—but there was something more. Standing between the tor and the hut, its branches silvered by the moonlight, quivering a little in the night breeze, stood the hazel tree I remembered from my dreams. My tiredness and hunger forgotten, I stood still and stared at the tree, stammering with excitement.

"The hazel tree. The tree in the dream. It's *here.*"

To which Euny, to whom I had said nothing about my dream, replied, "Well, of course. It's been here all along. You could have noticed it by daylight if you weren't so absent-minded. You'll have to do better than that." And she went on into the hut.

As I stood, still transfixed by my discovery, I heard the brush of wings overhead and looked up to see Moon, white and ghostlike, flying above me, seeking his food just as Euny had recommended.

"Moon!" I called to him softly. "I have found the hazel tree!" At which he circled around me twice in acknowledgment before continuing on his hunting trail.

8

AND SO MY LIFE with Euny began. She was an odd mixture of busyness and laziness. She did not care at all about the state of the hut and spent most of the day sitting in her chair in front of the fire, sometimes asleep, sometimes humming tunelessly, sometimes just still and quiet. Yet she had periods of extraordinary energy. Alone or taking me with her, she would walk for long distances, as on that first dreadful day (walking so quickly that I found I was out of breath trying to keep up). Often she was making for a hill, a forest, a ring of trees or of stones. Once there she would search diligently for some particular spot— I could never work out where it was going to be—and having found it would stay, singing a wild tuneless song, muttering words that sounded like poems. Her eyes would be closed, her face set and concentrated. She smiled to herself quite often, but sometimes her expression would change to one of pain. She never said anything to me before or after these occasions, just let me stand there on whatever windswept hill or moorland we happened to be, shivering and rather frightened. I wanted to ask her to explain these times to me but I never had the courage.

Soon after my arrival we had climbed our own tor—its sides were steep and gaunt like the ribs of a giant, and I arrived at the top with my heart pounding. I could see our tiny hut a mere speck at the bottom, and there was a wonderful view of forest and hill, with the tor of Glasweryn and a village with its plowed fields away in the distance. On this occasion Euny neither laughed nor wept but simply stood quietly. Then she led me to a small wattle-and-daub hut that stood on the crest of the hill. Within it, like a queen in a hovel, was an extraordinary carved and painted figure set in a kind of cave made of stone. Her face was black, her eyes dark and wild, and upon her head she wore a crown decorated with a moon and stars. Her gown was blue and red, and sitting upon her lap was a baby, awkward and doll-like. A wreath of hedgerow flowers—the last beautiful flowers of autumn entwined with berries—had been hung around her neck, and others were strewn at her feet or thrust into little pots. At her feet was a well, its ancient wooden lid beautifully carved with flowers and animals. There were candles too, set around the rim of the well, one or two still alight, the others burned out as if many people had visited the place and left a burning candle as a memento of their visit.

Euny, always so dry, so caustic, astounded me by suddenly prostrating herself on the floor while I stood awkwardly by. When she got up I saw that her face was wet with tears. Then she opened the well, threw in the dipper on its long chain, drank a little of the water, and replaced the dipper without offering any water to me. On the way back to the hut she was silent. Only when we had nearly reached it did she say sternly to me, "You are not to climb the tor, nor visit the place of the Mother unless I tell you to." Immediately I felt irritated and as if I might wish to do so, though that steep climb would not otherwise have been much of a temptation.

In fact, Euny was full of instructions about what I might and might not do. From the moment she woke me each day from my uncomfortable sleep, usually very early in the morning, she ordered me out to draw water, to grind meal, to start up the fire, to make porridge, to gather sticks, to sweep, to feed the chickens, and to chop up scraps for the pig. I did not much mind doing these things since they helped us to keep warm or fed, or meant that the plates and pots were cleaner than when *she* washed them; it did annoy me, however, to see her sitting in her rocking chair, not helping, while I swept or cooked or cleaned the ashes from the fire or staggered in with the pails of water. It made me feel that I was her servant, which I didn't like at all. Once, on a bad day, I mumbled my resentment at her, and she replied with one of her crows of glee, "Yes, you are my servant. That is exactly what you are." My only comfort was that I did at least keep the hut cleaner than she did and that I soon learned to cook nicer meals.

THE TWO MOST painful things about life with Euny, however, were cold and hunger. In my privileged life in the Wooden Palace there had always been a fire blazing on the hearth, and I had always been warmly dressed and well fed. Life in the hut was very different. The thin walls did not keep in the warmth of our fire, and every night I woke up shivering, so that I felt tired and miserable the next day. As the winter approached, I went out gloveless in all weather on my innumerable errands for Euny, and my cloak and boots, made for life at Castle Dore, were not thick enough to keep out the damp and the cold. Soon I had chilblains on my hands and feet, which became very sore and drove me half mad with irritation whenever I did get warm. Euny showed no sympathy for my shivers or my chilblains. Once when I complained she said, "You came here to make your life real. Cold, hunger, the hard floor to lie on—these are your teachers."

If they were my teachers, I reflected angrily, then they made me very miserable. Yet I could not help noticing when I next picked up my spoon to eat my soup that since I had had almost no food all day, the soup tasted better than any soup I had ever eaten in my life. It was as if my whole body had suddenly come alive and was singing. The flavor of every bean, grain, and vegetable in the soup spoke to me. Even the water I drank tasted wonderful. Was it just the purity of Euny's well, or was it that desperately hungry as I was, my mouth was wonderfully alert to enjoy all that entered it?

Similarly, when I came in half frozen from a series of trips to the well, there was a special kind of joy in letting the warmth of the fire steal through my cold body, though the torment of the chilblains spoiled it a little.

It also occurred to me that I had never noticed the change from autumn to winter as sharply as I did now. Before, I was dimly aware, as everyone is, of the falling of the leaves from the trees, the coming of the frost, and the short, dark days. Now, partly perhaps because of my fear of cold and hunger, I noticed that no two days were the same, that as the year declined, there were changes of sky and stars and the behavior of birds that I had never known before.

Not, of course, that I was ever observant enough for Euny.

"What were the clouds like?" she asked, as ever, when I returned from an expedition. "Did the wind change? What birds did you see? Which trees have lost all their leaves? What shrubs still have flowers upon them? What was the moon like?"

It had been my habit to walk through the world in a pleasant dream, remembering stories or conversations, going back over bits of the past I had enjoyed, or having romantic fantasies about the future. Euny did not seem to understand this at all.

"You are hopeless, hopeless," she told me angrily. "You will never make a *doran.*" I was wounded by this and sulkily tried to remember to notice the sort of things she asked about, but she had an unnerving way, after I had made a point of counting the birds or observing the clouds, of picking on something quite new—the shape of the landscape, the number of footpaths and the way they joined one another, the appearance of people we had met by the wayside, or animals. I tried harder, but it seemed to be no use at all.

In addition to hunger and cold I realized that I was also struggling with silence. Euny sometimes went all day without addressing a word to me. In desperation I had long conversations with Moon and with Borra, the pig, standing beside his sty and scratching his back with a stick. Euny often fed Borra scraps and sometimes I stole one or two of them for myself before giving them to him. He, after all, was very fat, whereas I was much thinner than I used to be. I enjoyed Borra's grunts, but I would rather have talked to another person.

"Do you ever feel lonely?" I asked Euny once. There was a long silence.

"Sometimes," she replied.

"Don't you mind?"

She made a gesture like pushing something away from her. "I am used to it. It doesn't matter."

When the chores were all done, Euny expected me to sit still as she did, she in her rocking chair, I on a cushion on the hearth. I hated doing this and soon learned to spin out the chores so that they kept me busy for much of the morning, but sooner or later there was nothing to do but to go back into the hut and sit down. Half a day would pass without conversation or movement. Sometimes I fell asleep—upright, since Euny saw no reason for me to lie down during the day. Always I yawned and fidgeted.

"It's very boring," I said unwarily once.

"Good," said Euny, and spoke no more. Not for the first time I hated her. I spent the time dreaming of food.

THERE WAS SOMETHING that I began to mind more than the cold and hunger. It was the feeling that while I was enduring all this discomfort and Euny's wounding sarcasm, I was learning nothing about the special sort of power that was the gift of the *doran*. I had supposed that Euny would sit me down and instruct me properly in the use of herbs and ointments, helping me to understand, as all my other teachers had done, instead of merely tossing off a comment about a plant now and then, but when I saw Euny working on her medicines and asked for information, she would wave me away with "It's not important," as if the whole thing were a secret, and suggest that it was time for me to get on with feeding the pig.

"How will I learn if you never teach me anything?" I asked crossly one day. She did not bother to reply.

9

THE WORST THING that ever happened in the first part of my stay with Euny was the day she spent a long time sharpening the big knife on a stone by the door and then handed it to me.

"Go on," she said to me, and I gazed at her in puzzlement.

"The pig," she said. "Kill it!"

I stared open-mouthed at her, looking from her face to the gleaming knife in her hand.

"I couldn't possibly," I said. I remembered the horrors of pig killing on the farms around Castle Dore—the squeals and the flowing blood. I had always shuddered and hurried by, back to the life of a princess.

"Someone has to do it!" said Euny. "So why not you?"

"Please don't make me," I begged her. (Already my experience of Euny should have taught me that this was the worst possible way of going about things.)

"I have noticed that you like to eat pig meat," Euny

said haughtily. "The old carcass is empty. If you don't kill this pig, there will be no meat for you to eat."

"You don't mean it!" I said. Fat bacon was most of our diet. I knew she did mean it. Furious with her, I snatched the knife out of her hand and went to the pigsty.

Borra had become a good friend of mine by now. At the sound of my footsteps he looked up expectantly. I hid the knife behind my back and talked kindly to him, noticing the life in the bright little eyes, the pleasure in his grunts. I went back to Euny.

"I can't do it!" I said, throwing down the knife. "It's cruel!"

"So we shall starve to death!" she said triumphantly, as if the prospect pleased her.

I tried to argue with her. "I don't understand. I thought the *doran*s loved the creatures of the world and wanted to care for them."

"What could show more love for an animal than eating it?" replied Euny.

"But you are taking its life away from it. All it has."

"For it to become part of the life in you. You are being false. What you will discover—*if* you ever stop being interested in yourself for long enough to notice the world around you—is that all life feeds off other life."

"But not Borra! He's so sweet, and I love him so much that I cannot kill him."

"But sweet or not you would eat him if I killed him. Is that not right?"

Shamefaced, I was forced to nod. I knew that I had only to smell bacon cooking to feel a wild hunger.

"So long as *you* don't have to feel responsible for killing him. So long as the princess does not get blood on her hands! Wonderful!"

Euny's scorn hurt me, but I minded it even more when she picked up the knife and handed it back to me.

"Hurry up! There is a lot of work to be done on the carcass, and we need to start while there is still plenty of daylight."

I left her again, but instead of going back to the sty I began to pace around the bottom of the tor. I had never been spoken to in my life in the way Euny spoke to me, and it left me helplessly angry. It was then that I noticed I was brandishing the knife furiously in the air—and suddenly I observed with a faint glimmer of unexpected amusement that what I was doing in my mind was plunging the knife into Euny. I couldn't kill a pig, but I had a secret longing, at least just for that moment, to kill her. Yet I knew that my future as a *doran* was linked to my obedience to Euny, that she would refuse to teach me if I did not do as she said. I paused outside Borra's pen, praying to his spirit to forgive me. This time I did not hide the knife, and he looked at it without fear. I held his head in one hand and with the other slipped the knife beneath his chin. My heart pounding, I pushed the knife against his throat. Immediately Borra began to struggle, and with tremendous force he threw me back against the wall. I had

not even cut him. Frightened now at the furious creature, I put the knife straight to his throat, shouting to
him, begging him at the top of my voice not to resist.
The knife made only the smallest cut, but suddenly
blood began to pour out of him and the knife itself was
slippery with it. Borra backed against the wall with
squeals that rang sickeningly through my head. I
wounded him again, but he was still full of fight and
began to come after me with his head lowered, making
a strange growling noise in his throat. For a while we
circled each other, Borra wanting to attack me but afraid
of the knife, me wanting to finish my terrible task but
afraid of his hoofs and his powerful snout. Desperate,
I lunged at him once more and knew from his scream
that I had hurt him, but also that this big angry animal
was now going to charge. I moved as quickly around
the little space of the pen as I could, until suddenly my
foot slipped in a puddle of blood. I fell. At that moment Borra also fell, and I could hear his dreadful labored breathing as he lay on his side. Swiftly I stood
up, bent over him, and cut his windpipe properly. Although his legs twitched a bit, I knew he was within
seconds of death.

"Borra, forgive me," I said to him. "This was not my
choice."

White, shaking, covered in blood, I went back to the
hut. For a moment I was too upset to notice that Euny
was not alone, indeed that the hut seemed to be full of
people. There was my mother looking her most beautiful, her delicate pale face framed in a collar of fox.
There was Erith, shocked at the sight of me. There was

Gamal standing by the hearth regarding me sympathet-
ically and beside him another boy about our own age
who stared at me in open amusement. I stood there
looking mutely at them, bloodstained, my hair falling
over my face, the knife in my hand. My mother made
a small, stifled exclamation as she caught sight of me
and then was silent. Erith was less restrained.

"You look awful," she said.

"I've killed the pig," I said unnecessarily to Euny,
not knowing what else to say. Euny, quite unruffled by
the company, nodded with a small, pleased expression,
took the knife from me, and suggested that I should
change my smock. Gamal, trying to act as if all was as
usual, introduced me to Finbar, a new page at my father's court who had come to carry food and warm
clothes, which my mother and Erith had prepared for
me. Even in these circumstances I noticed that he was
a very handsome boy, with brilliant blue eyes and black
hair. As I tried to speak to my mother, Finbar, where
she could not see him, was pointing at me and silently
pretending to hold his sides with laughter, like a mocking jester behind the throne. I thought he was the rud-
est boy I had ever met.

LATER, MY HAIR COMBED and wearing a cleaner smock,
I walked with my mother to the foot of the strange-
shaped hill. A jumble of feelings fought inside me—
humiliation at being caught looking so dreadful, anger
at Euny for making me kill the pig, triumph at finally
having done it, apprehension about what my mother
would say. Would she persuade me to return to Castle

Dore? I realized I had very mixed feelings about that.

For a long time neither of us spoke.

"So how is it?" my mother said at last.

I started to mumble some reply but could not speak for the sob in my throat.

My mother stood for a long time looking up at the steep sides of the hill as if trying to read something from it. Then she said, "Of course you must come home if it is too dreadful. But I don't know; I have a feeling that you want to be here. Awful as it is."

An extraordinary surge of gratitude ran through me, gratitude that although she was my mother, she could see and understand something that went beyond my thinness, my swollen fingers, and my own anger and perplexity. I began to cry in earnest because of her love for me, and she put her arms around me.

"Why do I have to?" I asked her.

"I don't know."

"I felt so ashamed," I said, "that you and Erith and the boys saw me all bloodstained from killing the pig. And that Euny and I live in such poverty."

She lifted up her white profile and, looking like the daughter of a prince that she was, said, "You were always a brave child, Ninnoc. Knowing you, I expected you would live this ordeal with courage. Life with Euny is hard, but it won't go on forever." She smiled at me. "Don't despair."

"I don't understand it," I said, "but I seem to need to be here. And yet it *is* awful."

"One good thing," went on Erlain, "we have brought

you some food, some sacks of wheat and oats. That should help. That and the pig." She smiled at me again. "And Erith put in some blankets and pillows and a thick woolen cloak."

"Good," I said.

"Gamal has brought you some cakes and some wine. You should get a decent supper tonight."

"You do understand," I said in gratitude.

I was humbled by my mother's generosity, at her willingness to let me, her only child, follow a strange path. I flung my arms around her and this time we both wept.

I also had time to talk with Gamal.

"I shall come and see you sometimes," he said. "And so will Finbar. He's become a good friend. I'm teaching him our language—his home is on an island a long way north of England. He wants to be a navigator."

I felt a pang of jealousy at Gamal's transparent enthusiasm for his friend.

"I don't like Finbar," I said. "I think he is very rude."

"You'll like him when you know him better. Everybody likes him. He's awfully funny, and he's brave."

It was impossible to ignore Finbar completely when the party left. I held out my hand coldly to him, and he kissed it, as was the custom, still taunting, it seemed to me, with mocking eyes.

"I hope *you* will come again, Gamal," I said pointedly.

I FELT very lonely when they had all gone away and I was back alone with Euny again, but I had no time to dwell on it since Euny and I spent the rest of the day cutting up the pig—a tiring, messy business—so that it could be salted. We did cook some of it at once, though, and had a marvelous supper, which I ate ravenously.

"We won't starve this winter," said Euny with satisfaction, looking at the sacks stored in the corner of the hut.

"What did you do in other winters?" I asked curiously.

"Survived," said Euny shortly.

"The trouble with being hungry or cold," I said thoughtfully, "is that you think of nothing else. It's like having a pain. On the other hand, you really appreciate it when there is food to eat or a warm fire. I never knew food to taste as good as it has these last few weeks."

Euny grunted.

"I didn't know I could kill anything," I said, still minding about Borra, even though he tasted very good.

Euny smiled a wrinkled, leathery smile that I had never seen before.

"You were a good, obedient girl," she said.

"You didn't give me much choice," I replied crossly.

"I am proud of you," she said, and I could scarcely believe my ears.

10

ONE DAY Euny said, "Tomorrow we go to see Angharad of the West."

"Who is she? Where does she live?"

"A long journey. You'll see."

"But suppose Gamal comes to see me while I'm gone."

"He'll just have to go home again, won't he?"

IT WAS a bright winter day when the two of us set off, with the sun winking on icy puddles and the sky blue and clear. The air seemed to sparkle. The prospect of a change had cheered me and I felt happier than I had for some time, even though Euny insisted on walking extremely fast. By now Moon was too big to fit in even the largest pocket, and I carried him in a special bag I had made for him out of an old shift.

My warm cloak was very comforting, but my boots felt too small for my swollen toes, and I could feel the

cold of the ground through the soles as they slipped
and slithered. My hands quickly became blue and numb,
and even with an old ragged blanket of Euny's around
my head and shoulders I could feel the wind biting me.
Euny, as usual, seemed not to notice the cold at all.

"Don't dawdle, girl," she said whenever I paused for
breath. We had not brought much food with us, just
some bread and some withered apples.

Much later we stopped at a farm and Euny begged
some milk. The farmer's wife was baking hot rolls and
the air was filled with the delicious smell of new bread.
She picked out two rolls each and gave them to us.
Seeing my wan face and frozen hands, she asked us in
to rest before the fire and then suggested that it was
too late to go on that night and that there was hay
enough in the barn to keep us warm. I slept well that
night in deep gratitude for her kindness, though Euny
roused me from a sound sleep before it was light and
insisted that we must be on our way. Rosy from the
nest of hay, my chilblains itching at the unaccustomed
warmth, I stumbled out yawning, ate my second roll
and drank the rest of the milk, and we set off again.

On this day we walked along a huge sea channel, a
giant estuary like a sea itself. From the cliffs we could
see dangerous rocks below—ships stayed well out in
the center. The blue-gray color of the sea was shot with
white, like a ripped garment with its lining showing
through.

Sustained by a good night's sleep and a breakfast, I
found that I walked faster and incurred fewer rebukes
from Euny, though the endless questions about what I

had seen on the walk—"How many ships?" and so on—continued. She had spoiled the pleasure of walking for me, filling it with anxieties about noticing and remembering. I did seem to be a little better at it than I had been, however.

By that evening, to my distress, we were miles from any human habitation. We drank water from a stream, but we had nothing to eat, and I was bitterly hungry. When it grew too dark and I was too tired for us to walk any farther, we sat on a log in a wood and simply waited for the night to pass. I took Moon from his traveling bag and watched with envy as he swooped over the moorland in search of food.

"I'm hungry," I said accusingly. And then when no reply was forthcoming, "Why didn't we prepare properly for this journey? We could have brought more bread with us, maybe some beer."

"But then you miss the pleasure," said Euny.

"What pleasure?"

"Of living as birds do from the hand of nature."

I thought of the starved birds I had often found lying dead on the ground in winter.

"Birds often die at the hand of nature."

"Sometimes. Mostly not."

I listened to the ravening eagle inside me demanding to be fed.

"I must have food," I said desperately.

"If there is no food, you simply have to be hungry."

"Don't you mind being hungry?"

Euny hesitated.

"Nowadays, not at all. It is like the weather—I live

with it. But when I was a child . . . yes, I wept a great deal about being hungry."

I was intrigued. Euny had never before told me anything about her past—I am not sure that I thought she had one, that she had not emerged into the world full-grown, wearing her greeny-black clothes. I hoped she would say more, but she did not, and I did not dare to press her.

"Tell me where we are going," I asked at last to distract myself from all my discomforts.

"To one of the greatest *doran*s in the land. This country, you know, has many women of power, but Angharad is one of great power, and she has offered to teach you."

"What sort of power will I have?"

"The mending sort, the healing kind," Euny said shortly and crossly. *"If* you are ever ready for it. *When* you can use it rightly."

That night seemed interminably long, and it was dreadful to have to set off walking again. My feet were now so swollen that I could only hobble along with difficulty. My hunger had mysteriously vanished, as it does when no food is in prospect, though I felt quite weak and occasionally a little faint. We paused only once to drink water from a spring.

Then in the late afternoon we breasted a hill overlooking the sea, and Euny pointed to a little house set in the valley, with the sparkling waters of a lake behind it. Smoke was rising from the smoke hole, and there was something about the house that was pleasing and reassuring. I quickened my painful steps.

When we got nearer I could see something bright-colored hanging over the wall of a storehouse. There were patches of vivid red and yellow and green, but I was almost too tired to wonder about them, still less to ask questions.

It took us a while longer to reach the house, and by the time we did it was nearly dark. Euny lifted the latch and we entered a shadowy fire-lit room in which Angharad, a woman of graceful middle age, rose to greet us. The large fire made the room deliciously warm. There was the scent of a rich, meaty stew in the air.

I unwrapped the blanket from my head and stood uncertainly in the soft firelight, feeling as if I might burst into tears. The room swirled disturbingly about me just when I wanted so much to look at it. I had a horrible feeling that I was going to be sick, and then I was aware of Angharad catching me as I fell.

When I came to from my faint, Angharad was very gently easing the boots from my swollen feet.

"When did you last eat?" she was asking Euny.

I was aware at once of the comfort and refinement of life in Angharad's house and felt ashamed of my dirty clothes and ragged blanket. But Angharad showed no sign of despising us. When I felt better it was lovely to be drawn forward to the fire—though the heat caused my toes to itch furiously—to sit in a comfortable chair and fill my hungry stomach (my appetite had sprung back to life at the first sniff of the stew).

There was a sort of step with cushions on it around the hearth, and a big chair. In one corner stood a loom strung in brilliant colors, and in another corner a lad-

der passed up into a shadowy chamber. The chair, the
table, and the cushions were covered in bright fabric,
in the palest pink, rosy orange, a deep inky blue, all of
them glowing like jewels in the half-dark of the firelight. The color, the comfort, and the rich taste of the
stew could not have been more different from the
hardships of Euny's hut. There was also a smell of roses,
one that, I would later know, seemed to pervade
Angharad's house. To this day I can never smell a rose
without remembering her.

Angharad, wearing a pretty red gown, with her shining fair hair and her gentle apple-cheeked face, was not
in the least like Euny. She reminded me a little of my
mother, and I was instantly drawn to her. While she
talked to Euny—a conversation about people who were
unknown to me—I was aware of her readiness to in-
clude me, the way her gray eyes turned to me and smiled
with a sympathy to which I had grown unaccustomed.
At the same time her hands were busy with her spindle. Gradually I grew warmer and relaxed on my cushion, but was immediately aware of a desperate need to
sleep. Suddenly Angharad interrupted the conversation
with Euny and stood up.

"Come!" she said to me. "You are tired out."

She picked up a candleholder, lit a candle from the
fire, and led the way up the ladder. Above were two
chambers, a big one and a small one. She took me to
the small one, where there were two beds upon the
floor, straw-filled pallets covered with bright-colored
blankets, and pointed to the one that had a thin white
sleeping shift folded on it. She left me and I undressed,

settled Moon comfortably on a beam, and crept into the nest of rustling straw. Then Angharad came back carrying bandages and a jar of ointment. She tended the open sores on my feet. Then she tucked the blankets around me and kissed me gently.

"I hope you'll be very happy in my house!" she said. Then the waves of sleep were lapping around me.

11

I WAS WOKEN by a voice saying insistently, *"Please
wake up. I want to talk to you."* With a start I
came to, saw sunlight brilliant on the white walls
of the room, and could not think where I was. I turned
my head and saw a girl about my own age, a very pretty
girl sitting cross-legged by the bed, watching me intently. She had long fair hair, braided, falling down over
her shoulders, and her eyes were a vivid green.

"Who are you?" I asked in surprise.

"Trewyn," she said. "I live with Angharad. I'm a sort
of apprentice. Didn't they tell you about me?"

It seemed useless to explain that Euny never told me
anything, so I simply smiled at her.

"I'm longing to talk to you," she said, full of eager-
ness. "Angharad said you were a princess!"

I must confess that I felt pleased that Trewyn was
obviously impressed by this, but I still felt too shy to
launch into a long description of my life.

"Do you sleep in here too?" I asked, seeing the other bed disarranged.

"Yes. It *is* going to be nice having you. I was longing to wake you up and talk to you when I got home last night. I was out looking for a plant Angharad needed to make a dye. But she wouldn't let me wake you up." Trewyn paused for a moment. "Are you hungry?"

I nodded. She got up and went out of the room, and for a moment I caught sight of her lovely profile and long neck—it was she, not I, who looked like a princess, I thought. I lay back, propped on my pillow, still quite tired but enjoying the warmth of my bed, the simple lines of the room, and the fact that for the first time in months I was to have a companion of my own age.

In a little while Trewyn was back with an oatcake and a drink they make in those parts by fermenting the whey of milk. The good plain taste of the oatcake— delicious like all Angharad's cooking—and the fiery warmth of the drink put new energy into me. While I ate, Trewyn asked about Moon and tried to talk to him, but he blinked stupidly at her.

I climbed down the ladder to the room where the two *doran*s were sitting in front of the fire together. Euny, usually so pale, looked a little flushed from the fire. She looked up at me, saying, "Tomorrow I will travel north. I will be gone for two months. Angharad will teach you in that time." The pleasure must have shown in my face, because she said rather crossly, "I hope she won't spoil you too much."

"Nonsense!" said Angharad. "She's a sensible girl, and she and Trewyn will be company for each other. Come back and fetch her in the spring."

I THINK my obvious preference for Angharad must have rankled Euny. The next day I walked a little way with her on her journey. Then she stopped.

"Go back now." She hesitated. "You think I am hard on you, maybe that I do not care about you. I can only be a *doran* in the way that is natural for me." Euny waited, as if she were trying to say more but could not manage it. Then she kissed me roughly on the cheek, turned, and marched away. I was touched by her speech but could not wait to get back to Angharad and Trewyn.

One of the reasons that Angharad had offered to keep me for a while, I think now, was that she believed Euny was starving me and wanted to feed me up. The food was generous and delicious, and she encouraged me to enjoy it, occasionally saying things like, "Young girls need proper nourishment," which I took to be an oblique criticism of Euny. Not that I felt she disliked Euny.

"You have one of the most remarkable *doran*s in the country as your teacher," Angharad said to me one day, when she and I were out gathering docks to make a green dye.

"How do you mean?" I asked with bitterness. "What is it that is so remarkable?"

"Among the *doran*s we speak of people having power, you know. We don't mean power like kings or popes have power, of course, but power to bring things back into a sort of harmony, like tuning an instrument that's gone flat."

"And Euny can do that?" I said disbelievingly.

"In a most unusual way, yes. She sees to the heart of things."

There was something I wanted to say to Angharad, only it was difficult because it felt disloyal.

"She's very hard on me."

Angharad was silent for a long while, and then she said, "Did Euny ever tell you the story of her life?" I shook my head.

"When Euny was a tiny little girl her parents were killed in a raid. Some of the tribes were very brutal in those days. They didn't just take cattle and crops. . . . Some say Euny's mother was killed in front of her—that she escaped only because she was hidden in the roof of the barn but that she peeked out and saw what happened. Two or three of the children were left, but their house was destroyed and they had nowhere to go. They lived as they could, roaming the countryside, or-phaned and homeless, begging food or work here and there, sleeping wherever they could be warm. Euny's whole childhood was like that. Only when she was fourteen, a famous *doran* called Phrene took Euny in. She was starved and sick like a little wild animal in winter, but Phrene was very gentle with her, and slowly Euny became strong and well. I know this"—Angharad gave me her sweet smile—"because I was Phrene's ap-prentice, and Euny and I were sister *doran*s-in-training, just like you and Trewyn are. Phrene reckoned," she went on, "that Euny was the best pupil she ever had, and as you know, good *doran*s are made by good teach-ers. You will be a good—perhaps great—*doran* partly because Euny trained you."

"But she *doesn't* train me," I said obstinately, although I was very moved by this tragic story.

"Child," said Angharad slowly, and there was a long pause, "open your eyes."

WHEN WE were back in the house, we boiled a vat of the dock leaves with vinegar, and I pushed skeins of white wool into it.

"Without the vinegar—what is called the mordant," Angharad said, "the dye would run as soon as you washed the wool. It is the biting acid that makes the color fast. It was brave of you to leave home to go and live with Euny. I know what Euny's housekeeping is like. You must often have been frozen as well as hungry."

The pleasure of Angharad's sympathy made it possible to swallow my resentment.

"It was rather cold," I admitted. "But I wasn't really brave. I just couldn't help myself. Also I know that Euny has something to teach me . . . if she only would."

Angharad turned and looked at me. "Perhaps you think learning to be a *doran* is like learning French or mathematics. But it isn't. It's quite different."

"But I've only got a year and a day," I reminded her, "and so far I haven't learned anything."

"Well, after today you will have learned how to dye wool with dock leaves."

Later, when we fished the shining green skeins out of the vat and hung them over the storehouse wall to dry in the sun, I had a sense of achievement but thought, "It's nothing to do with being a *doran*."

Although Angharad fed me properly and kept me warm, she expected me to work hard. To begin with she taught me how to tease wool, the process of preparing it for spinning. I learned to pull the wool off the fleece, take out the dirty and tangled bits, part the wool between my fingers until it was of even texture, and then comb it into delicate little rolls.

"It's the preparation that counts in spinning," Angharad said. "If you are lazy about that, you will never spin an even thread."

Then she showed me how to knot some thread onto the spindle and, spinning it between my feet, twist the combed wool onto it while the spindle revolved. It was very difficult at first because the thread kept breaking and going into lumps. It was nothing like the perfect, even thread that Angharad made so rhythmically. I persisted though, and eventually, to my great pride, a cone of spun wool rested on the spindle. Then, instead of letting me whirl the spindle between my feet, she stood a spinning dish on the floor beside me, and I found I could spin much faster and more easily than before. I was delighted at first, then I got bored and began to spin more carelessly, wanting to be done with it. The result was rather poor. Angharad did not scold me. She simply expected that I would go on practicing.

"Wool is a living thing," she said once. "That is why you cannot spin wool from a dead sheep."

Watching her spin, I noticed how as she joined one piece of wool to another the little hairs of the wool clung together to make a strong thread with no trace of a join. As we teased the wool plucked from the fleece,

I suddenly saw it with new eyes, noticing the tiny black flecks of peat in it and the yellow waxy substance that made my hands soft. As we carded it and made it into long webs of wool, I felt its softness, its delicate strength. Angharad's long slim fingers twirling the distaff and making a fine even thread made it seem almost as if she spun it out of herself. I caught myself trying to match her rhythm, to move into the kind of easy concentration that produced a thread without lumps, but I kept finding that either I tensed myself and squeezed the unspun wool so hard that it would not flow properly into the thread or that I pulled the threads out so far that they thinned and broke. It was more difficult than I had thought at first.

"It's how you feel, isn't it?" I said to Angharad one day in a moment of insight. "That's what makes the evenness of the thread. You need to concentrate yet not notice that you're concentrating." I suddenly remembered what she had said about learning to be a *doran* being different from learning French.

"Do you think spinning could be helpful in learning how to be a *doran?*" I asked.

Angharad laughed. "It's exactly the same thing," she said.

I frowned.

"How can it be the same thing? Every old woman sitting spinning on her doorstep knows how to do this. They're not all *doran*s?"

"No, not all, but don't underestimate their wisdom. When you are wise it won't make them stupid."

12

GRADUALLY ANGHARAD taught me to dye with many different plants—with leaves and roots and berries. On almost every sunny day the wall was hung with wool in jewel colors—the pink, orange, and red of madder and lichen, the blue and purple of woad, the yellow of dandelions, marsh marigolds, and heather, each carefully set with its mordant. When I looked at the wool dyed a wonderful delicate yellow from lichen, I remembered with amusement the frustrating morning I had spent trying to collect urine from Betsy the goat—goat's urine being the best mordant for lichen.

Mornings were spent cleaning the house, drawing water, building a fire, preparing food, finding herbs, making and using dyes. In the afternoons the three of us sat down to our spinning, often whiling away the time with stories and songs. Trewyn and I would have an hour or two to ourselves in the late afternoon, and then after supper we returned to our spinning.

"When you have enough wool," Angharad said to me, "I shall teach you to weave."

"What shall I weave?" I asked her.

Angharad nodded to Trewyn, who left the room and came back with a cloak over her arm. At a further signal from Angharad, Trewyn put the cloak on over her simple brown smock and fastened it with a gold clasp. The cloak was a deep dark green, lit here and there with a vivid flash of pink, a fish or a flower that floated in its dusky depths. Trewyn's slim body, long neck, and beautiful profile with its perfect cheekbones seemed to take on dignity and mystery. Somehow the cloak seemed to reveal everything about her that I already knew as well as other things about her that I had only guessed at.

"This is the cloak of a *doran*," said Angharad. "Every *doran* has one, and it needs to be carefully made because one day it will be your protection against the magic of sorcerers. It must be as perfect as it can be."

"Will mine be like that?" I asked, amazed that Angharad might think me capable of making such a cloak.

"No. Your cloak will be as you make it. When you thread the loom, you will know which colors to use. That is why you need to prepare a good stock of colors now, so that you will have what you need."

I RETURNED to my spinning with a new zeal, determined now to make the thread as perfect as I could. It reflected my mood continually. It broke when I was tired or angry or impatient and flowed effortlessly when

I was calm and happy. Angharad gave me a shelf to store the wool for my cloak, and every day I added to the colored skeins.

It was a real relief to me that I was no longer cold or hungry. Even when the sleeping chamber grew cold on the frostiest nights, it was always possible to creep down and sit by the dying embers of the fire. And there was always enough food, though it was simple—milk and goat cheese, porridge, bread, beer. I was no longer tortured by chilblains, nor weary from hunger. It felt like a very precious sort of freedom.

One day Angharad said to me, "It is time to start weaving now. You must choose the threads with which to make the warp of your cloth."

I looked helplessly at the shelf with its many colored skeins and balls of wool.

"I don't know how to choose," I said lamely.

"Look inside yourself," Angharad said. "You do know really."

I looked inside myself but no knowledge came, only a sort of panic.

"I don't know," I said again. "You choose."

Angharad did not reply, but began moving around the house, preparing supper. Trewyn was out on some errand of her own. Moon stared down at me from the beam above my head, at a time when he was usually out hunting for food. I sat feeling bewildered at what was expected of me, and when supper came I was grateful for the diversion.

After supper, I turned to pick up my spindle, but Angharad shook her head.

"Weaving," she said emphatically. I continued to sit

on my stool, feeling silly. Much later Angharad and
Trewyn rose to go to bed. Angharad looked at me, her
gentle motherly face unexpectedly determined.

"No point in going to bed till you've solved it," she
said. Trewyn threw me a sympathetic glance as the two
of them left me there.

When they had gone I straightened my aching back
and wondered what to do. I could, of course, sleep in
Angharad's chair and she would be none the wiser, but
this would bring me no closer to solving my problem.
I looked again at the wool on the shelf and felt more
puzzled than ever. I stared at each color in turn—the
pinks, the reds, the oranges, the blues, the purples, the
yellows, the browns, the greens—and tried to imagine
beginning work with them, but none of them claimed
me.

I wiped away a tear. I could see that I would still be
sitting here at breakfast time and that even Angharad,
who was always kind, would sternly force me to wait
until inspiration struck. I could, of course, just take up
whichever color came to hand and start work with that.
Angharad would not know (or would she?) that I had
cheated. Exasperated, as my hand hovered over the shelf,
I thought that I might choose one of the colors blind-
folded.

Yet immediately my hand fell back to my side.
However tired I was, however hopeless it seemed, there
was simply no point in cheating. If this cloak was
somehow to be my protection, it needed to be woven
with truth. Both Euny and Angharad, so very different
from each other, had taught me that.

For a few moments I felt lonely and rather cross, as if someone ought to be telling me what to do. The feeling of crossness grew and grew until I slapped the side of the loom in rage. Why didn't my teachers help me? Almost at once I saw the answer. It was that like a small child taking its first steps, there was something I needed to try out, something only I could teach myself.

Now I was very still, trying to notice something in myself that I had never noticed before. Sweating a little, with a sense of growing excitement and trembling a little too, I heard myself suddenly say out loud, "Who are you?" And then, quite firmly, as if I had never properly understood this before, I answered myself, "You are Juniper." As I said this, my hand, completely sure of itself, reached out and picked up wool of the deepest midnight blue and luminous gray-blue. My hand reached out again and this time it took up white un-dyed wool. On its third journey to the shelf it chose two yellowy colors—a deep amber and a lighter yellow. Did I really know that these were the "right" colors? Yes, I did, but I did not know how I knew. I began reaching the midnight-blue wool around the loom, knotting it, weighting it, too concentrated on what I was doing to find it odd that it was now the middle of the night. At one point, however, I looked up and saw that Moon's amber eyes were still fixed unwinkingly upon me. When Angharad got up to milk Betsy the next morning, there were many threads on the loom. She came straight across the room to look, nodded with pleasure, and said, "You got it right. I knew you would."

13

"DO YOU *want* to be a *doran?*" I remember
Trewyn asking me one day as we sat high on
the branch of a tree.

"I want to *understand* all kinds of things," I said.
"Maybe more than some people do. Or maybe they do
it differently. And I don't want to be pushed into getting married just for the sake of it."

"I'm a bit scared about being a *doran,*" Trewyn admitted. "Angharad can do real magic, you know, though
she doesn't bother very often."

"Yes, I think Euny can too," I said. "I suppose that
means that eventually we will do magic."

"I used to think when I was little that it would be
lovely to do magic—imagine being able to fly or get
the house to clean itself up all on its own, or have
something good to eat just when you felt like it."

"Or get to a place quickly without having to walk all
the way," I said.

"Now I'm not so sure," said Trewyn. "Exciting in a way, but maybe something I'd rather not meddle with. I mean, I like to feel that you can *depend* on things being predictable—apples falling downward, a bowl of porridge being empty when it *is* empty, people being there or not being there."

Trewyn was silent for a while. Then she began to tell me of an extraordinary experience.

"I went to Caerleon on an errand for Angharad one morning," she began, "and on the road I met a terrifying dog. It was very big—the biggest dog I had ever seen—black, with great teeth, a slavering tongue, and a strange smell. It would not let me move. Every time I took a step forward it growled and looked as if it would attack me, but when I started walking slowly backward the way I had come, the same thing happened. I stood there until noon, too frightened to move. Then it was as if I talked to Angharad inside myself, asking her what I should do. Suddenly there she was, right beside me on the road, though she did not look at me or talk to me. She spoke to the dog in a language I did not understand. Then she took me by the hand and led me right past it. I turned around to see what the dog was doing, but it had disappeared. When I turned back, Angharad had disappeared too.

"When I got home I asked her about it, of course. I half hoped she would deny it, say it had all been my imagination, but she simply nodded her head and said, 'You needed help.' Then, and this was the worst bit, she added, 'That was no ordinary dog.'

" 'It was bigger than any dog I ever saw,' I agreed.

" 'I mean—it wasn't a dog at all,' Angharad said. 'I have a great enemy in Caerleon. I supposed he was away and that it was safe to send you. But I was mistaken. He had returned to Caerleon and he recognized you as being my apprentice.'

" 'How could he recognize me?' I asked. 'He had never seen me.'

" 'Sorcerers recognize anything or anyone that belongs to a *doran*—their clothes, their animals, or their apprentices.'

" 'How?' I asked, and I could not believe Angharad's answer. 'By their *smell,*' she said."

I was struck by this story of Trewyn's. I was also trying to see if I could smell Trewyn or remember whether any special smell came from Angharad. Yes, I thought, she smelled of roses. Euny's house certainly had a distinctive smell—damp and musty—and her person also had a smell—of garlic, and spice, and of unwashed skin—but I didn't smell like that. Or at least I hoped I didn't.

"Somehow," Trewyn finished, "that whole episode scared me. Up till then I thought magic was exciting, but then I knew that there was real danger."

"What danger?"

"That sorcerers could kill you or enslave you. They can take the spirit out of you, you know—they call it ghosting—and you wander around not knowing who you are. Sometimes now I just want to go back home and lead an ordinary life and not get mixed up in magic."

Finally, hesitantly, I told Trewyn about the time I had done some magic myself—how I had healed Gamal.

Yet when later I had tried to cure my own chilblains, it had not worked.

"Do you think it just works when you do it for other people?" asked Trewyn. "I mean, I've never seen Angharad use magic to make her own life easier—to save bothering to grind any more meal, say, or to avoid the labor of threading up a loom."

PERHAPS THE TALK of magic influenced me in some way. A few days before, Angharad had been showing me how to weave, and that afternoon, standing alone at the big loom while the other two were out somewhere, I had the strangest feeling that the feathery white figures I was weaving into the midnight-blue background were three-dimensional, that they were just as solidly part of the world as the stool or the loom itself. Later, when I took up the spindle, I felt as if the thread was flowing not just from the puff of wool hanging over my left shoulder, but through my arm and indeed through my whole body. For the first time the thread was perfectly even. It looked like the thread that Angharad spun, and what was more, I knew that I was spinning somewhat as Angharad did, in an effortless rhythm.

When Angharad came back, she looked at the weaving I had done and at the thread I had spun.

"So!" she said. "You are ready!"

"Ready for what?" I asked.

"You must work hard at your cloak. Euny will be back soon."

As so often, that day when it all seemed so easy was

followed by one in which it all seemed impossibly difficult. I realized that I had made a slight mistake in
following the pattern of my weaving, but it was a long
way back and I simply couldn't be bothered to undo it.
In any case, the error was so tiny that it scarcely showed
at all.

"WHAT DID Angharad mean, 'ready'?" I asked Trewyn
in our white and timber sleeping chamber. "Ready for
what?"

Trewyn's lovely face looked troubled.

"I don't know," she said. "Some sort of ceremony,
maybe. Or an ordeal—*doran*s are said to train their apprentices with ordeals."

"What do you mean?" I asked, uneasy now myself.

"They want to find out if you are strong enough,
brave enough," she said.

"But Angharad and Euny wouldn't do anything really
cruel to us, would they?" I asked.

"They might if they thought it would be good for
us," Trewyn replied gloomily.

I often thought about this conversation in the days
that followed, as I finished the rich material of my cloak.
Yet I would look across the room at Angharad's kind
motherly face, and I could not believe that she wished
me any ill. And even Euny, hard as life with her had
been, had never set out to hurt or frighten me—she
was just not very good at imagining what I was feeling.
I felt that I trusted both *doran*s.

Trewyn, however, felt far less confident than I did.
She was plainly frightened of the coming ordeal—

whatever it was—and she began to sleep badly. Occasionally she would wake me with her tossing and turning. Twice she had bad dreams and began to shout in her sleep. In the morning she was pale and heavy-eyed. I saw Angharad look thoughtfully at her, and I wondered if she would give her a word of comfort, but she did not.

Angharad spoke only once about what was to come, on the day we cut the heavy material from the loom. Joyful that my long task was done, I picked up the material and draped it for a moment around my shoulders. It was very heavy. Angharad glanced at me, then lowered her eyes as if she had seen more than she wanted to see.

"Take it off," she said quite sharply. "It is not time."

"When will it be time?" I inquired.

"There will be a . . . ceremony," she said. "For you and Trewyn. When Euny returns."

"What will it be like?"

"I cannot tell you."

"Trewyn is very scared about it," I said disloyally, wanting a little comfort myself.

"I know," Angharad said, and turned to poke the fire. I was not reassured.

THERE WAS STILL a lot of work to be done on the cloak. From the wooden chest Angharad produced a bolt of dusky orange silk for the lining. She also gave me two topaz stones set in silver with which to make a clasp. And finally I had to embroider a collar for it. I spent several days drawing patterns on a piece of slate, until one pattern—a design that grew unexpectedly from the look of Moon's claws—seemed exactly right to me. Angharad gave me some seed pearls to sew into the pattern, and they represented claws very convincingly.

"This will be the most precious thing you will ever own," she said, "and you will keep it all your life."

ON THE DAY that I sewed the last stitch of my cloak and Angharad folded it safely away for me in the big chest, Euny came back. It was a raw March day with a bitter east wind cutting across the moor, and Trewyn and I were glad to come home from our walk, back to the fire and a hot drink. And there was Euny, sitting on the hearth as if she had never been away.

14

ONCE OR TWICE on my walks with Trewyn I had noticed an odd-shaped building near the circle of standing stones where she often liked to go and sit. It was made of stone with curving walls that bent upward toward the ridge of the roof. The line of the ridge, I had noticed once, pointed to the center of the stone circle. One day, when rain was pelting down, we had pushed open the creaking wooden door and gone inside. It was much bigger than it appeared from the outside, with a plain earth floor that looked as if it had been recently raked and a center hearth with a fire already laid upon it. We could see this only by leaving the door open since there were no slits or holes in the walls to give light.

"Someone uses this place," I remarked to Trewyn. "But who? And for what?" She made some reply about it being a shepherd's hut, but I knew what they looked like—tiny rudely constructed wooden buildings with just room for a man to curl up and sleep out of the wind and the rain. Not like this at all.

Back at home I noticed that Angharad was no longer pushing us to continual spinning and weaving—she gave us time to idle the day away as she had never done before. She and Euny were often deep in conversation—not always agreeing, I suspect—the sort of conversation that breaks off as soon as you come into the room.

"Something funny's going on," I said to Trewyn.

"It's the ceremony," she replied anxiously. "They are getting us ready for it."

One April afternoon they called us in. We had been punting on the lake on a raft we had laboriously nailed together. Trewyn had pondweed clinging around one leg from pushing the raft out with me on it, and her clothes were wringing wet. I was scarcely looking better. I had torn my smock, and my hair was wild and knotted from blowing in the wind. We were a dreadful sight.

"You must both be bathed," Angharad said, and I could see enormous cauldrons of water already steaming on the fire. "Wash every part of yourselves, including your hair."

We took turns using the tub and washing each other's backs. I could feel Trewyn's hands trembling as she said to me in a quiet voice, "It's going to happen." Certainly there did seem to be something odd going on. When we got out of the tub, we were each given a big cloth on which to dry ourselves. There was no sign of clean clothes.

"Shall I go up and get a clean smock?" I asked at last.

Instead of replying Angharad simply handed me a huge sheet, and she gave another to Trewyn.

We were combing out our wet hair in front of the fire when I said, "Is supper going to be soon?"

"You are fasting," said Euny.

"We are all fasting," Angharad amended.

Trewyn and I exchanged nervous glances.

"Why?" Trewyn finally croaked out.

Angharad shook her head as if she could not answer, and Euny looked out the door as she had done several times already. It was dark outside, and a wind was blowing, whining ominously around Angharad's house. I wished that if something frightening had to happen to us, it could happen on some other night, or better yet, by day. Trewyn and I had already speculated on every possibility—would they beat us or torture us? Make us eat or drink horrible substances? Both of us were sure we had heard stories of such things. We sat by the fire, two substantial ghosts, and after a bit a full moon, huge and brilliant, appeared in the sky. Euny nodded to Angharad. "Time to go," she said.

They stood up, took the sheets from us, and said, "We are going out."

"Where are our clothes?" asked Trewyn, her slim body tense with distress.

"No clothes," said Angharad. "You will go just like that."

"I can't," Trewyn wailed. "We might meet some- one."

"We won't meet anyone," said Euny definitely. "Come along. There is work to be done."

Trewyn threw an agonized glance in my direction, hoping, perhaps, that I would join her in a rebellion. For some reason I was less fearful than she. I simply followed Angharad and Euny to the door. Once outside the stones hurt my feet, the wind, which was cold, blew painfully on my bare flesh, and quite soon my teeth were chattering. Even the soft tickle of my loose hair on my bare shoulders felt unfamiliar. What were we doing? And why? The moon, a huge yellow disk at the end of the path we were following, lit the landscape in precise lines without shadow. Trewyn's trembling naked body in front of me shone in a gold light.

Only when we reached the stone hut did I realize that that was where we were heading. It was a relief to march our cold bodies out of the bitter wind, though the only place on which to sit was a cold stone. There was an unlit fire laid on the center hearth and two big piles of wood beside it. I looked wistfully at it, my body shaking and shuddering with cold.

The four of us sat down and Angharad and Euny lit a rush lamp and began reciting, by heart, a long and very tedious poem. It spoke of dead heroes and heroines, most of whom I had never heard of; it was a recital of the interminable history of the *dorans*, whose wisdom had been frequently persecuted. At the end the words began to be addressed to me and Trewyn, admonitions that we should be worthy of our high calling, should enter into harmony with the world, should care for others, should never work magic for our own aggrandizement.

Then Euny bade us to lie facedown full-length upon the ground.

"Think before you answer these questions," she told us. "Do you wish to be admitted to the order of *doran?*" she wanted to know.

Lying shivering on the cold ground, I wished that I were safely home in bed. If this was what being a *doran* was all about, it was hard to see why anyone would wish to be one. Yet when I thought of the hazel tree, of the strange way that Euny and I had come together, and of my experiences at Angharad's house as I wove the cloth for my cloak, I knew that life was pushing me toward the particular sort of wisdom that Euny and Angharad had. I felt that I had no real choice.

"I wish to become a *doran,*" I said through chattering teeth.

I waited for Trewyn to make a similar declaration, but she lay in silence.

"Trewyn?" Angharad asked at last.

"I don't know," Trewyn wailed. "I'm frightened."

I could hear Angharad and Euny conferring.

"Very well," Angharad said finally. "We will continue with the ritual. At the end of it, Trewyn, we will ask you the question again, and if then you answer no, you will leave us and never mention to anyone what you have seen here."

One of them had touched a light to the fire on the hearth and I could hear twigs crackling.

"You may get up and come to the fire," Euny said to us, and we sat on our haunches beside it. Trewyn was weeping, whereas I felt a kind of sullen anger.

Euny took a handful of herbs from a bowl on the ground and began to chew them. Then she passed the bowl to Angharad, who followed her example.

I was surprised to see Euny now piling green wood on the fire, when there was a perfectly good supply of dry wood. Inevitably, the stone hut quickly filled with acrid smoke. My eyes brimmed with tears, I began to cough convulsively, and for a few moments I lost sight of the others in the smoke. Feeling that I was suffocating, I made for the door but found that I could not open it. To my surprise, it appeared to be bolted from the outside.

Groping my way back in the smoke, I bumped into Trewyn and we sat with our arms around each other, still shaking with cold, as far from the fire as we could get. Then the smoke cleared a little, and to our astonishment Angharad and Euny had disappeared!

I noticed that the green wood had been placed in a separate pile, and I had no doubt that the two *doran*s had deliberately filled the hut with smoke. But there was another huge pile of dry wood next to it, and I put two large logs on the fire. Trewyn crept back to the hearth, still coughing.

"Why did they do it?" she asked. "Is it part of the test?"

I was so angry at being locked in the hut that I could scarcely speak.

"You do suppose they intend to come back?" Trewyn asked tremulously. "They wouldn't just leave us here?"

"Of course they'll come back," I said with a confidence that was not entirely real. Suppose the two of us were destined to be some sort of sacrifice? Suppose they were going to leave us to starve?

I noticed a shabby wooden chest in the far corner of the hut and dragged it closer to the fire. For a while Trewyn and I sat on it—it was warmer than the cold stones—then slid down to the earth floor and sat leaning against each other, propped up by the chest, our feet comfortably toasting by the fire. Its flames now burned in a deep old-rose color shot through at moments with vivid blue. There was a sweet smell so pure and fragrant that for a moment I almost forgot where I was. I closed my eyes to enjoy it and when I opened them again, everything seemed a little bigger and clearer, as if I could suddenly see better.

"Do you see anything?" Trewyn asked hesitatingly after a while.

"Not exactly. Things just look more beautiful. I think the smoke must be magic. And I feel a lot warmer."

Even as I spoke, I noticed the grain in the wooden door as the firelight flickered over it. It looked like the markings on a snake's back, and like a snake, it moved. I did not feel threatened, simply delighted at the beauty of the design.

"The door!" I said to Trewyn.

"Snakes!" she said cheerfully, and I felt full of love for her that she could share this vision with me. I now noticed that the stones on the walls shone with a sort of golden light. The shadows between them were deep and lustrous, and there were faces—not ugly or frightening faces as sometimes in dreams, but very ancient faces, some in profile with hooked noses, some with gentle smiles and closed eyes. Tracing out these faces fascinated me so much that I was silent for a long time.

The fire was a continuing source of wonder. Gazing into its shifting and hissing depths, I saw an extraordinary sight. There was a branch with buds of apple blossom upon it, probably culled from one of Angharad's old trees. As I watched, the warmth caused the buds to open. For a moment I gazed at the perfect flowers, until the flames caught them too and quickly reduced the whole branch to ashes. I felt that Trewyn and I were like the buds coming into flower in our youth and beauty, one day achieving our moment of perfection, then returning to the nothingness from which we came.

"Are you still frightened?" I asked her.

"Oh, no, not at all. Well, not of being a *doran.* It's what we have to be, isn't it? You and me. It's what we're meant for, don't you think?"

WARM FROM THE HEAT of the fire, busy in the caverns and passages of our own minds, Trewyn and I dozed, propped up against the wooden chest. When I at last awoke, Angharad and Euny were sitting once more on the far side of the fire, looking as if they had never disappeared. They sat still and silent, without a glance in our direction.

They were different, however, as everything else was

different. Both of them had the same golden glow that I had noticed in the stones. The folds of the yellow shawl that Angharad wore seemed deep with mystery. Even Euny's worn black garments had a luminous sheen to them. Angharad's face, always full of kindness, now seemed so pure, generous, and good that I felt full of reverence as I looked at it. Euny's dark stern face held the desperate sadness of a lost little girl, yet I could see how gradually, painfully, that loneliness had grown into a great strength. Euny, I saw (though I felt I had always known this about her), was totally without fear. Whatever this strange uncomfortable ceremony was about, I decided that Angharad and Euny were to be trusted.

Euny was now building up the fire, though it was already hot in the hut, and Angharad had begun to chant a slow rhythmic melody. Trewyn and I had been taught the words and automatically joined in. As the heat grew in the hut, I could feel perspiration running down my face. Trewyn too looked desperately hot and turned anguished eyes to me. Yet Euny was still pushing twigs and logs into the fire.

Angharad and Euny now rose to their feet, and with Angharad making the mouth music that is common in her country, they began a sort of dance. It was nothing like the kind of merry occasion in which young men and women dance together. Rather it was as if Euny and Angharad were tracing out a pattern on the floor, seeking some knowledge with their feet. Occasionally they touched hands, turned toward or away from each other, led by the strange crooning cry of Angharad's singing, weaving the shape of the dance. First Trewyn, then I, got up and found ourselves irresistibly dancing with them with sure steps that no one had ever taught us. We danced, it seemed to me, for hours, weaving and dipping, turning and touching hands. Sometimes we danced—sometimes the dance danced us.

I think after this we all slept in total exhaustion. I was aware of waking once, cold since the fire had died down, stiff from the iron hardness of the ground, and desperately hungry. I could see daylight under the door, and I longed briefly to be part of that world outside, but sleep mercifully drew me back again into its embrace.

MUCH LATER, Trewyn was shaking me.

"Wake up! Look, the door's open!"

With an enormous effort I threw off the web of sleep. I could smell sweet fresh air through the open door—though both Trewyn and I were shivering with cold. We could see the dark sky with a few stars twinkling in it. There was no sign of Angharad or Euny.

"What do we do now?" I asked.

Without further conversation we left the hut with its dead embers. High up on the hill by the standing stones we caught sight of a bonfire and moved toward it. Cold and disheveled, wondering what fresh ordeals awaited us, we stumbled into the ring of standing stones and then stopped in astonishment. Angharad and Euny stood by the fire, as if waiting. Angharad wore a shining brown cloak clasped with yellow stones, and Euny wore a cloak figured in green and yellow and black. They signaled us to join them by the fire. Each had a bundle at her feet, and I was surprised to recognize the cloak I had so laboriously woven lying on the ground beside Euny. She came to me with a soft white tunic which she lifted over my head so that the folds fell to my feet. She fastened it at the neck, tied a girdle around my waist, then took a comb made of bone and combed the earth and tangles from my hair. She placed a pair of deerskin slippers on my feet, then lifted the heavy cloak and, easing it over my shoulders, joined the topaz clasp. It was lovely to feel the cloak's warmth and weight.

Meanwhile Angharad had also dressed Trewyn. When all was done, they embraced both of us, and Trewyn, in her warm, affectionate way, turned and hugged me. I could see in her eyes the thought that now we were really sisters.

Angharad took a loaf of wheaten bread and broke it in her strong fingers. She handed each of us a piece, and I ate mine eagerly. Even in my hungriest days with Euny food had never tasted as good as this. I could smell the wheat and the yeast in it, taste the salt. Then Angharad passed us a big cup of wine, and we each took a long drink. There was a spicy taste to it, and I guessed that she had added some secret herb. Just then, white and ghostlike in the starlight, I saw great wings floating above me, and there, big and silent, was Moon.

15

ACK IN Angharad's house the next morning, Trewyn and I made an odd discovery. "Watch this," she said to me. "I've just discovered it."

There was a moment's pause and then her smock, which was lying over a chair, got up—that is the only word for it—moved across the room, and flopped down on the floor. There was another pause, during which I could feel her concentrating hard, and then her smock rose up again and returned to the place it had come from.

I was impressed and at once determined to outdo her. A candle stood on the table, the one that had lighted us to bed the night before. I closed my eyes and concentrated, thinking only of the candle. When I opened them again, the candle was alight! Trewyn then extinguished the candle without moving from her bed, I lit it again, and she put it out.

"I know," said Trewyn, "let's see if we can make something. Both of us together." We agreed on a spider and almost at once a spider ran across the floor.

In the days that followed, both of us had a passion for trying out our new skills. We hid this from Angharad and Euny, sensing that they would think us very frivolous, but we simply could not stop. As soon as we were alone together or out for a walk, we would start on our trumpery magic. It was the greatest fun and we found it difficult to believe that we would ever tire of it. I am sure that Angharad at least, hearing the shouts of laughter that came from our room, knew very well what we were up to, but she never said a word. Perhaps she reflected that our time together was coming to an end.

We had changed in another way too since the day of the ceremony.

"Do you notice something different about your sense of smell?" I asked Trewyn tentatively one day. She nodded.

"I can smell you and Angharad and Euny—not just the usual human smells, but *something else.* It's as if they tell me something, just as the expression on a person's face tells you something about them. I can smell Angharad's goodness and Euny's strength. I can smell your healing wisdom."

"And I can smell your beauty!"

We asked Angharad about it and she confirmed, as if surprised that we would even ask, that smell was one of the skills of a *doran.*

IT WAS EARLY SUMMER when Euny and I set off for home, and our journey this time was pleasant. The hedgerows were fragrant with roses and honeysuckle, the meadowsweet billowed beneath them, the sky was a wide, cloudless blue, and we heard the cuckoo sing its late song. As we crossed the meadows, skylarks high above us rinsed our ears with their joyful din. We walked along the edges of cornfields full of young grain, past gardens from which we helped ourselves to tender pea pods, through misty blue woods, through dim forests, and over gentle hills. Sometimes, far away, we could see the glimmer of the sea. This time we slept warmly at night, full of Angharad's oatcake and fermented whey. One evening, as we ate our supper, Euny surprised me.

"Angharad said I did not feed you properly. Because I eat little I forget that young things need their food. I'll try to do better."

Euny said this without embarrassment or shame, but just as a fact. Angharad had pointed it out to her, and now she understood. I was touched.

"It's all right," I said awkwardly.

I had felt very sad at leaving Trewyn and Angharad, not to mention the comfort of Angharad's house, but I found that I took pleasure in being alone again with Euny, that although no word of affection was expressed and there were no embraces, her austere warmth toward me gladdened and pleased me. Since the time in the stone hut she seemed a little more friendly, as if she was sure of me in some way. The long days in the open air and nights of sound sleep made me feel extraordinarily well.

As we came out of the forest near Euny's hut and I saw the great shadow of the tor above us, I felt a little shiver of excitement and joy. It was not dark, but already a brilliant sliver of moon hung in the sky over the tor. Rain had made a pool on the grass in front of the hill and sitting upon it were twelve swans, their beautiful heads and wings mirrored in the water. The sun shone upon the tor at an angle that lit it strangely. Its bare, terraced sides were shadowed, its outline haloed. Euny and I stood quite still and Euny made some exclamation under her breath—it might have been an incantation or a prayer.

After a few moments she walked on, and I followed. The hut, with its dead embers, some moldering pig hanging on a hook from the ceiling, threadbare rug, and pathetic bits of furniture seemed unwelcoming, dusty, and cold, and for a moment my heart sank. Bearing the rotting carcass outside under Euny's orders, however, I saw the moon through the branches of the hazel tree and the outline of the hill springing behind it, and I knew that this was the place where I should be.

Euny had seated herself with unusual weariness in her old rocking chair. I lit a fire, swept and dusted, and made soup with the remains of the vegetables that Angharad had given us. Going outside to gather herbs, I saw the empty pigsty and remembered the incident before we had left home.

After supper I counted on my fingers. "Three months before I go back to my parents," I said. Euny nodded.

"There is a lot to do," she said. As always with Euny,

I could not bring myself to ask *what* there was to do, and she never explained.

WITHIN A FEW DAYS Euny and I had fallen straight back into our old routines. There were the household chores, the long silences, the meager meals. But Angharad's words had driven her to try harder to feed me. On the day after we returned home she disappeared without a word and came back several hours later laden with a large sack of wheaten flour. I immediately started making bread and cakes with it, as Angharad had taught me. On other days she returned with eggs and honey and cabbages and a set of newly hatched chicks, which she gave to me to rear. I was enchanted by their furry little bodies and loved to pick them up in my hands. When some of them died, as chicks do, I grieved over them, to Euny's irritation.

It seems to me now that I needed someone, something, to love. I missed Angharad and Trewyn badly. Though Euny noticed every flower and berry and cloud and turn of the wind, it felt as if she could live with *me* only by forgetting and ignoring me for much of the time.

Angharad had given me some material to make a pallet for myself, and after I stuffed the bag with straw I was able to sleep much more comfortably and warmly at night. She had also made me a blanket, in a brilliant pattern of dusky orange and midnight blue. I was never cold beneath it and it hung over the back of the rocking chair by day, giving the room a vivid focus. I picked flowers too, taking one of our few bowls to set them in.

I was out in the meadow near the hut one day picking some wild lilies when I heard the sound of hoofs
on the trail. And there was my beloved Gamal! I was
so thrilled to see him that it took me a few moments
to notice that there was another rider behind him. To
my dismay it was Finbar. Gamal gave a whoop of pleasure at seeing me, shouted to Finbar, and came across
the field. Then Gamal and I began to talk. He wanted
to know where I had been—he had come several times
in search of me. I wanted to hear about everyone
at Castle Dore. He had brought me a present from
Meroot—some wind-dried meat that was a special del-
icacy among our people. Finbar listened patiently,
smiling. Since their last visit, I had considered Finbar a
sort of enemy, but he seemed perfectly friendly toward
me. It was disconcerting.

"We thought we could stay here overnight and then
spend tomorrow together," said Gamal. My heart sank
slightly. How would I persuade Euny to let me have
the day to myself?

"I'll go and ask Euny," I said nervously.

Euny was sitting and rocking herself placidly in the
hut, and in the way that was typical of her she knew
what I had come to ask before I asked it.

"They needn't think I'm going to feed them," she
said.

"Couldn't we?" I pleaded. "We've plenty of meal."

Euny did not answer.

"I could make some porridge or something . . ."

"And you can't have the time off to play with them.
We have a lot of work to do."

I felt furious both at her lack of hospitality and her

unfairness. I went out, slamming the hut door behind me.

Gamal noticed my crestfallen expression at once.

"It's all right," he said. "We can sleep out in the meadow in our blankets."

"She won't give you any food," I said. I had grown up in a tradition that treated the guest as sacred, and I felt humiliated.

"We've got enough in our saddlebags."

"But I *will* come out with you tomorrow. I'll pretend to be going to the well to get water and then I'll run off with you."

Finbar, I could see, admired me for this, but Gamal looked a bit worried.

"Won't you get into awful trouble?" he asked.

I shrugged. The thought of a day's fun was worth it.

The next morning I set off with my buckets, left them lying by the well, and ran off with Gamal and Finbar. We rode to a distant beach, splashed in the sea for hours, climbed rocks, and sunned ourselves. Gamal played to us on his flute. Then I rode Gamal's pony along the sand. It was wonderful to feel the motion of a horse beneath me.

"You do ride well," Finbar said admiringly, and my heart slightly softened toward him, though I gave no indication of this. Also, when he caught a fish he came and presented it to me as if giving me a present. But I scarcely acknowledged it. I could not forget the shame of the occasion when I had killed the pig, and the mockery in Finbar's eyes at a moment when I was so unhappy. In any case, I wanted Gamal to myself. As if sensing my wish to be alone with Gamal, Finbar went off for a long ride by himself.

"How's Meroot?" I asked Gamal. A shadow crossed his face and he shrugged without replying. What he wanted to talk about was music. A new musician had come to court since I had left and was secretly teaching Gamal.

"It's not so much playing that interests me now. I have started to make up music. One night at dinner Evert sang a song I had composed and Meroot said how beautiful it was—without knowing it was mine, of course."

"She would never let you be a musician, would she?"

"No one can stop me from thinking of music—not even Meroot," said Gamal.

As the afternoon wore on, I grew a bit fearful of going back to confront Euny.

"Do you want us to come with you?" Gamal asked.

"No, go on home," I said. Gamal promised to come again, but I felt very sad as they cantered off along the beach.

I noticed as I passed the well that the buckets were still lying there, so I filled them and took them back with me. Euny was sitting in the rocking chair as if she had spent the whole day there. I braced myself for a scolding, but none came. In fact, I had an odd sort of feeling that she was rather pleased with me. I could not understand it at all. In fact, it was quite disturbing.

THREE

16

THE NEXT DAY Euny suddenly started to instruct me in the way I had longed for at the beginning, sitting me down and giving me long hours of teaching about spells, herbs, good magic, and bad magic. First she made me give demonstrations of the sort of skills Trewyn and I had practiced—making things move, appear, and disappear—then told me sternly that that was quite enough and that she hoped I would never waste my energies with that kind of thing again.

"Different *doran*s have different gifts," she said. "Yours will be to do with healing people, which is partly about a special kind of knowing and partly about a long and difficult study of herbs."

I was surprised that Euny took my healing gifts seriously.

"Oh, I knew about the healing because of the white owl," she said. "It was perfectly obvious. All those under the protection of the owl know about healing."

"What is the special kind of knowing?" I asked her.

"Being able to pay attention to people. Not just with your mind but with every part of you. Then you see the sickness quite clearly. I cannot help you with that. What I can teach you before you go home is the lore of herbs. As well as some other healing skills."

Euny had, of course, taught me to recognize many herbs in my first weeks with her. Now the task was to learn their uses by heart, to discover how to combine them, how to make them into pills and ointments, decoctions, tinctures, and teas. She had me reciting endlessly.

"Elecampane root, powdered, for coughs, and for those who cannot breathe . . . tincture of dwarf elder for dropsy . . . horsebane for piles. Dock for a purgative. Comfrey root boiled for inward hurts and for the spitting of blood . . . fresh comfrey root upon fresh wounds, cuts, and broken bones. Dried coltsfoot leaves and roots to be burned and the smoke drawn into the mouth through a reed with wine for a persistent cough. Culverwort to be used for sore throats. Yellow bugle, if you can obtain it, to cleanse the urine. Bistort to cure worms in children, catnip for colds . . ." It went on and on, hour after hour.

She taught me to make clearwater, the colorless liquid that protects a *doran* against sorcery, steeping rowan leaves with herbs in water where gold has lain. She explained to me about the terrible curses used by sorcerers which bring slow and miserable death to those who are their victims, and then recounted some of the rituals great *doran*s have used to dissolve the curses.

"There is no one way of doing it—you just have to use your wits and your imagination—but remember that earth, air, fire, and water are your allies . . ."

She taught me what to do for someone who has had a "sad" spell laid on them by a sorcerer, or the kind of spell that makes all places and people strike deadly fear. Even more important, she said, was to know what to do for a person who was "ghosted"—that is, captured and enslaved by a sorcerer in such a way that they no longer had a will or mind of their own. She told me of sorcerers who gave drinks to their enemies that made them appear like dead people. Their relatives buried them in great sadness. Then the "corpse" woke up in the coffin, was dug up and spirited away by the sorcerer, and forced to work as a slave in a distant place. Of course, nobody wondered what had happened to them. Suddenly I remembered Gamal's description of the dreadful picture in Meroot's parchments.

The spells and recipes Euny taught me were long and complicated, but all of them were to bring about good or prevent evil. The only way to be sure of them was to learn them by heart and then to repeat them to her time after time, which she made me do endlessly, until she was quite sure I had mastered them. She would not permit me to change even unimportant words, but insisted that I repeat the words she used, even, it seemed to me, in her exact tone of voice. I was so interested in what she was teaching me that I found this laborious learning quite pleasurable.

Now the weeks passed very quickly. Once or twice Gamal came again, this time alone.

"Tell me truly about Meroot," I said, remembering his reluctance to speak of her. "Is something wrong with her? Is she ill?"

"Not as you mean it. Only I think there *is* something wrong with her."

"Can you explain?"

"I will tell you what I think. It is that she still dreams that one day, when your father is dead, I will take over his kingdom."

Embarrassed, Gamal looked away from me out over the countryside.

"Would you want to do that?" I asked, my voice wobbling at the thought of my father dead.

"That is not the point. Last birthday I swore my allegiance to the king. Plotting against him is against the rule of the knights."

I was silent, not knowing what to say.

"There is something else." Gamal's voice cracked with shame and anguish. "You know that Meroot can do magic, is . . . perhaps . . . a sorcerer. I'm afraid of what she might do."

I shivered with fear of Meroot but put out a hand and patted Gamal's hand.

"I will be back home soon," I said. "Then we can talk more of these things. Perhaps I could warn my father." Gamal shook his head gloomily, as if in doubt that we could save the situation.

That night I told Euny about the conversation, and she listened with her head on one side like a bird.

"Your magic is at least as strong as Meroot's magic,"

she said. "You have been well taught. There is perhaps only one other who may be stronger."

"Who is the other?"

"A sorcerer in Caerleon."

"Angharad's old enemy!"

I shivered at the dangers hidden in her words. "I must try to oppose Meroot, then?"

Euny spoke dryly. "Perhaps it was for this that you were born."

The relationship between Euny and me had suddenly become quite different. Instead of treating me as her servant, Euny now did her full share of the household chores—fetching water from the well, cleaning out the fire, preparing meals, sweeping and tidying. There was a note of respect, of listening to what I said, which I did not remember from before. For the first time since I had come to live with her there was a sense of peace, of pleasantness and ease, which reminded me of the life of Angharad and Trewyn.

As day by day Euny imparted her secrets to me, I knew that the seasons were wheeling to the place when I must soon again return to my parents, though I knew too that at some time in the future I would come back to Euny for the rituals that would complete my training as a *doran*.

"What will happen when I go back home?" I asked Euny. "Must I marry?"

"Do you want to marry?" she asked.

"I don't know. Not yet, anyway. I'm only a child."

"Who will rule the kingdom when your father dies?" Euny asked sharply. "Will it be you?"

I shrugged. "Because women are not warriors, it is difficult for them to rule."

"I don't see why," said Euny. "There are other important things in kingship besides warfare."

"I'm not sure if I could rule," I said uncertainly. "What difference will being a *doran* make? I thought it was a vocation of its own."

"You will have to see," said Euny unhelpfully.

"Will you miss me when I am gone?" I rashly asked her.

Euny tossed her head in a gesture I knew well.

"I need nobody," she said. "Certainly not you."

I was not as crushed as I would formerly have been.

"Well, I will miss you," I said, "and I believe that you will miss me." I could see by the obstinate gleam in her eye that she had no intention of giving me the satisfaction of telling me she cared for me.

On the day of my departure for Castle Dore, Euny watched me as I lowered Moon gently from his perch and put him into his traveling bag.

"I am coming with you to help you carry your things," Euny said suddenly. Since I had nothing but my *doran*'s cloak, and Angharad's blanket, and a little food and water for the journey, that was scarcely necessary, and I knew she was merely using it as an excuse.

"I will miss the hut," I said, looking around it for the last time.

"It will still be here," said Euny pettishly. "You can come and see it when you can spare the time from your grand life."

I wept a little as we walked through the forest. I felt as if nothing would console me for the loss of those hard days which now, I realized, had taught me a great deal. I would not see the tor, nor the hazel tree, when I woke up each morning. I would not see Euny.

When Castle Dore appeared in the distance Euny stopped. She put her hands into the folds of her gown and brought out two large flasks and some other objects and laid them on the ground in front of her.

"Here are your 'protections,'" she told me, using the *doran* word. "If there is the slightest chance of your running into danger, you must carry them with you at all times."

One of the protections was a crescent moon on a leather string, and Euny put it over my head with the air of investing me with an honor. The next thing she gave me was a black egg.

"If you are in danger of your life you may break this egg," she said. "But be careful. If you do it when the danger is not severe, you will be unprotected when the real danger comes. As come it will, early or late. So use it wisely."

"But how will I *know?*" I said in a sort of wail, already certain that I would break the egg at the wrong moment. Euny gave me a withering look and did not deign to answer.

"Clearwater you know about," she added, giving me the two flasks. "After this you must make your own."

I tucked away all the protections into my bundle and then looked up to speak to Euny, but she was gone!

The long straight path was quite empty, only it seemed to me that I could hear her cackle of laughter echoing in the air.

I walked on soberly. I was nervous about my return. As I approached Castle Dore, I was surprised to see a great flock of rooks wheeling about the place. I had never seen rooks there before, and their black wings and persistent cries gave an air of menace.

The guards saluted when I reached the entrance—I found my way quickly through the trick of the maze and into the big enclosure of the castle. The doors of the hall and the council chamber stood open wide, so I knew my father must be elsewhere. I went straight to my parents' quarters and found my mother reading and my father writing on his tablet. The glimpse I caught of him through the lattice before he saw me suggested that he was worried—he looked older, bent with care.

I stood in the doorway.

"I have come back."

My mother and father embraced me and made me feel that I was glad to be back at the Wooden Palace after all.

"Tell me," said the king, "did Euny teach you all that you hoped?"

"It was very hard," I told him. "But I learned more, much more than I knew there was to learn."

"And you have come back here to marry?"

"I don't know," I said. "Do you wish me to marry?"

My father hesitated, exchanging glances with my mother as if weighing up different ideas in his mind, then said, "We will talk of this later. Tonight we will have a feast for your return. See that you wear a fine gown—not that rag you have on your back—and that your hair is dressed with jewels."

I bowed before him because, after all, he was the king, and I went to my old apartment.

It was strange to be back in the comforts of Castle Dore. Although my own chamber was cold and empty, Erith soon bustled in, embraced me with joy, and lit a fire. While I waited, she had a servant bring me a plate of chicken and some white bread, which I ate hungrily. She summoned other servants, who brought water heated in the kitchen. As she had done so often in the past, she bathed me—exclaiming in horror at the calluses on my hands and the blisters on my feet and observing how thin I was—then she dressed me in a yellow silk gown that went well with my dark hair. She found a fillet of silver and bound my hair with it, then placed a torque of silver around my neck and bracelets on my arms. When I looked at myself in the big bronze mirror, I saw how grown-up I had become—very different from the child who had last sought her reflection there. I was slender and pretty, I thought with youthful pride, and the heat of the fire had brought a pleasing pink to my cheeks. When I went to join my father I held my head high. King Mark's daughter had come home.

My father was expecting me and gave me a long appreciative look and a smile. He was obviously pleased. Together we walked to the Great Hall, where his knights waited to dine with him, and together we walked through the big room while the pipes and drums played for us. I sat beside his carved chair in my smaller one, and when he took up his knife he cut a piece of roast swan and presented it to me—the custom used by my people to make a guest welcome.

The evening proceeded as I remembered many evenings doing in the past—the slow meal that I had always found so tedious once my appetite was satisfied. There were a number of courses, but—was it my imagination?—there seemed to be less food than there had been in the past. While we ate, a bard sang a song of love and adventure.

Perhaps because I had lived such a simple life with Euny, because I was genuinely hungry, or because my recent experiences had made me look at the world with a fresh eye, everything tonight seemed wonderfully interesting. I enjoyed the faces of the knights—some of them old and scarred with battle, others still in the pride of young manhood. I savored the bright colors of the clothes and jewels, the harmonies of the music, the glorious taste and smell of the food, the rich scent and ruby tint of the wine, the beauty and intelligence of the dogs that crouched beside my father. I laid my hand upon my father's.

"It is good to be back," I told him.

Afterward, as we sat near the fire, the knights came up and talked to me—men who had known me as a child. The young squires, no older than I was myself, who had sat at the lowest table, eyed me shyly, one or two of them looking as if they would like to talk. I went about the room, enjoying the lively company and the handsome young men. Yet . . . many of them had a pallor, a kind of weariness about them that puzzled me. Surely they had not always been like that?

Even after my father had left the hall I stayed, talking and laughing. At one moment my eyes strayed toward the door. Two tall boys were leaving and one of them was half turned, laughing, to catch a comment the other had made. It was Gamal and Finbar. Gamal waved and Finbar bowed with just the faintest suggestion of friendly mockery. I grinned back at them.

Later, in my parents' quarters, I sat on a footstool between them, as I had often done as a child. In reply to their questions I told them a little more of my life with Euny and asked them about life at Castle Dore.

But I could see a shadow cross my mother's face, and my father moved like an old man in his chair. He was very thin, I noticed.

"There is trouble?" I asked him, expecting a story of raids and plundering, of the need to lead his young men to some horrific battle from which many would not return. He clasped and unclasped his hands in a wretchedness I had not seen before. He was not a fearful man, and had always had a certain appetite for the excitement of war, though he grieved at the human cost.

A look of shame and pain crossed his face.

"The crops have done badly," said my mother. "Many animals have died for no reason that we can discover."

"Is it magic?" I asked.

"There have always been years when the crops failed," said my father crossly, "and years when the animals have been sick."

"Not often both together," said my mother pointedly.

"Do you suspect anyone?" I asked her. She did not answer, but again exchanged a glance with my father, and I guessed that they had had many conversations on this subject.

"We cannot speak of it tonight," she said. "It is late. Come and see us tomorrow and I will say more."

17

THE NEXT MORNING there was a light tap on my door at dawn. Accustomed to early rising, I was already awake. I opened the door quietly, so I would not disturb Erith, and found Gamal waiting outside.

"Come out for a ride!" he whispered. In a few moments I was dressed. He had two horses saddled and ready, and soon we were miles away on a hillside overlooking the sea. We breakfasted out of the wind in a hollow—Gamal had thoughtfully brought bread and some cold meat.

"Is it good to be back?" he asked me.

I hesitated.

"It is lovely to be home, but . . . my father seems ill, and he tells me that the harvest was so bad he fears famine."

Gamal nodded. He looked miserable, I thought.

"Something is very wrong," I added. He was silent,

but I felt that there was more he could have said if he had chosen to. Then he mentioned a piece of court news that I had already heard: Meroot intended to marry again.

"A knight from Caerleon," he said. The name stirred some troubling memory in me, though I could not think what it was.

"She will marry in December," said Gamal shortly. "The king is to give a great feast for her."

As we returned home, I noticed a sort of bleakness about the countryside that I did not remember from previous autumns. The sheep looked sickly and listless, the people gray and afraid. Even at Castle Dore, now that I was no longer excited to be back, I saw that everyone looked pale, tired, and dispirited.

The next day I called upon Meroot, as etiquette dictated, to greet her upon my return and to congratulate her upon her marriage. She received me in the little house my father had built for her—she had never ceased complaining about its smallness—and we drank a sweet tawny wine from across the sea and ate honey biscuits. The room was very bare, save for an odd-looking leather stick that stood propped against the wall.

Meroot wore a gray gown with a turquoise and silver collar; her wrists were heavy with jewelry of jet and silver. She was accompanied by a huge black hound that I had never seen before, collared, like her, in turquoise and silver. The hound was so big I could not take my eyes off it. A pastille burned in a dish, giving the room a scent of lilies, yet somewhere beneath that

scent there were other smells, sharp and sour and sickening.

"So what did Euny teach you?" Meroot wished to
know. Though it was the same question my father had
asked, the way it was asked was quite different.

"She taught me healing arts," I said carefully. "She
taught me the doses for sicknesses and the way of
touching to make people well. And Angharad of the
West taught me to spin and weave."

"Angharad!" she said in obvious surprise.

"Do you know her?"

"I did once."

The silence fell heavily between us, until Meroot left
the room to fetch more wine. She closed the door behind her and I glanced around. The leather stick caught
my eye again and I stood up and moved toward it. Immediately the black hound growled softly in its throat
and moved between me and the stick. I sat down
uneasily. Suddenly I had the oddest feeling that I was
being watched, that through a knot in the door or a
hole in the tapestry Meroot's cold blue eye was fixed
upon me. I composed myself as unselfconsciously as
possible and wondered why she would do such a thing.
What could she see that she could not observe when
she sat in front of me?

At that moment the outer door opened and Gamal
came in, hot and weary, wearing parts of his armor and
carrying the rest over his arm. He smiled and started
telling me of his latest lesson, then sat down, filthy as
he was from the practice field. It seemed to me that
once again I heard the dog growl softly in its throat,

though it did not move. But then Meroot came back, the dog slunk into a corner, and Gamal and I fell silent. I was glad when I could go home without appearing rude.

My mother was alone that afternoon when I called upon my parents.

"It's Meroot, isn't it?" I said without delay. "You are afraid she is laying a curse upon Castle Dore."

Erlain nodded.

"Your father won't hear of it. He is loyal to her, and it is destroying the kingdom." Erlain's eyes filled with tears. "I was wondering, Ninnoc. Do you know any magic that might help us?"

My first thought was to send for Euny, but then I remembered that she had gone away on a visit to Angharad. I felt both excited and frightened. I had not dreamed that I might need to use my new skills so soon. "Let me think about it," I said. Before I left Erlain, I gave her a flask of Euny's clearwater and told her how to anoint herself with it.

"See if you can persuade Father to use it too," I said, not very hopefully. Lying in bed, I thought about the careful schooling I had had in magic—how I had learned all that my wise teacher could tell me. Now I would find out if my education was equal to the challenge. Just as I was falling asleep I remembered, with a start that woke me right up again, that it was at Caerleon that Trewyn had encountered a sorcerer and been saved by Angharad. Who was the sinister enemy of Angharad Trewyn had once described to me? Suppose, just suppose, it was Meroot's new husband. Was this why

Meroot was startled to hear Angharad's name? If she had not known it before, Meroot now knew that Angharad and Euny were friends.

ALREADY THE PLANS were going forward for Meroot's wedding. Wines were being taken from our cellars; pigs, chickens, and swans were being fattened; deer were being hunted. Soon we would start making pies, baking, and roasting.

Gifts for the bride from the Gray Knight of Caerleon began to arrive: silks and spices, scents and rare fruits, inlaid boxes containing jewels, nightingales in cages, fine hunting hawks, beautiful ponies with snowy coats and bright enameled harnesses. The knight's presents were so many and frequent that they became the object of jokes around the Wooden Palace—there was not much to joke about just then—but it was evident that the knight either loved Meroot or needed her good will. It was clear too that he was a rich man.

I can still remember the set look on Gamal's face as the knight's servants arrived day after day bearing gifts.

"You know, they wish me to go with them to live at Caerleon," he said.

"You won't go?"

"I don't want to . . ." I knew of Gamal's loyalty to his mother, a loyalty I had only once seen waver.

THE PREPARATIONS at Castle Dore speeded up—the bards composed new songs and the smell of roasting meat pervaded everything. The kingdom was short of food, yet the rules of hospitality demanded that guests

should be richly entertained. On the night before
the Gray Knight's arrival, my father gave a feast for
Meroot in the Great Hall and she sat beside him in the
seat where my mother or I usually sat. Her pale face
was flushed, her eyes sparkled, and there was an odd
sort of triumph about her that troubled me. Sitting directly opposite her, I could not avoid her gaze, nor the
need to make conversation.

"You will live at the house of the Gray Knight?" I
asked her. She described it to me and it sounded very
splendid. Yet gazing into her strange light eyes, so
lacking in depth or feeling, I felt as I had felt as a small
child: her apparent amiability concealed an intense hatred
of me. I remembered my father telling me of Meroot's
longing, as a little girl, to outstrip him at everything—
at running, at shooting with a bow, at climbing trees,
or at the civilized arts of singing and oration. For the
first time I felt sympathy for Meroot—it was hard to
be a girl in a royal family and see your younger brother
preferred to you for no better reason than that he was
a boy. I, who had no brothers, was far luckier than
she—I am sure she thought this. All the same, because
I was a girl I was vulnerable to Meroot's scheming.

I slept fitfully, tossing and turning, and woke just
before the cold, gray dawn. I got up quietly and went
out, as I had done so often when I was restless or anxious, to walk around the ramparts and the big ditch
beyond them. I hailed the sleepy sentries and began a
slow pacing. It was bitter cold, and I drew my cloak
warmly around me, but I enjoyed watching the light
gradually ascending over the valleys. Then, with a sense

of shock, I saw the figure of a woman in a field outside, her face turned to the Wooden Palace. I realized it was Meroot. She could not see me—I was no more than a small face above the parapet and it was still fairly dark—and she went on with what she was doing, moving widdershins, holding up her hand and making signs in the direction of the palace, occasionally dipping her fingers into a bowl she held in her other hand. As the dawn gradually replaced the dark, I saw that her upraised hand was stained a dull red; the bowl must contain blood. I could not hear her voice or see her mouth move, but I had no doubt at all that she was uttering spells.

18

THAT DAY the Gray Knight arrived, celebrated by a trumpeter as he entered our gates and surrounded by pages who carried more presents for Meroot, including a magnificent collar of pearls. He was received by my father, and they spent half the day talking together. I met the knight when the evening brought us all together in the Great Hall.

He was a tall, handsome man, carrying, as many of the knights did, scars of battle on his face. In his case, they only added to his good looks. He had piercing black eyes, and when he was introduced to me, I felt as if he looked right through me and knew everything about me. For the first time since my return I felt afraid. The sight of Gamal's miserable face as he stood beside Meroot did not reassure me.

The wedding was celebrated with great splendor, and as was our custom, the feast went on for days. Like most of the younger people, I got bored with the endless drinking and storytelling and soon slipped away to talk and have fun. Freed from Meroot's supervision, Gamal and I spent a lot of time together. Quite often we were joined by Finbar, who, despite myself, I was beginning to like. Gamal often played his flute, pausing from time to time to share the thoughts that troubled him.

"They'll make me go back to Caerleon with them," he said. "The trouble is, I'm not old enough to refuse."

"One of the knights could make you his squire," Finbar suggested.

Gamal shook his head. Both of us knew the reason this was unlikely: if Meroot wanted him to accompany her, none of the knights would wish to defy her.

"Do you think now that Meroot is married she will give up her plans for Castle Dore—you know, the ones you told me about that time at the shore?"

This was not quite honest of me. The memory of Meroot cursing us all in the winter dawn did not suggest that her ambitions had changed.

Gamal shook his head and flushed.

"She has never forgiven your father for inheriting the kingdom and taking it from her. She believes it is rightly hers—and eventually mine." He hesitated for a long while. "She thinks only of how to get it back. She will not forgive me for refusing to help her. I think that is why she bore me and why she insists I must be a soldier. So that somehow I can avenge her."

"What will she do to get what she believes is hers? Will she fight for it, or will she prefer to use spells?" I tried to keep my voice as even as possible, as if we were discussing something that did not matter very much.

Gamal shrugged.

"I have no doubt she is using spells already. As to war . . . I do not know."

"For a moment, the other night, I felt sorry for Meroot," I said. "It is not fair that she was robbed of the throne. I would not like it if a younger brother was preferred before me—if I wanted to be queen, that is."

"But she swore loyalty to King Mark, as we all did. He has been good to us and . . . you are my cousin and friend."

I put out a hand and grasped Gamal's.

"In any case, curses are no way to get what you want." So Gamal really did think, as I did, that Meroot's curse was what ailed the country.

It was a great relief when Meroot and the Gray Knight rode back to Caerleon along with their retinue of servants. The knight's servants had been rude and arrogant, and the feast had strained the slender resources of Castle Dore. Though, of course, I watched Gamal ride away with a sad heart. My friend and ally had left us.

Yet almost immediately I was distracted by a new piece of information. Visiting my mother, I found her in a strange state, both elated and anxious.

"Ninnoc, it is unmistakable . . . I am to have a baby!"

I knew that she had longed to have another child, and that although she loved me, her only daughter, she had felt somehow to blame for not providing the warrior-heir that kings preferred. I also knew that if

she did have a boy, it meant that I would never become queen. I felt a pang of jealousy. I tried to crush
it beneath the protective feelings I had about my mother.

"Don't tell anyone for as long as possible in case
Meroot finds out," I cautioned.

"That is why I am afraid," said Erlain, her great gray
eyes filled with dread. "That she may know already and
have damaged my child."

"You used the clearwater?"

"Yes. Every day."

"It will be all right. This comes at a good time. It
will comfort people that something—someone—can live
and grow despite Meroot's curse."

I had been giving a lot of thought to Meroot's curse,
and as a result, I was sleeping badly. My nightmares
were about Meroot, clad all in gray, and, more terrible,
of a huge unblinking eye watching me through a hole
in a wall. If only Euny were at home, I kept thinking,
to give me advice. How could I undo the curse and
turn Meroot's corrupting, killing hate into the love that
made all things grow?

I turned over in my mind all that I had been taught.
"Earth, air, fire, and water are your allies," Euny had
said.

I planned the ritual and asked my mother to accompany me. The next morning I woke with a sense of
fear—I felt as if I were directly challenging Meroot—
but I got up, put on Euny's crescent moon necklace
and my *doran*'s cloak, and lowered Moon onto my
shoulder. Erlain and I went out before dawn to the
place beyond the walls where I had seen Meroot. I stood

still and thought of the mother goddess before whom Euny had bowed in her shrine high on the tor.

Then I took earth and crumbled it between my fingers.

"Mother, let sun and rain make this earth fertile. Let it yield crops to feed our animals and provide food for our children. Let the plants flower and the trees bear fruit. And let no human blood be spilled upon this earth."

I took water and poured it out on the ground.

"Mother," I said, "let our springs and streams and rivers run pure so that all may drink. Let this water wash away the curse of violence."

I lit a small fire.

"Mother, let this fire burn away all that is wicked and corrupt."

I stood and looked up into the dark sky.

"Mother, let the air of this place not be filled with cries of pain."

I turned to Erlain, the mother whom I knew and loved. Putting my hands gently on her belly, I thought of the baby within.

"Mother, keep this one safe," I asked. "May this child be born strong and healthy and grow up in a kingdom that knows peace."

Then, as Angharad and Euny had taught me, I danced the dance that is the harmony of all creation, and as I did so, I uttered the great words that keep sorrow and sickness within bounds. Finally I bowed low in the direction of the Wooden Palace.

When it was over, I felt desperately tired, almost too

weary to climb the path to Castle Dore. I had given my strength to the anticurse, and it had left me feeling weak and afraid. As we returned, I noticed with a sense of pleasure and relief that the rooks were rising from the trees on one side with noisy cries and flapping indignantly away.

WITHIN A FEW WEEKS it was plain that something was very different in the kingdom. The ewes and cows and horses began to conceive, and the people to regain their old vitality. My mother had a new piece of information for me.

"Ninnoc, I don't know what you will say. The astrologers tell me that the baby will be a boy!" Again I felt that pang of jealousy and anger. It had not been difficult to utter a *doran*'s blessing upon the new baby— I could not possibly wish my mother any harm—yet I knew that in my heart I had hoped the baby would be a girl.

The winter months slipped away and the sun returned. That year we had a wonderful spring. The air seemed full of the calling of birds, and the woods shone with primroses, violets, and bluebells. Trees and hedgerows were covered with blossoms, the sowing produced strong green shoots, and the lambing was the best we had ever had. After the fear and darkness of the winter, people were lighthearted and joyous. They were thin and short of food after their ordeals, but their eyes were full of hope, and my father walked with a light step. Meroot had gone, and her curse had gone with her.

19

I HEARD NOTHING of Gamal for many weeks, and I missed him sorely. I worried that if Meroot's schemes were defeated, loyal Gamal might be made to suffer for it in some way. I could scarcely imagine that he was happy in the house of Meroot and the Gray Knight, knowing well that the best parts of his childhood had all been at moments when he was away from his mother.

Now that the immediate danger to Castle Dore had been averted, there seemed no real task for me there, nothing worthy of my energies or of my training as a *doran*. Euny, I reckoned, might be back by now from her visit to Angharad. I decided to go and see her, to tell her of what had passed since I left her and see whether she would give me any guidance about my future. Goodness knows she was obstinate enough in what she would and would not talk about, yet I was certain, somehow, that if my need was urgent enough, she would relent and tell me what I had to know.

I suppose I could have taken my pony and traveled faster, yet it seemed proper to approach Euny on foot, as I had done in the past. With little more than a change of clothing I made my way to her hut, navigating by the tor, passing through the forest without the fear I had once known. If she was not at home, I thought, I could spend a day or two at the hut and return, though I would be very disappointed not to see her. I was delighted, at the end of my long walk, to see smoke rising from her hut. Just as if she were awaiting me after an afternoon of herb gathering, she was sitting in her rocking chair, and one of her strange-smelling soups was bubbling on the fire.

I could tell from her smile that she was very glad to see me, though, as always, she did her best to hide her pleasure.

"Nothing better to do, I suppose," she said with a sniff.

"I was longing to see you, and I need your advice," I said.

"I know," she said. "I made the soup because you were coming."

"How did you know?" I asked, more for the pleasure of hearing what she would say than because I doubted her.

"I dreamed it," she said airily.

I had my familiar sense of being surprised by Euny—of always being on the wrong foot yet of rather enjoying it—and I laughed to myself as I sat down by the hearth. It seemed a long time since the day I had sat there with my swollen ankle and wept at the misery of becoming her apprentice.

Over supper I told her of the anticurse and how well it had worked. She listened attentively, her dark eyes watching me, and when I was done she gave a nod of approval.

"But I do not think Meroot has finished with us," I added. "I believe she means to take my father's kingdom by one means or another. There is the baby too. If my mother has a boy, then I shall not become queen." I tried to say this calmly, without feeling, but Euny was not deceived.

"You're jealous!" she said.

For a moment I hated her. Then I nodded.

"I am," I said.

Euny was silent for a long time. I had forgotten how slowly life moved around her.

"It is time to fly," she said at last. I knew that flying was an important adventure in the *doran* world—that it was a way of discovering where one's true vocation lay. I took a deep breath—the idea scared me—and said, "When?"

"The day after tomorrow. You will need to fast."

IN ORDER TO FLY you had to have a special brown ointment spread all over your skin. Then you sat very still and concentrated, usually with the help of your teacher, and if all went well you found yourself in another place. What you had to do there was to keep your eyes and ears open, and if you did it properly, then you often learned about the future, not so much ordinary details about what might happen to you—the sort that soothsayers provide—as a sense of the shape and meaning of it. It was easy to get frightened and will oneself back into ordinary life long before the end. I was determined that no matter what I saw, I would wait for the flying dream to leave me of its own accord rather than run away from it.

The day of fasting seemed very long, but as nighttime came, Euny helped me bathe and then anointed me all over with the brown ointment, of which she kept a jar on a shelf. Then the two of us waited, standing face to face before the fire, our eyes fixed on each other. I felt a little sick, a little faint, but Euny willed me to stand upright while I waited for the moment of change. I would have given a lot to be somewhere else just then, but I tried to calm myself and wait. What changed everything was a sound like a tremendous cracking—the sort of sound a tree makes if it is snapped off in a winter gale—a noise so loud that I felt I lost consciousness for a moment. Then there was a strong pulling sensation, as if a hurricane were blowing me away and I was whirling through space so fast that it was hard to breathe. Not for long.

Almost at once, it seemed, I was in a dark place that reminded me of my old dream. I could hardly see, but I was running over sharp, slippery stones, and something was coming after me, making a noise of splashing and snuffling. An appalling stench was in my nostrils, one I felt I ought to know but could not quite identify. Almost before the horror of this overtook me, the vision changed. Now I could see clearly, and what I saw was Gamal's face, but it was upside down. At the same time I heard the sound of a child crying.

Then once again the pulling feeling had me in its power. I was being lifted, dragged, blown off the earth and had to submit again to being whirled in space. From high in the sky I looked down upon an island, and then I was standing on the island in front of a house. The house was white and stood upon a sort of inland cliff. I entered it, and there was a great hearth in the center of the room, the heart, I thought, of a place full of peace. Behind it were shelves with jars full of liquid, and when I looked out I could see a garden with neat rows of herbs. On the other side I could see that the land fell away, and in the distance was a view of a village and sea and shore. Feeling almost as if I were trespassing in someone's house and the owner might come home and catch me, I sat in a big chair by the hearth, watched thoughtfully by an owl—not Moon—who perched on a shelf. As I did so, my fears subsided. I knew that this was my chair and my house, that I fitted it perfectly and was completely comfortable, that this was the place in the world that I was seeking. It was a place in which there was no dread. From it I returned, after a while, to Euny's hut.

"I've found it," I reported with joy to Euny.

"What?"

"The place where I must be."

"Where is it?"

I described to her the house and the island, the inland cliff and the distant sea, and she nodded.

"I think I know where it is."

"Where?" I was breathless.

"If the flying dream wanted you to know that, it would

have told you," she said maddeningly. "In any case, that is far in the future. Was that all you saw?"

Much less happily I told her of the terror that had pursued me in the tunnel, of Gamal's face, and of the sound of crying. She looked grave.

"Do flying dreams make something happen to you, or are they what would have happened anyway?" I asked Euny.

"There is a part of you," said Euny, "that knows the future as well as it knows the past. It is not concerned with time. So that if you consult that part, which flying does, it can give you a memory of the future, just as your ordinary memory tells you about the past." She hesitated, her eyes fixed on mine as both of us struggled with this memory, a very fleeting and vague memory, in my case, of the future. I had a sense that something was being asked of me, some act of love or generosity that felt unbearably difficult.

"Something must be given up," I heard myself say to Euny, and she nodded encouragingly, as if that was just what she had seen herself, and she quoted under her breath a *doran* poem about "seeking with purity of spirit."

"How do you mean?" I asked, but she simply stared at me in reply, as if she had said quite enough.

"Gamal? How does he come into it? Why is he upside down?"

"Your love and friendship for him will be tested. Meroot, or perhaps the knight—they have power over Gamal at present." Euny looked past me now, as if painfully fixed on the future.

"And the terror in the tunnel?" I finally asked.

"You are a *doran*," said Euny. "A *good* one. I have seen to that. To be able to encounter evil, naked evil, that is your business. Not every day, not often, but when it is necessary. And now that you have found your place—through the flying—that makes it much easier. That is your center. It waits for you, and one day it will find you."

I RETURNED to Castle Dore scarcely knowing whether to feel pleased or sad. The joy and calm I had felt in my dream house with the great hearth taught me that one day I would truly find my place and my own peace in the world. How could anyone not rejoice at that? Yet somewhere in my life—presumably before I found my way to the island—lay the prospect of terror, with the unknown significance of the crying child. I didn't like that thought at all.

So not very cheerfully I set off on the long walk home. It felt comforting to see dear Castle Dore looking particularly beautiful as the evening sun shone upon its steep walls and low roofs.

"Your father wants you," Erith said as I was washing off the dust of my journey.

Something different about the king's face struck me as soon as I came into his chamber, and without asking anything about my visit to Euny he came straight to the point.

"I have heard from Meroot," he said. "Gamal is proposing marriage to you."

20

I WAS SO SURPRISED I sat down on a stool and stared
at him dumbly.

"We're not old enough," I said at last. I knew
very well, of course, that children my age, particularly
royal children, did get married, but because Gamal was
a friend I had always known, it had never occurred to
me to think of him as a husband.

"In many ways it would be good," the king went on,
ignoring my remark. "Meroot, I am sure, has minded
that my birth robbed her of the throne. By this marriage of cousins she would feel gratified, and Castle
Dore would have the protection of a warrior."

"As well as of a *doran*," I said crossly. At that moment I felt hurt and angry that my father so clearly
preferred a boy as his successor. "But if Mother has a
boy, Meroot won't get her wish anyway."

"That is true. We must consider both possibilities."

"Why don't we wait and see? There's no hurry, is there?"

I could see the king trying to decide how much to tell me, though the gravity of his expression told me much before he spoke.

"I am told," he said, "that the Gray Knight is pressing the countryside for soldiers. No one is quite sure"—his tone was very dry—"why he is recruiting them, but the rumor is that he means to attack Castle Dore."

I knew how painful this news must be to the king for several reasons, but I also saw how it affected my own position. The Gray Knight had let news of his activity reach us, but at the same time a marriage was suggested between Gamal and me. If I agreed, there would be no war. If I refused . . .

"You love Aunt Meroot, and you believe she loves you. Would she let the knight attack us?" I felt angry at my father's blindness about his sister. He did not reply, but a look of mingled shame and pain crossed his face.

"You *like* Gamal," he said. "He has been your dearest friend."

I thought of my dear friend with his honest eyes and his truthful tongue.

"I take it there is no word from Gamal himself," I said. There was not. Both of us fell silent, each thinking our thoughts. I was beginning to wonder why the flying dream had given me no hint of marriage, when the king startled me out of my reverie with his next words.

"Your aunt Meroot suggested that you visit

Caerleon, and I accepted the invitation on your behalf."

I reacted to this news with shock and disbelief.

"Father, these people wish to fight us! How can you send me to visit them?"

"There will be no danger to the kingdom if you marry Gamal. And I am certain that Meroot will take care of you." Nothing, I could see, would ever convince my father that Meroot was not to be trusted. All the same, I thought I would try once more.

"I don't trust Meroot. She is a dangerous woman. All she wants is to put Gamal on the throne. I don't want to go to Caerleon."

My father's face grew dark with rage. "You will do as I say."

I got up, inclined my head as etiquette demanded, and went out. Without hesitation I went in search of my mother.

"You know about the marriage suggestion? And that Meroot has invited me to Caerleon?"

She nodded. "I am sure the king knows it is wrong, but also that he fears to lose the kingdom to the Gray Knight."

"So I am to be the sacrifice?" I asked bitterly.

"We women are not asked whom we will marry. I was lucky that I loved your father. You could do worse than Gamal."

"And become the tool of Meroot and the Gray Knight?" My mother was silent.

In my anger I went out and paced around the Great Ditch. What I resented most was having no control over my life, of being a mere pawn, indeed a lost pawn, in the game being played between Meroot and my father. Suddenly an arrow whistled past my ear. I looked up, and there, fifty paces away, was Finbar grinning at me.

"That's dangerous," I said crossly. In my heart I had never quite forgiven Finbar.

"Let me come with you."

"What?"

"Let me come with you to Caerleon."

"How on earth do you know about that?" Castle Dore was always alive with gossip, but I knew my father had kept his moves fairly secret.

"I have been your father's messenger."

"Why do you want to go?"

"Because I am Gamal's friend and because . . ." With a slightly nervous gesture he looked up at the walls around us. He knew, as I did, that someone lying on the other side of the mound could hear every word that was said while remaining unseen. "Is there some-where we could talk in private?"

We returned to my chamber and sat there together as Gamal and I had done so often in the past.

"I carried a message for your father to Caerleon. It is a grim place. Naturally, when my business was done, I asked to see Gamal. At first Meroot said that I could not see him. Then I told her that I had a message for him from you. And that you had said I must deliver it only to Gamal. She kept me waiting for ages and then he came. . . . He was led . . . into the room where I was." A look of pain crossed Finbar's brown face. "He was . . . I don't know words for it . . . he was *not there.* He was like somebody sleepwalking. I am not even sure he knew me."

"He was ghosted," I said.

"What's that?"

"It is when you take the spirit out of somebody so that you can control them body and soul."

"Can it be cured?"

"Yes."

There was a long silence between us. Now, instead of resenting being forced to visit Caerleon, I wanted to go, to reach Gamal and see what ailed him. How bravely he must have resisted for them to resort to such a desperate measure.

"Could you cure him?"

"Perhaps. Going there . . . trying to help him . . . might be dangerous, you know."

Finbar nodded, as if the thought of danger gave him pleasure. I was surprised to hear myself add, "It would be good to have you with me . . . someone who cares about Gamal as much as I do."

Finbar looked me in the eyes and said, "I am sorry I was rude to you that time at Euny's. I don't know why I did it. It was not the way to treat the king's daughter, and it was ungallant of me. I like you a lot, and I'd like to help you on this visit. You can trust me, and you will need people you can trust there."

He was not alone. That night, when I mentioned the visit to Erith, she said almost the same thing.

"I never liked your auntie Meroot. I don't trust that

one as far as I can see her." I sketched for her Finbar's description of Gamal.

"That poor boy!" Erith said indignantly.

IN THE DAYS that followed I made my preparations. I rehearsed spells in my head, made several flasks of clearwater, took Euny's black egg from its wrappings, and prepared herbs with a number of magic properties. I carried a little package of tidbits for Moon—Erith was disbelieving when I said that I must take the owl, but I was quite sure that I must—and of course I took my cloak and my moon amulet, which nowadays I wore all the time.

The little band that set off for Caerleon included not only Finbar but four soldiers, a bard to sing the praises of the young couple, and an astrologer-magician named Winan.

I had scant respect for the official magic of my father's court, but I thought that if I seemed to consult someone like Winan it might lull Meroot into a sense of false security about my knowledge.

So not without fear I set out for Caerleon.

The journey took us several days, but the weather was fine. At night, wrapping ourselves in our blankets, we slept under the stars. At dawn we woke to the scent of the soldiers' fire and the smell of bacon cooking. Between Finbar and me a special closeness sprang up— we were drawn together by our love for Gamal, by our sense of the dark magic that threatened all of us, and by our awareness of the dangers that might lie ahead. Our love and trust in each other, together with my largely untried magic, were nearly all the protection that we had. I insisted that Finbar use the clearwater. He laughed, but I suspected that he was glad enough of whatever protection it might afford.

Now that I had time to think about it, I was surprised at how my feelings toward Finbar had changed. The rude boy who had hurt my feelings and made me jealous was now quite different—a companion whose loyalty had been proved, whose laughter and jokes were very comforting, whose brilliant blue eyes seemed to me to see farther than most.

Even Finbar was silent, however, when we first saw the outline of Castle Caerleon against the sky. I suspect he was wondering, as I was, whether any of us would come out of it alive—or at least without the damage of spells.

I put on my cloak, which made me feel safer. As we got closer to Caerleon, we saw how grim and fortified it was, and I wondered what Gamal had felt the first time he approached it with the Gray Knight and Meroot. The guards at the gate allowed us to enter, and we rode into a courtyard where our horses were taken from us.

21

IN MY FATHER'S HOUSE the practice was for guests to be shown immediately into his presence, or if that was impossible, to be greeted by an ealdor and offered refreshment. In the Gray Knight's house, in contrast, we were left standing in the courtyard, tired and dirty. At Castle Dore you were always aware of life going on around you—you could hear chatter, laughter, and singing as people went about their work. At Castle Caerleon there was an ominous silence that grew as we waited, a silence so oppressive that our conversation fell to a whisper.

"Do you think we are being watched?" Finbar asked me quietly. I nodded. Somewhere, I knew, from the stairways and balconies above, eyes were looking coldly down upon us. I shivered.

At that moment a servant appeared and bore away all my possessions to the room I would occupy. He returned shortly to lead the soldiers to the barracks. He tried to shepherd Finbar out with the soldiers, but

Finbar stood fast, and I said firmly, "Finbar comes with me."

"My lady asked only for you," the servant said nervously.

"And I will not go without Finbar. I will explain it to your lady."

Meroot was sitting in a huge chair on a dais in the middle of a long room, which gave her the appearance of a queen awaiting her subjects. Herbs were strewn on the floor, scenting the room. The great black hound sat at her feet watching us alertly. Meroot was dressed in a silk gown of brilliant red; at her neck was a chain with flashing stones. I advanced several steps into the room, very conscious that she was studying me. She knew, I was sure, that I had the protection of my *doran*'s cloak and probably also that my skin had been bathed with clearwater. Then, as if she had only just noticed me, she rose to her feet with a small cry of simulated delight. She held out her arms to me, kissed me, and drew me to a seat beside her grand chair. It was placed lower, I noticed, on a step.

"You remember Gamal's friend Finbar," I said. Meroot gave him a bleak stare.

"I had hoped that we might speak alone," she replied.

"There is nothing that Finbar may not hear," I said. "He is my father's messenger."

Meroot hesitated and then, plainly not wishing to cross me so early in our meeting, said, "Very well."

"We were kept waiting by your servants," I said, "and we need to wash after our journey."

"Later, later," she said indifferently.

There was a pause, and again I had the unpleasant sensation of being watched. I looked around the room. Hanging tapestries might conceal a watcher. A door at the far end of the room was ajar also.

"Where is Gamal?" I asked in a loud voice. By all means, let any eavesdropper hear the conversation.

"He is unwell," Meroot said.

I stared at her. My expression showed plainly enough that I knew this statement to be a lie.

"What ails him?" I asked.

"He has a rash and a fever," she replied. "He is not well enough to see you."

"Perhaps I could help. I am trained in healing."

A look of contempt crossed Meroot's face.

"I have no doubt that you know all the old wives have to teach."

I controlled my temper, remembering the need to find a way to help Gamal.

"You know that Gamal's choice of you, Ninnoc, has brought great joy to the Gray Knight and me. As my brother's daughter, you were always dear to me, and now we shall move into a closer friendship, to which I look forward with happiness."

"And Gamal? What does he feel?"

"How can you ask? You know that he has always adored you."

"We have been friends . . ."

Her eyes flickered hypnotically. She had an oddly snakelike quality, I thought.

"You will wish to see your room. It is what we call the eastern apartment. Finbar will have a room in the barracks."

"Finbar," I said, "is part of my retinue and must have a room near me. My father was concerned about my taking so long a journey virtually alone, and I promised him that Finbar would be my bodyguard and stay always within earshot."

Meroot's eyes flickered again.

"You think yourself in danger in the Gray Knight's house?"

"There are dangers everywhere."

"When I was a girl," Meroot said icily, "such an arrangement would have caused unpleasant gossip."

"My honor and Finbar's," I said, "are beyond doubt. And I am still a child. I am surprised at you, Aunt Meroot."

Finbar had listened to this exchange with his habitual look of faint amusement, but he flashed an admiring glance at me when it became clear that I had won the argument. I was very relieved to know he would be close at hand in that sinister castle.

The two of us went with Meroot to the eastern apartment. It was large and sunlit with a big silk-hung bed. There were fine tapestries of gods and goddesses; in the one opposite the bed a goddess who seemed to be the spirit of spring was strewing flowers over a barren winter landscape. A servant had unpacked my baggage, and everything was stored neatly away. I lifted Moon out of the bag I was carrying and set him, sleepy as ever, on a beam.

I noticed a door set in one of the walls and asked for it to be opened. I sensed the servant's reluctance and thought I could detect the sound of movement in the next room. Finally Meroot nodded. The door, I saw, opened into a small, bare chamber in which there would be room to place a bed for Finbar. There was a clean patch in the dust on the floor, as if a chair had been set close to the door of my chamber and then removed. My guess was that someone had been preparing to spy.

Finally Meroot went away with her servants, leaving me alone with Finbar. We looked searchingly at each other but knew better than to speak our thoughts.

"I need to wash and rest," I said, "and so do you. But I would like to see the environs of Caerleon before dark. Later we will ride together."

Finbar nodded and went out.

When we did meet, there was something I needed to report to him immediately.

"They took the clearwater," I told him. "I questioned the servant and she swore that the flasks were not in the baggage."

"That leaves us unprotected." Finbar's face was grave. He no longer thought the clearwater a foolish notion.

"Not at all," I said. "Look." And I produced a flask from under my cloak.

"I brought one for each of us just to be sure. Use it carefully."

WITH THE REST of the retinue we attended the formal dinner that Meroot gave in welcome that night. I had taken pains with my appearance and was slightly dismayed when just before I went to the hall Moon clambered up my arm and sat firmly on my shoulder. I lifted him off gently, saying, "No, Moon," but he returned imperturbably and I knew that he meant to accompany me. I must have looked very odd when I entered the hall, but when I sat down Moon hopped on the floor and dozed off again under my chair. I sat beside the Gray Knight. He was beautifully dressed in velvet and fur and scented with a sweet rich oil. Did the scent conceal some other less pleasant odor? I suspected that it did. As I soon discovered from his conversation, the knight was well educated and had studied the astronomical wisdom of the ancients at length. He was also very courteous and I must say I was charmed by him. He had huge dark eyes that I found very attractive; every time I looked into them they reminded me of someone, though I could not think of who it was. I retired for the night more than a little under his spell.

The next morning Finbar and I were taken to see the Gray Knight's soldiers practicing on a nearby field. I was appalled by their number—they were a small army— and I knew that I was intended to be impressed by this display of might.

Three days passed. Meroot said more than once that it was a pity Gamal was too ill to meet me on this visit. There was nothing, however, to prevent us from making all the necessary plans for the wedding, though Gamal and I might not meet again until the actual day of the ceremony.

I did not know where Gamal's chamber was, closely as I watched the servants for clues, but I did know that Meroot and the Gray Knight had their private rooms in the western wing of the castle.

So it was that I formed the desperate plan of visiting

Meroot's rooms in her absence to see whether I could find Gamal or simply discover some secret about Meroot—I knew not what—that would help save him. Every afternoon, I observed, Meroot and the Gray Knight rode out together, yet I knew that her servants might be at work in her absence.

After the midday meal I pleaded a headache and a need to rest and went to my room. Later, knowing that Meroot would have left, I put on my *doran*'s cloak, and with my heart beating quite fast I went to the western wing. Meroot had a suite of rooms, and in the first of them her fat servant was asleep upon a daybed, snoring loudly. I slid silently past her into another room. This was a day room, comfortably appointed, and through an open door on the far side of it I could see Meroot's sleeping chamber. Inside there was nothing of interest except a troubling smell. Partly it was the smell of Meroot's dog—I was surprised that she allowed such a large dog in her room and also that its smell lingered even in its absence, though I was relieved that she had not left it behind to guard her quarters. Yet beyond the dog smell there was another smell that I half recognized but could not place. There was no time to think about it, however. When I opened a door on the far side of the chamber, I found myself in a workroom full of flasks and jars. A cock in a crate on the floor began to protest at the sight of me. I recognized many herbs whose uses I knew well, but everything was placed tidily on a shelf and there was nothing to indicate which jars were in use. Meroot's leather stick stood against the wall, and I picked it up and examined it with interest. It had the look and feel of a magical object, but I could not imagine what Meroot used it for.

Yet another door opened out of this room, and without much hope of finding further clues about Meroot, I opened it. For a wild moment I simply could not take in what I saw, it was so extraordinary. For there, sitting up in bed and staring straight at me, wild-eyed, was Gamal! Not only did his face show no sign of recognition of me, but he seemed unaware that anyone had come into the room. I went to the bed and took his hand.

"Gamal! It is I, Ninnoc. Do you remember?"

But as if he were deaf, blind, and without feeling, Gamal continued to stare straight ahead. I squeezed his hand, touched his white face, talked to him, but I might as well have talked to a chair. Yet I could feel that his hand trembled, see that he was sweating, smell the odor of foreboding that his body gave off. I longed to stay with him, but I knew that I could not risk it. Quietly I slid out of his room and began the journey back through Meroot's rooms toward the corridor and safety. I had gotten as far as Meroot's sleeping chamber when to my horror I heard Meroot loudly scolding her servant. I could not escape!

I was so frightened when I heard Meroot's voice coming closer that at first I could not move. Then very quickly I began to retreat toward Gamal's room. There, without thinking about it, I crawled under the bed. I was well hidden by the draperies of the bed, but I was shaking with terror at the thought of being caught. I had no idea why she had returned early from her ride, but I feared that somehow she had guessed what I had done.

She came into the room so quietly that at first I was not even sure she was there. I scarcely dared to breathe as I waited for her to lift the draperies and expose me. Then I heard her walk across the room and pour something into a goblet. She walked back to the bed, and it sounded as if she was giving Gamal a drink. There was a clink as she put the goblet down, then a long silence. After an interminable wait, Meroot to my horror said, "You can come out from under the bed, Ninnoc."

Red-faced, I crawled out, saying the first thing that came into my head.

"I thought perhaps I could help Gamal. Being a healer."

Meroot looked at me with a mixture of amused contempt and anger that made me feel not at all like a *doran* but like a very silly little girl.

"If we need your help, Ninnoc, we shall ask for it. In the meantime I shall let your father know about your appalling manners and suggest that he teach you the rudiments of what it means to be a guest. Since you have forfeited that right, I shall treat you as what you are—a naughty child. Go to your room. We shall not expect to see you at the table until tomorrow."

I went to my room fuming at Meroot's speech. Yet despite my anger I knew that there was something much more important at stake than my hurt feelings. I could not forget Gamal's staring eyes and blank white face.

22

WHEN I DID NOT appear for our evening ride, Finbar came in search of me, and it was a relief to be able to tell him what had happened. Before I spoke a word he went around the tapestries, poking them and looking behind them, and even then we spoke to each other in whispers. I could see that Finbar was impressed by my courage. I was pleased too when he decided that if I was to go without my dinner he would share my exile.

"Her anger was calculated," he said, "to distract you from what you had seen. She must be frightened now."

"The trouble is that now Meroot knows I know. What I long to do is kidnap Gamal and take him to Angharad's house. It is less than a day's ride from here. But Meroot's guards would never let him through the gate."

"Suppose we pretend that we have not noticed anything—that we believe her story about the fever. You agree to marry Gamal on the day Meroot ap-

points. We leave and go home. Then we return secretly and steal Gamal away. They won't know we are
coming back, and he won't be guarded."

"We would never get through the gate."

"We might climb up the outside somehow," Finbar
said doubtfully.

"And take Gamal out that way? In his present state?"

"What we really need is a path that leads into the
heart of the house. They say that all such castles have
a secret way in and out, so that if there is a siege the
ealdors and their ladies can escape."

We were both silent, trying to think how, even if
such a path existed, we could possibly discover it. The
next day I begged Meroot's pardon, and after that I
went out of my way to be nice to her, pretending to
enjoy my stay and to take an interest in hawking, a
hateful, bloody sport to which both she and the Gray
Knight seemed addicted. I could not tell whether she
was taken in—I would catch her eyes resting thoughtfully upon me, but in the days that followed Finbar and
I became extraordinarily good actors. We swallowed
Meroot's thinly veiled insults and the Gray Knight's
cold speeches with smiles and soft words. I proclaimed
that the prospect of marrying Gamal pleased me immensely, and a date was set three months hence. I let
Meroot believe that though at first I had thought I was
too young, my father had prevailed on me to agree,
and his word was law. Perhaps I overdid it; I don't know.

Meanwhile Finbar and I spent more and more time
in the countryside searching in copses and on rocky
outcrops for anything that looked like a cave that might

lead into a passage. Armed with candles, a tinderbox, and a makeshift lantern, we searched with ever-declining hope. On one such day—a rather hot day—we were sitting under some trees to give ourselves and our sweating horses a little shade, when I idly picked up a stick and twirled it in my fingers as we talked. Suddenly, to my great surprise, a familiar feeling ran through my hands and arms, and I felt the twig, of its own accord, move downward. As I gave an involuntary gasp, Finbar looked at my hands and saw the twig move. "It's nothing," I said, slightly embarrassed. "It may mean that water runs beneath here or that some precious stone—"

I broke off because Finbar sat up sharply, his brilliant eyes staring into mine.

"Water!" he said.

"What about it?"

"Water runs beneath the castle, does it not? There is a place in the foundations where the servants draw water from an underground stream. On my first visit, when I slept with the servants, I went there to wash myself, as we all did. The underground stream runs into the castle but it does not appear to run out again. It must stay underground for some distance; then perhaps it emerges. Could the stream lead us in?"

We were both so excited by the idea that we set off at once, riding along slowly so that we could watch the action of the twig. It took us across several fields, across a moor, and through a wood. I was just beginning to think that this was foolish—that we might follow the indications of the twig for miles—when we began to hear the gurgling noise of a stream. There, tumbling out in a waterfall from beneath a rocky outcrop, was the water we had so faithfully searched for. It gushed out so quickly that we knew it must also flow quickly underground. There would be no chance of swimming against that fast current. The only faint possibility might be of a path or tunnel, left behind perhaps from a time when the water level was higher, that we could walk or crawl along in the direction of the castle. There was no sign of such an entrance from where we stood. So together we climbed up some slippery moss-covered rocks beside the waterfall. Eventually we pulled ourselves up onto a smooth clean rock near the top. Standing there, a dizzying distance from the ground, Finbar and I both gasped. For now we could see just to the left of the waterfall a dark hole that led into the stony embankment beside the rushing water. Both of us shouted with triumph.

When we entered it we could see that the path wound back into the darkness, into a rocky tunnel. We smiled at each other and Finbar lit the candle we had brought and put it into his lantern. Picking our way with care, we began to walk along the stream in the underground tunnel, sometimes passing through rocky caverns, sometimes having to bend low to avoid bumping our heads. I felt excited and exhilarated by our discovery. If only it led to the castle!

Quite soon I noticed something that surprised me: a subdued light of a delicate greenish color came from the amulet Euny had given me. Even without a lantern it gave enough light, I thought.

Just as I was beginning to worry that the path might end anywhere, and that however interesting the tunnel we were unlikely to be helping Gamal, Finbar suddenly stopped and pointed at the upper part of the rock walls.

"What? What?" I said, unable to see anything unusual.

"It's red," he said. "The rock is red. Just like the rocks around the castle."

The path led on for another five hundred paces. Then it curved and light appeared dimly at the end of it. As we got closer to the source of the light, we could see that a great rock blocked the path but that light shone down onto the water of the stream.

"I think we have reached the castle," Finbar said, "but we will have to make sure that we can get into it from here."

The water looked dark and uninviting, and it was flowing fairly swiftly away from the castle.

"I think we could use the rock to hold on to," said Finbar. "Do you want me to see if I can do it?" It was tempting to let him try by himself, but I knew that this was my adventure just as much as Finbar's. Gamal's white face, staring eyes, and shaking hand came vividly into my mind.

"Let's stay together," I said more bravely than I felt. We waded down into the water, which was cold and deep, but I was comforted by handholds on the rock. Half walking, half swimming, we groped our way around it. Suddenly the huge bulk of the castle stood above us, and we could see two of the castle servants standing in the wash place scrubbing linen. Fortunately they were too busy working and chattering to notice our arrival. We turned and crept silently back the way we had come. We had found the way to save Gamal.

NOW WE WERE READY to make the plans for our departure. Remembering Euny's instructions, I sewed myself a belt with small pouches in it to take the protections she had given me, and I kept the moon amulet around my neck. I chatted with Meroot about the wedding and plans for the future, and still I wondered whether she believed me.

The day came for kidnapping Gamal—a perfect summer day to which I woke with a feeling of sickening fear inside me. I longed for it to be time to go, but I knew that I must appear calm and controlled, as if nothing unusual was afoot.

I said farewell to Meroot with what I prayed was convincing affection and exchanged courteous pleasantries with the Gray Knight. Our party set off on the route home—in a different direction from that of the stream.

Somehow I persuaded our retinue to leave us. Perhaps because all of us were so relieved to be away from Caerleon it was not difficult. I told them that I wished to visit my old teacher Angharad and that I would join them in two days' time. Scarcely believing our good luck, Finbar and I cantered away, soon finding the path back to the wood and the waterfall.

The worst part of that day was waiting for darkness to fall. Both of us tried to talk of other things.

"I am glad to be having this adventure with you,"

Finbar said. "I trust you." By now I trusted him too, though I was also frightened at the thought of entering the castle at its very heart. Would there be guards outside Meroot's rooms? Would any of her servants wake up? Most terrifying of all, would Meroot or the Gray Knight awaken as we passed through their bedchamber? Then would Gamal come with us, and how difficult would it be to get him to walk? Suddenly something else occurred to me, and I gasped.

"The dog, Finbar!" I said. "What about the dog?"

"I've already thought of that. There is a kennel outside in the stables, and all the dogs are kept there at night. I slept near it on my last visit and was always being woken up by their barking."

"We cannot put clearwater on before we go in case the water washes it off," I said, raising another worry. "I shall carry a flask of it for us to use when we get out of the water."

Finbar nodded, not at all sorry, I thought, to have a little magic working for him. I suspected that he was just as frightened as I was, though sometimes when we discussed the adventure, his eyes would flash with a touch of his old carefree humor.

23

I SUPPOSE WHEN we worry about things it is a way of preparing for all possible disasters in advance. What often seems to happen then is that those particular disasters never occur, but that others undreamed of do. It was like that in our rescue of Gamal.

We tethered our horses in the wood, with Moon in his bag on my saddle. Then, as before, we set off along the tunnel. It felt very different setting off on a dark night instead of on a summer afternoon, and I was glad for my belt, my *doran*'s cloak, and Euny's amulet. Soon after we entered the tunnel there was a swish of wings about our heads. We both ducked, thinking a bat was above us. To my astonishment, I saw the great white sweep of Moon's wings instead. He settled on my shoulder for the rest of the journey, clutching me hard when I slipped or stumbled, sitting on my arm when the ceiling got low. It was oddly comforting having his company.

We managed the dive, leaving Moon behind in the cave—I solemnly instructed him to wait, and he seemed to understand. Once inside the castle walls we heaved our dripping bodies onto the bank, removed our cloaks and outer garments, and anointed ourselves with clear-water. Then, with the amulet as our guide, we set off again. I could feel my heart thudding; oddly, though, I felt excited and cheerful, not terrified as I had expected.

There was no sign of a guard as we made our way to the western side. Quietly we opened the door of the antechamber, which was empty. To my relief no servants lay snoring in the outer room and no hound was in sight. On through Meroot's sinister workroom and then, much more terrifying, into Meroot's bedchamber. The two of us paused in the doorway, ready to run at any moment. If necessary, I thought, we could dash down the stairs, into the water, and back into the tunnel before they could catch us. But the only sound we heard was quiet breathing. Moonlight lit one corner of the room; the rest was in darkness. Its rays illuminated something—the turquoise collar that the hound had worn, lying on a table as if only just taken off. As I saw the collar there, a hideous smell reached my nostrils and a piercing realization came to me—what I was reminded of when the Gray Knight looked into my eyes. It was a terrible shock, but I came back to my present errand when Finbar took my hand and the two of us stole into Gamal's room. Closing the door behind us, we turned to look at Gamal, who was sitting up in bed staring in front of him, exactly as he had been on my other visit. It was terribly uncanny. Did he never sleep?

Finbar threw back the covers of the bed and, putting his arms around Gamal, half lifted him out of it. Gamal slipped down until he was crouching on the floor. Finbar and I exchanged frightened glances. But we lifted him up, each slipping an arm through one of his, and without signals or words—we felt so tuned to each other that night that there was no need of them—we began to walk toward the door. Gamal offered no resistance. On the threshold we hesitated, dreading the ordeal of walking through Meroot's bedchamber. But I took a deep breath and we set off again, the three of us walking as one, and without a glance in the direction of the bed, we passed through and into the other room as silently as we had come. By the time we got to the steps my legs had begun to shake so badly that it was quite hard to keep going, but Gamal needed more help from us there and I pulled myself together.

Finbar and I discussed at length how we would get Gamal into the tunnel. We could do nothing but push him into the water and, with one of us in front of him and one behind, ease him along as best we could. Our great fear was that not understanding what was going on, he would struggle with us—a nasty prospect in that fast-flowing water—but he did not. In fact, I had a feeling that although Gamal's mind was not with us his body was responding as well as it could. We pushed and pulled him between us onto the bank in the tunnel. I wrapped my cloak around my wet body and we set off once more along the path. To begin with I felt much safer, but gradually a hateful feeling of unease spread over me. Soon I traced it to its source—seeing the turquoise collar in the bedchamber and realizing where I had seen the look in the Gray Knight's eyes.

Just then, however, the small ancient voice of Moon began to speak in my ear.

"Run, run . . . Run fast!"

"Why, Moon?"

"He's coming! Run. Run!"

"Who's coming?"

"The dog . . . the dog . . . the dog."

I turned desperately to Finbar, who did not understand Moon's language and heard only owl noises.

"Moon says the dog is coming. We must run, Finbar!"

Finbar must have been tempted to argue with me, but he did not.

Together we tried to run, each of us holding one of Gamal's arms. But he was so inert that he slowed us to little more than a fast walk.

"We *must* run, Gamal," I said to him desperately, but I knew my words meant nothing to him. We stumbled over the slippery, sharp rocks, and more than once one of us fell, yet despite pain and the dead weight of Gamal, we dared not go slower. I was still hoping, as I am sure Finbar was, that it was all a mistake when suddenly, far behind us, I heard a terrifying bark, and a few moments later the sound of the dog panting and running and snuffling as it leaped over the rocks. A choking, evil smell reached my nose, and it came back to me—the experience of terror in the tunnel that I had known in my flying dream. With mounting horror I heard the great hound draw closer. His monstrous baying echoed like thunder in the rocky tunnel.

Even as I heard the great dog draw closer, I remembered with dismay that in our haste we had forgotten to reanoint ourselves with clearwater when we emerged from the water. What I knew now—had known ever since I saw the collar in the bedchamber—was that the dog was the Gray Knight in his magical form. In the few seconds it took me to think this I remembered in detail when Trewyn told me how she had been threatened on the road by a huge black dog who was an enemy of Angharad's in disguise. It was terrifying enough to be chased by a huge savage beast; it was much worse knowing that it had human and magical powers as well.

The three of us continued at our slow, stumbling pace—though it was clear, at least to me, that we had no hope of outrunning the dog. As the hound drew near, Finbar, in a last desperate attempt to save us, indicated a ledge above the path. Finbar leaped and scrambled onto it, and standing below, I tried desperately to push Gamal up to him while Finbar grabbed Gamal's shirt and pulled on it. The shirt tore and Gamal dropped down on me, knocking my breath out so that for a moment I was helpless.

Then, hearing Moon's little voice chant a litany of "Try again . . . try again," I seized Gamal, and with a strength that at other times would have been impossible for me, I picked him up and lifted and pushed him up toward Finbar. This time Finbar caught Gamal beneath the arms and somehow dragged him up to sit on the ledge beside him. The dog was now very near—the

noise it made was deafening. I did not know how to
find the strength to scramble up to the ledge—I was
trembling so much. Whether Finbar managed to pull
me—I remember his arms reaching down to me as my
feet slipped—or whether some help reached me from
my *doran* allies, I do not know. But one moment I was
staring up hopelessly and the next I stood on the ledge
beside Finbar. To my surprise I was suddenly much
less afraid. Finbar pulled Gamal farther back on the
ledge so that his legs no longer hung down, and I pulled
my cloak around me and turned to confront the terror
that pursued us. I noticed that my amulet now burned
with a clear red light.

In the brief time before the dog reached us, when I
could see its great red tongue hanging out, its eyes
rolling, hear its baying cries, I reached into my pouch
and took Euny's black egg in my hand. Within moments the suffocating smell of the beast seemed to sur-
round us, so that I thought I would choke. I was aware
of it crouching to spring, of its huge paw reaching up
to drag me from the ledge, of its claws penetrating my
cloak and piercing my leg. At that moment I threw the
egg.

Later, Finbar and I had different recollections of what
happened next. I thought there was a sort of flash, but
Finbar said that the air seemed almost to split open;
what both of us watched, unbelieving, was a beast slowly
changing into a man, as the black hound became the
Gray Knight. Deathly pale, he tottered on his feet,
clutching his throat as if unable to breathe. He struggled like that for some moments, his face turning blue

with the effort, until he collapsed on the ground, rolling to and fro in agony. Grotesquely, the front of his gray tunic was covered in egg yolk, as if I had thrown a perfectly ordinary egg at him.

I was so fascinated by the spectacle that I could do nothing but stand and watch. Finbar, however, nudged me. "Let's get away." While the Gray Knight gasped and struggled and groaned, we lowered Gamal over the edge as if he were a sack of corn, and then, still not taking our eyes off the knight, we two scrambled down. Once more the three of us set off half running, but this time there was no sound of pursuit, only the sound of Moon's wings as he glided along beside us.

24

I T WAS NOT till late afternoon that we reached
Angharad's house. All day, since we had only two
horses, Finbar and I had taken turns walking, and
my right leg had gradually become very painful. The
deep scratch, which the dog's claw had inflicted, was a
livid purple, and the leg itself was beginning to swell.
The terrors of the night came back to me all through
the day; at such times I could not believe that we were
not pursued. More than once I found myself turning
around and looking over my shoulder, as if the dog
were chasing us once more. Finbar too was pale and
nervous and spoke little.

All this was bad enough, but at the moment when
my hand went to my neck to feel the comfort of Euny's
amulet, I found nothing there. I groped frantically beneath my cloak where the leather thong had been, but
it was gone, and the silver moon with it. I stopped,
appalled.

"It's gone. What shall I do? What *shall* I *do?*"

Finbar was kind and sympathetic, but I knew that he had no idea of the power of such a gift.

"We can't go back. There's nothing we can do, Ninnoc." I began to long passionately for Angharad's kindness and wisdom, for the comfort of her house and the pleasure of seeing her gentle face.

It was with near despair, therefore, as we breasted the hill and moved down into the valley, that I noticed that no smoke came from her smoke hole, that no wool hung drying on her storehouse walls. As we arrived at the house, I knew in my bones that it was empty—that Angharad was away on a journey. I was so disappointed that I began to cry. I thought I could not go on.

Of course, it felt good to reach the house and look once more upon the big room where I had learned to spin and weave and where Trewyn and I had worked and laughed. What was odd was that everything seemed ready for us—peats and wood piled beside the fire, fresh milk and bread as well as other food on the table, the loom itself with a shuttleful of green wool, as if at any moment Angharad might come in and take it up. That encouraged me. Angharad must mean to return soon. With a lighter spirit than I had felt all day I made one further exhausted effort. I laid and lit the fire and set about preparing a supper of porridge.

Finbar and I had not eaten for a day, and once we had dined (and painstakingly fed spoonfuls of porridge into Gamal), we both cheered up. I had taken the precaution of fastening the bolts on Angharad's doors; sitting comfortably by the fire with Gamal safe between us, everything suddenly felt much better. Finbar and I smiled at each other.

"We did it!" he said softly to me.

I climbed into my old bed and spread my *doran*'s cloak on top of me. Fingering the long tear the dog had made in it, I noticed something odd. The place in the front of the cloak where the tear began was the place where all those months ago I could not be bothered to go back to correct the mistake in the weaving.

No one will notice, I had thought, and no one had noticed. Yet it had given the dog his chance to wound me. My throbbing leg made me regret my carelessness bitterly.

I slept late the next morning—Gamal, Finbar said, never slept at all but sat staring unseeing in front of him. My leg had swollen further in the night, so that I could barely walk, and Finbar waited upon me and Gamal. Seeing my desire to keep the door bolted all the time, Finbar was reassuring.

"Meroot could not possibly know we are here, you know. Nor the Gray Knight. If he survived, which seems unlikely."

I wished I believed him. I had been trying to remember conversations between Euny and Angharad about the ability of *doran*s and sorcerers to "smell out" their enemies. My own heightened sense of smell since the *doran* ceremony made it seem only too likely that a person more experienced with magic than I might possess advanced skills of this kind. I could not recall exactly what my teachers had said, but my fear was that although it might take time, a quarry was always found in the end. My fervent hope was that Angharad would return before Meroot found us.

In the meantime we had to care for Gamal. It was unnerving having him sit with us all the time, speechless and unseeing. I loved the tender way Finbar washed his face and hands, combed his hair, tidied his clothes, and fed him. Lying weakly beside the hearth, bothered by increasing pain in my leg and full of fears and dark thoughts, I decided to distract myself by thinking about Gamal's problem and how he might be healed. I traced my way back through the long lessons in healing that Euny had led me through during our last weeks together.

"What we have to do," I told Finbar, "is find 'a path to his heart'—that's what the *doran*s say. We must think of something that matters so much to him that it will lure him out of his hiding place."

"Hiding place?" said Finbar, looking thoughtfully at Gamal. "You mean that he is in there somewhere but is too frightened to come out? I had thought that somehow he might just be . . . gone."

Certainly, looking at Gamal, he did seem to be gone. Even physically he seemed to bear less resemblance to the boy we had known. He looked wizened and faintly yellow, and when he was not completely still, he had a nervous mannerism of twitching his fingers. Occasionally a tear rolled down his cheek, which was all the more disturbing since he showed no other sign of feeling.

We sat in silence for a while, racking our brains for ideas to tempt Gamal.

"I think I know what to do," said Finbar quietly. "Music. That's what Gamal liked . . . likes . . . better than anything."

I remembered then that Trewyn had owned a rough flute, and with a bit of a search we found it. For the rest of the afternoon Finbar and I took turns picking out tunes on it. Did the music make any difference to Gamal? It was hard to be sure. His fingers moved more convulsively, and there were more tears than when we did not play, but there was no sign of the old Gamal returning. Late in the afternoon, when the pain in my leg was becoming so bad that I could no longer ignore it, I had a fleeting, shameful longing to shake Gamal, as if to force him to talk to us.

Finbar, at my request, had started dipping rags in cold water and spreading them over my badly swollen leg, alternating them with others as hot as I could bear. I began to shiver, and he put a hand on my forehead.

"You've got a fever," he said gravely. As he helped me up the ladder to my bedchamber, I suddenly looked around the big room.

"Where's Moon?" I asked. The previous night Moon had slept on his beam, but I suddenly realized that I had not seen him all day. He had never stayed away during the day before. I began to weep.

"First the amulet, now Moon," I said. I could not bear it.

Lying in bed, I could hear Finbar playing tunes to

Gamal and could picture the blank look on Gamal's face. As my pain grew worse and worse, I cried and shivered and sweated with fever. Although we had gotten Gamal away from Meroot, I felt that I had failed in my *doran*'s power. I had let the dog tear me, and the poison of the wound might easily kill me. Tossing and moaning, I knew that I had not wanted power with the "purity of spirit" of which Euny had once spoken, but in order to be superior to others. This reminded me of how hard it had been to relinquish the idea of inheriting my father's throne, of how jealous I had been of the unborn child who would supplant me. I had wanted the throne as much as I had wanted to be a famous and successful *doran.* Now it was too late to be anything at all.

As the pain grew worse, at times I seemed to be no longer in the white room but back in the dreadful tunnel with the sound of snuffling and baying pursuing me. I would be conscious for a while of the bed and my pain and then would be off once again down the dark, fearful corridors of my own mind. This torment went on, I believe, for hours. The house was quiet now—Finbar must have been asleep.

Suddenly I heard a baby cry. It was the cry of a very tiny child, a babe newborn, and it was as close as if it were in the room with me. I was so surprised that I sat up. The room shone with a blue-white light, and within it I saw the great throne in the council chamber and my father in his kingly robes sitting upon it. What I saw was power—a certain sort of power—and it was attractive to me. It could be used well, I knew, not to gratify one's own vanity or to make oneself rich, but to make a country safe and prosperous and to dispense justice. I had seen my father exercise his power in just this way. I knew I wanted it—I wanted the dignity, the respect, the sense of being the one to whom attention was paid and to whom others had to listen. I wanted my father's throne.

Just then I heard the baby's cry again, weak but piercing. Its pathos moved me deeply. As I thought of it, I could see the baby, a little naked boy child wrinkling his face as he cried, feebly moving his tiny hands. I felt an unbearable longing to comfort and protect him, to use my grown-up strength and knowledge as a safeguard until he grew big and strong. *This* was my rival, this frail, innocent thing? My mind moved unexpectedly away from the baby to Meroot. Meroot had wanted kingly power, had let her whole life be shaped into corruption by jealousy of her younger brother. She had not seen that her brother loved her, only that he had what she had not.

Questions and visions roiled in my mind. I felt myself coming to some difficult, reluctant decision. Something had to be surrendered or understood by me—I had to be different, but I did not know how. Pain, like an unwelcome visitor, lingered in the room. Sometimes I was wholly caught up in it, so that I could think of nothing else. Sometimes it withdrew a little from me, and I was desperate to escape from it. What helped somewhat was the memory of Euny and her way of dealing with hunger; she did not fight it, but accepted it calmly. I tried, not very successfully, to welcome it as if instead of being an intruder it was a favored guest.

Eventually—was it part of the delirium or not?—I thought I heard Moon's wings sweeping around the room and felt the breeze of his flight cooling my hot forehead. Soon afterward my pain eased, and I fell at last into a peaceful sleep.

It was morning when I awoke—a bright, sunny morning—and feeling weak after my fevered night, I lay motionless, conscious that the terrible pain had sunk to a mild throbbing. The sun winked on something on the floor beside the bed, and I blinked, then put out my hand, disbelieving. For there on the boards, with the broken leather thong still attached to it, was the silver amulet. Had it been caught in my clothing and fallen out when I undressed? No. I would have found it the night before. Then the memory of the sound of wings in the night came back to me, and I looked around the room. Moon sat comfortably on a beam, sound asleep. Only one explanation seemed possible. He had gone back for the amulet and brought it to me.

"I think you may have saved my life, Moon," I remarked shakily. Moon, who usually ignored my attempts to talk to him, opened his huge amber eyes, regarded me sternly for a moment, shuffled his feet, and went back to sleep.

25

Y MOTHER has had a son," I told Finbar.

"How on earth do you know that?"

"I saw it," I said. "In a kind of dream." The swelling of my leg was gradually going down; the pain had almost ceased. Finbar and I sat opposite each other at Angharad's hearth with Gamal between us.

"That will mean you won't become *regulus*," Finbar said carefully.

"I know. I saw that too. I think now that part of the reason I am a *doran* is so I can protect the baby and the kingdom."

"Don't you mind? It's unfair that you cannot rule because you are a girl."

"It *is* unfair, and I *did* mind very much," I said truthfully. "But something has changed in me. . . ." I hesitated, trying to put difficult thoughts into words. "It was Euny, of course. You see, I had grown up with *things*—clothes and jewels, fine ponies, cups set with precious stones, delicious food and drink . . . they were part of my father's power, a way of showing that he was rich and strong and could defeat his enemies. When I went to Euny, she had nothing—not enough food to eat, nor kindling to keep us warm—no possessions, really, at all. We just used exactly what we needed to keep alive—that and no more. We lived almost as simply as the wild creatures around us."

I caught Finbar's eye and remembered the dreadful day when I killed Borra.

"Part of Euny's power came from her simplicity. In the end I knew I'd rather have her sort of power than all my father's possessions."

"So will you end up living like Euny?"

I laughed. "I hope not. My upbringing taught me to take pleasure in many things Euny does not care about— in learning and music, in the taste of food, in keeping warm enough and well-fed enough not to be utterly miserable. But because of Euny, I don't want to live in a palace like my father, with all those precious things and an army. I don't want his sort of power. Not that his sort is wrong, but it is not what I am called to. I want something simpler where I can work out what being a *doran* means."

"Meanwhile your brother will rule at Castle Dore," Finbar reminded me.

"Probably not half as well as I would have done," I said. It annoyed me that my brother's birth automatically excluded me, even though in my heart I wanted something very different from being *regulus*. "But I will use my power in a different way."

There was silence between us, and we both looked at Gamal, wishing that my power might do something more for him. Finbar's patient work with the flute had had no effect on Gamal at all. Suddenly I had an idea.

"The tune!" I said. "There was a special tune, a rather beautiful lullaby that Gamal remembered someone singing to him when he was a little boy. I think I know how it went." Not stopping to pick out the notes on the flute, I began to sing Gamal's tune to him slowly as I fumbled to recall it, my eyes fixed on his face. When I finished, not getting it quite right, I sang it again, this time remembering it completely. Now Finbar took up the tune, and the two of us sang it together, pouring into it our love and concern for Gamal. Then I noticed a flicker of interest in Gamal's blank face. It made me exclaim with surprise, but immediately it was gone, and I decided that the next time it happened—if it did happen again—I would ignore it and carry on as if nothing had occurred.

Later that day, quite casually, Gamal put up a hand and touched his own hair. Finbar and I pretended not to notice, but nothing more happened. That evening Gamal was as lost as ever.

"All the same," Finbar pointed out, "it does make you think that someone's in there."

The next morning Gamal coughed in such an ordinary, natural way that we both turned to him, expecting him to speak. As I fed him, I thought I saw, just for an instant, a flicker of recognition in his eyes, though at once he stared in front of him as if it were not safe to acknowledge me. Again and again that day we sang his childhood song, feeling sure now that something was beginning to change inside him.

"If he has come out of his hiding place, he needs to pretend he is still there," I thought.

We were growing short of food now, and the next morning Finbar offered to go off on a foraging expedition to try to buy meal and do some fishing. It was quiet in the house without him, and it was hard work washing and feeding Gamal all by myself. I busied myself cleaning Angharad's house—it would never do if she came home and found it dirty—and I kept the door bolted most of the time.

I was scrubbing the pots one morning a week later when I heard Finbar calling me.

"Come and see what I've got, Juniper!"

I was so delighted that he had returned that I rushed to the door and unbolted it. Even as I swung the door open it came into my mind that Finbar always called me Ninnoc. There, just a short way from the house, stood Meroot, holding her leather stick.

THE TWO OF US stood and looked at each other—accomplished sorcerer and raw *doran*. I trembled. How could I fight her experience and her cruelty? Yet I knew too that I carried within me the good inheritance of all *doran*s and that this gave me a special strength.

"What do you want?" I asked weakly.

"My son!" she said. "I want Gamal."

"You ghosted him," I said boldly. "You do not deserve to have him."

"You are speaking of things you do not understand," she said. "I know you have him here, and I have come to take him home."

I was surprised to notice then that although I was frightened of Meroot, I was much more frightened that Gamal would be taken by her and destroyed.

"You know that if a sorcerer steps on a *doran*'s territory she is in the power of the other. I have power and I shall use it," I told her, trying to keep the wobble out of my voice.

For a moment she was transfixed by surprise at my apparent confidence. Then her voice rang out imperiously. "I want my son."

Just then, as the two of us stood and glared at each other, something totally unexpected happened. From inside the house came the sound of Gamal's lullaby, played with the hesitancy of someone who has not played the flute for a long time. Meroot was as startled as I was.

"What's that?" she said.

I had heard the melody many times before, played by Gamal on various instruments and hummed by Finbar and me, yet it was as if I heard it for the first time and was struck by its extraordinary power. It spoke to me of the simplest and best kind of magic, the magic of human love, the love of the woman who had taught Gamal the song, the love of Finbar and I, who had longed so much to help our friend, the love I had begun to feel for the newborn little baby at Castle Dore. Suddenly I saw the pathos of Meroot's desperate

scheming life and her unreachable loneliness. She could
have enjoyed the love of Gamal and instead had nearly
destroyed him.

To my surprise I found tears in my eyes when I
looked at her.

"It was hard for you when your brother took the
throne instead of you," I said softly. But Meroot would
have none of my pity.

"And what will you do when *your* brother takes the
throne instead of you?" she asked tauntingly.

"You know about that?"

"If you return Gamal to me, I will help you get your
father's throne."

"If my brother is the rightful king, he shall reign at
Castle Dore," I said, "and I shall do everything in my
power to help him. As for Gamal, he shall choose for
himself whether to return with you, since you have
forfeited your natural right to care for him."

Suddenly Gamal stood in the doorway beside me.

"I am not your son," he said to Meroot, "and I shall
not return with you."

At this Meroot flinched as if he had struck her, but
he went on.

"I have now remembered what I could not bear to
remember—that when I was a small child you took me
by force from the fair-haired woman who was my mother
and claimed I was your child. She was a *doran* and a
woman of great goodness, but you destroyed her. You
had no child, but you thought you would use me to
obtain King Mark's throne. You trained me as a soldier
and you bullied and threatened me to try to make me

fit in with your schemes. Later you let the evil knight
work his spells on me. You thought it better that he
should torment me than that your plans should be frustrated. But now I am free, and I will never come back
with you. I am no longer your son."

The look of mingled rage and pain on Meroot's face
was a dreadful sight. She threw her leather stick at me.
One moment it was a stick, but the next it had hit the
earth and turned into a snake, its head near me, its
tongue flicking in and out of its mouth. Gamal and I
stood as if turned to stone. I had neither my cloak nor
clearwater to protect me, though I was wearing Euny's
amulet. Now, I knew, was the moment of power, the
shift in the balance of things between Meroot's magic
and the magic of the *dorans*. I picked up the snake in
my right hand and held it high above my head.

"The snake is now my snake," I said. "It will do as I
bid it. If you do not leave at once, without Gamal and
without troubling us any further, I will order it to follow you wherever you may go, anywhere upon the earth,
and to bite you. If you leave now, without spells or
tricks, you will go with my blessing. The choice is yours."

Meroot hesitated, her cold eyes fixed upon mine.
Then, unbelievably, she turned and shuffled away. I
lowered my arm and let go of the snake, which almost
at once became the leather-covered stick I remembered so well from Meroot's room at Castle Dore. For
a moment I stood trying to take in all that had just
happened. Then full of joy I turned to embrace Gamal.

The two of us went back inside Angharad's cottage
and there—how could we believe our eyes?—were

Angharad and Euny sitting by the hearth as if they had been there all along.

"You took your time in dispatching her," said Euny, "and you nearly spoiled everything with the flaw in the cloak." But her face shone with pride in me.

Angharad got up and hugged me with her old warmth. "You did well," she said.

"The black egg worked," I told Euny gratefully. "It saved our lives. I don't know what happened to the Gray Knight, though. Do you think he died?"

Euny looked rather wickedly smug.

"Oh, he lived," she replied. "But it will be a while before he troubles a *doran* again. He has been very ill since the day in the tunnel—that particular bit of magic is very effective—and even now, I suspect, he is only well enough to take little walks around his garden."

"Does that mean one day I may meet him again?" I asked nervously.

"If your life happens that way," Euny answered. "Meeting with sorcerers is part of your job. What did you imagine? But if and when it happens, you will know what to do."

THERE WAS FEASTING in Angharad's cottage that night—Finbar returned in time to join us—and I think that I have never felt happier in my life. I loved sitting between the two *dorans*—I felt so beautifully *safe*. I looked at Gamal. He was thin and pale, but life had returned to his face and his limbs, and he was again the boy I had ridden with and climbed with so often.

Angharad remembered the fair-haired *doran* who had

been Gamal's mother and answered many questions about her. Euny had visited my mother, had reassured her as to my whereabouts, and had seen the strong baby boy who was born on the night of my delirium. She insisted on looking at the scar on my leg, which bore an odd resemblance to a crescent moon. She touched the scar and murmured a spell over it, explaining that like the flaw in my cloak, if I was not careful, this could be a place where in the future dangerous magic might enter.

"What will happen to me now?" I asked the two *dorans*.

"You tell us," said Angharad.

I considered.

"I want to go home first. I must see my brother and my parents. Then . . . well, they're not really going to need me, are they? I want to travel, to see strange places, to learn more . . ." I was thinking of the need to find the place I had seen in my dream, the house by the inland cliff. I had completely forgotten Meroot's plan that I should marry Gamal, but suddenly I wondered what Gamal would do and where he would go now that he had broken with Meroot.

"I am going to become a musician at last," Gamal said, catching my eye. "There is a monastery at Streaneshalch, far in the north, in Northumbria, where they are famous for their singing and the tunes they compose. I will go there and ask if I can learn from them."

Finbar grinned. The quiet life of a monastery would not appeal to him.

"I could go back to being a page at your father's court," he said, "but really what I want to do is go to sea. I'd like to become a navigator. I will travel to the coast and persuade a ship's captain to let me join his crew."

We lifted our wine cups.

"To the mending of that which is broken," said Euny.

To which Angharad replied, "And to the finding of that which is lost."

As the youngest *doran* present, I said, "It shall be so," silently promising to do the work of the *doran*s as well as I knew how.

Monica Furlong

has been a journalist and a television producer, and is the author of several note-
worthy biographies of prominent spiritual
figures, including Thomas Merton, Alan
Watts, and Saint Thérèse of Lisieux, as well
as the critically acclaimed young adult novel
Wise Child. Ms. Furlong lives in London.